WOMEN ON TOP

WOMEN
ON TOP

The Quiet Revolution
That's Rocking the
American Music Industry

JAMES DICKERSON

BILLBOARD BOOKS
An imprint of Watson-Guptill Publications/New York

James Dickerson has worked for almost 30 years as a magazine editor, newspaper editor, reporter, columnist, book critic, and photographer, and has written five books. These titles include *Going Back to Memphis: A Century of Blues, Rock 'n' Roll, and Glorious Soul,* for which he was nominated for a Ralph J. Gleason Music Book Award; *Coming Home: 21 Conversations About Memphis Music;* and *That's Alright, Elvis,* the co-written autobiography of Scotty Moore, Elvis Presley's first manager and guitarist.

Senior Editor: Bob Nirkind
Editor: Liz Harvey
Designer: Areta Buk
Production Manager: Hector Campbell

First published in 1998 in New York by Billboard Books,
an imprint of Watson-Guptill Publications,
a division of BPI Communications,
1515 Broadway, New York, NY 10036

Library of Congress Cataloging in Publication Data
Dickerson, James.
    Women on top : the quiet revolution that's rocking the American
music industry.
        p.   cm.
    Includes bibliographical references and index.
    ISBN 0-8230-8489-2 (hc.)
    1. Women musicians—United States. 2. Popular music—United
States—History and criticism. 3. Sound recording industry—United
States—History. I. Title
ML82.D53   1998
781.64'082'0973—dc21   98-19826
                                                                                    CIP
                                                                                    MN

Manufactured in the United States

1 2 3 4 5 6 7 8 9 / 06 05 04 03 02 01 00 99 98

IN MEMORY:
EILEEN MARGARET DOOLEY

ACKNOWLEDGMENTS

I would like to thank the following for helping me with this book: my hard-working research assistant, Ginger Rezy; the editors at Glamour; Ed Frank of the Mississippi Valley Collection at the University of Memphis; Roberta Streeter, for opening new vistas; my agent, Debra Rodman, for sending holiday muffins; the Jean and Alexander Heard Library at Vanderbilt University Library; Bob Nirkind at Billboard Books; the Public Library of Nashville and Davidson County; John Bakke at the University of Memphis; Deana Carter; Pat Benatar; Kathy Mattea; Pam Lewis; Sandy Neese; Frances Preston; Terri Clark; Sheila Shipley Biddy; Brenda Lee; Anita Mandell; Tracey Edmonds; Tena Clark; Pam Lewis; Tiffany; Kathy Mattea; Abra Moore; Marilyn Arthur; Twana Burns; Renee Bell; and Anita Mandell.

CONTENTS

CHAPTER 1

THE BEGINNING OF THE REVOLUTION

Elvis Presley, the man Madonna once called God, stood in a certain place when he listened to playbacks in the early days at Memphis Recording Service. He always stood in the same spot, his hand braced against the wall for support. One day his hands were dirty—maybe from his job at Crown Electric, or maybe from his poking around the dark corners of the studio—and he left his handprint on the light-colored wall. For years afterward, young girls came into the studio to gaze at the handprint. Sometimes they stood in awe, breathless, as if they were at a religious shrine. Other times they touched, caressed, and kissed the handprint. Sometimes they measured their own hand against it. Always, they talked to it as if it could hear and understand and care. Then one day the handprint was gone, painted over by an unsentimental house painter.

Those looking for a starting point for the women's revolution in music— the precise moment when the little girls' dreams began to grow into the reality of womanhood, and the precise place where the dream began to take root— don't have to look any farther than Presley's handprint. That it no longer exists hardly matters. That it took precisely 40 years for the dream to be realized matters even less.

Today, women are doing more than topping the charts; they're transmuting popular music. They're taking it to a new level, just as Presley transmuted country and blues in the 1950s. This is as much a creative struggle as it is one of equality between the sexes.

Rock 'n' roll was in big trouble even before the women's revolution began. Sales have been declining for years, leading Val Azzoli, co-chairman of the Atlantic Records Group, to characterize 1996 as the year the music industry finally ran out of gold. It isn't hard to figure out why. You can manufacture cars or refrigerators or stereos, you can advertise them as anti-female products, and maybe you'll sell a few—but you won't stay in business for long. Music, for all its artistic components, is a product like any other, and it is susceptible to the same market influences.

Change was inevitable. Just as the empire that the Soviet Union had built ran its course and was replaced by a kinder, gentler form of government, so will rock 'n' roll—at least the male-driven version that has dominated for four decades—evolve into something entirely different. It is clear now that women will engineer these changes, which have already been set in motion.

EILEEN TWAIN: PREPARING FOR BATTLE

When Eileen Twain came to Nashville in 1991 from her native Canada, she was armed with little more than raw singing talent, a dazzling natural beauty,

Shania Twain

and a manager named Mary Bailey. It was hardly a potent arsenal with which to do battle with the granddaddy of all "good ole boy" networks. The 26-year-old brunette resembled a feisty magazine cover girl more than she did a country singer: elegant, reserved, above the fray. She certainly didn't look like someone about to step into the vanguard of a music revolution.

With two notable exceptions—Pam Lewis, Garth Brooks's co-manager, and Lib Hatcher, Randy Travis's manager—female managers were a rarity among successful recording artists on either side of the pop-country fence. But what did a country singer from Timmins, Ontario, know about the gender politics of stardom? Mary Bailey, herself a well-known country singer in Canada, had discovered Twain in the Canadian north country about 400 miles north of Toronto, where she'd been singing since childhood in restaurants and small-town nightclubs. Twain sang mostly pop and Top 40 material, but she was no stranger to country music, and it was well represented in her repertoire.

As a teenager, Twain worked in the Canadian bush planting trees with her stepfather, Jerry Twain, a full-blooded Ojibway Indian who had married her mother when Eileen was two. She had no memory of her natural father, Clarence Edwards, a man of French-Irish descent. As far as she was concerned, Jerry was her father—her only father. His crew went into the bush in teams of a dozen or more, with Eileen the only female among them. That didn't seem to bother her since she'd grown up a tomboy, with no real concept of gender differences. The only concession she made to her femininity was the large wash tub she loaded into Jerry's pickup when they headed out to camp. She filled the tub with water and parked the truck where it would receive direct sunlight while she was away at work. When she returned to camp at sunset, the water was warm enough to bathe in, so she stripped, climbed into the tub, and unselfconsciously washed herself under the open skies without fear of violation from the men in the crew. If anything, Twain's tomboyishness made her more trusting of men than was perhaps the norm for her age. She thought of herself as just another one of the guys.

If it was Jerry who helped Eileen define herself as a woman, it was her mother, Sharon, who helped her develop her musical talents. Sharon was a tall, no-nonsense woman of Irish stock who had an eccentric "British air" about her. "She couldn't sing a note, but she was such a wonderful, wonderful lady," Twain says of the mother she nicknamed Angel. "Everywhere she walked, she was definitely going somewhere. She was certainly not the sort of person to kinda saunter around."

Sharon instilled a sense of self-worth and self-confidence in Eileen at an early age. Just as Jerry taught her that she could do anything a man could do and could work alongside any of them with a sense of equanimity, Sharon convinced Eileen that she could sing as well as any of the women she heard on the radio. Sharon just knew her daughter could be a star. Eileen grew up believing stardom was her destiny.

The Twain family was poor by American middle-class standards, but so were most of the working class families in northern Ontario. Although the family didn't always have enough food to eat, according to Twain's recollections, her parents managed to scrape together enough money to send her to Toronto for voice lessons. After years of county fairs and local talent contests, Sharon finally got the break she dreamed of for Eileen and booked her on "The Tommy Hunter Show," a nationally broadcast variety show. It was that booking that brought Twain to Mary Bailey's attention.

Unfortunately, just as it appeared that Twain's career was about to move to another level, Jerry and Sharon were killed in a car accident in 1987 when their Chevy Suburban slammed head-on into a logging truck. Twain was devastated. Since her older sister, Jill, was married and had children of her own, she took responsibility for her three teenage siblings—two brothers and a sister—and became their surrogate parent. They moved to Huntsville, Ontario, where Twain found work as a singer at a resort lodge. She did three shows a day, seven days a week, singing everything from Broadway show tunes to country ballads. And just as Twain became a parent to her siblings, Mary Bailey became a parent to Eileen, replacing Sharon as her primary dreamweaver.

For three years, Twain worked as a cabaret singer, supporting her siblings and making a name for herself in the resort communities of northern Ontario. In 1991, Bailey arranged a meeting with Nashville attorney Dick Frank, who put her in touch with Norro Wilson, a successful Nashville producer/songwriter, and Buddy Cannon, the head of A & R, which stands for "artists and repertoire," for Mercury Nashville Records. Bailey paid Wilson and Cannon to record a three-song demo, which she could pitch to the record labels. Then, in the blink of an eye, or so it seemed, Twain had a contract as a singer/songwriter with Mercury Records.

This was a fortuitous union, although just how fortuitous she wouldn't understand right away. Mercury had signed Kathy Mattea several years earlier and was gaining a reputation as a female-friendly label for new-wave artists. One reason was label head Luke Lewis, who didn't share the traditional view that female artists couldn't sell records. The second was Sandy Neese, the vice president of media relations. Neese had gotten into the record business by way of radio, following a stint as a reporter at *The Nashville Tennessean,* a newspaper that had a reputation for supporting liberal causes.

Neese has a reputation for giving her all to her work. She works as hard for male artists as she does for female artists, but it is the latter who have a special place in her heart. Unknown to Twain, Neese was a member of a loosely organized "good ole girl" network in Nashville that years ago had pledged its membership to give breaks to female artists who were deserving of a helping hand. In time, she would have a profound influence on Twain's career, although the singer would never quite understand why.

The first thing Twain did upon moving to Nashville was to change her first name. She dropped the name Eileen and adopted the name Shania, an Ojibwa name that means "I'm on my way." She took the name out of tribute to Jerry and led reporters to believe it was a product of her Ojibwa heritage. Later, when the truth came out, she was roasted by the press for "lying" about her Indian heritage. In fairness to Twain, it must be said that she'd come to identify totally with this heritage. She had no memory of her natural father and considered Jerry to be her father. What possible interest would the media—or music fans—have in disassociating her from the man she regarded as her father? Eventually she would learn that the media and music fans have a penchant for tearing down people they build up, but at that point in her career it simply never occurred to her that her family life would be anyone's business but her own.

Most people who move to Nashville from New York or California experience a certain amount of culture shock, but this is based largely on the laid-back and rural folkways of the city. Not so for Twain. Her introduction to Nashville was her introduction to the United States, so she experienced a different type of culture shock. When working out in the bush with Jerry, Shania lived in a camp similar to what hunters call home in the United States. Father and daughter killed deer for food and butchered the animals on the spot. Because the Twains had no refrigeration, they buried the meat in the cold tundra while they worked in the bush. This effectively preserved the meat and protected it from wild animals.

"There's a big difference just in the culture," says Shania. "When I first moved to Nashville, going into the grocery and everything was real different because of the labeling and things like that. There were 30 or 50 different types of beans. It was, 'Where do I start? What kind of butter do I buy?' Just going to a restaurant was different. If you ordered a tea and didn't specify you wanted hot tea, they would give you an iced tea. I'm not used to that, you know. I ordered a country fried steak one time, because at home country fried steak would be a piece of ham. Here it's deep fried steak that's battered. I couldn't believe it. I said, 'I can't eat this. What is it?'"

Since Twain had been signed as a singer/songwriter, she turned in a slate of original songs for her first album. All but one of the songs were turned down by co-producers Wilson and Harold Shedd, the vice president of creative development for Mercury. She was crushed. Those songs represented her own unique view of country music. Wilson and Shedd felt more comfortable with the traditional songs that Music Row tunesmiths penned. This response represented a male view prevalent at the time: the records that female artists recorded that sold well were all variations of the "he done me wrong" theme. Twain's songs didn't fit into that genre. They were all about strong women taking charge of their lives. They weren't feminist in point of view, but they were unmistakably from the heart of a woman who hadn't been brought up to feel she had been put on earth to please men.

When Twain's self-titled album was released in 1993, it didn't do well on radio or in the stores. The two singles, "What Made You Say That' and "Dance With the One That Brought You," never cracked the Top 50. She was sent out on tour with two of Mercury's new male artists, Toby Keith and John Brannen. By the end of the tour it was Keith—not Twain—who was the star. Despite the disappointing public reaction to the album, it wasn't a total loss because rock producer John "Mutt" Lange was listening. He liked what he heard and called Mercury to get Twain's telephone number. After several phone conversations, they met for the first time in June at that year's Fan Fair, a yearly musical festival held in Nashville to promote country music artists. Mutt, who had grown up in his native South Africa listening to country music, suggested they collaborate on her next album for Mercury. That sounded like a great idea to Twain—and to the label executives who signed Mutt on as producer. But the singer and the producer collaborated on more than music and ended up getting married before work on the album was completed.

This time around, Mutt told Twain that, as her producer, he wanted to record only songs she'd written herself. He asked her to go through her catalog and select 10 songs she felt defined her as an artist. All of the songs she chose were keepers. Ironically, all of the songs had been submitted for her first album—and had been rejected as being unsuitable. Mutt wrote one song himself for the album, and Twain added a twelfth, a song fragment sung without accompaniment.

When the album was turned in, label executives were stunned. First, they'd previously turned down the songs. Second, the album didn't sound like anything else on the country market. It was an upbeat, instrumentally potent collection of songs that expressed a fresh approach to country music. Lewis knew it was special, but was it too special? He asked for confirmation from the Mercury staff that his gut instinct was right. Neese knew in her heart it was a hit album.

The first problem was what to name the album. Twain recalls: "Mutt and I went through everything possible for the title. Then Sandy came out one day and said, '*The Woman In Me* should be the one.' Just the way she said it, I said, 'Yep, that's it.'"

"Whose Bed Have Your Boots Been Under?" was the first single released from *The Woman In Me*. Radio wasn't sure what to do with the album. It was an upbeat, aggressive record that had a female narrator telling her unfaithful man to hit the road. "So the next time you're lonely, don't call on me," sang Twain. "Try the operator. Maybe she'll be free." It was a far cry from Tammy Wynette urging women to stand by their man.

"We really had a struggle with that first single," recalls Neese. "Radio didn't want to play it. It was too pop. It was too this, too that. Luke went back and pounded week after week on the promotion department. 'I know this is a hit. I know we've got something phenomenal going here.' He wouldn't let go. So what we finally did, we went to, oh, I don't know, maybe six stations, who had given [Twain] some support on her first album and talked them into airing it enough to get reaction from the listeners. When the phones started blowing off the wall, then that's when they woke up and listened."

Those callers, for the most part, were women.

Unknown to Twain, the "good ole girl" network fell in behind *The Woman In Me*. If there was one album that could rally the troops, it was *The Woman In Me*. Behind the scenes, women worked hard to make the album a success. Their hopes were riding high with Twain's own hopes.

Soon it became clear that the success of the album was due to female record buyers. Promotions targeted that audience like never before. Twain didn't want to do a concert tour to promote the album because she felt she didn't have enough songs under her belt to merit a full-scale concert performance. Instead, she performed on television and focused on the media, doing hundreds of interviews. In a throwback to pop star Tiffany's wildly successful mall tour in the late 1980s, Twain did appearances at malls where large numbers of women could be expected to gather. For example, at the Mall of America in Minneapolis, more than 10,000 fans gathered to meet her. She didn't sing. She simply appeared.

The success of *The Woman In Me* was a dream come true for Twain, but for women in the music industry it was one of the early warning shots fired in the quiet revolution taking place in American music. By September 1995, *The Woman In Me* had peaked at Number 6 on the pop charts, putting her in the same company as hitmakers Alanis Morissette and Natalie Merchant. By 1996, *The Woman In Me* had sold more than 12 million copies, making it the biggest selling album by a female country artist, ever.

The revolution was underway.

1996: ROCK'S BERLIN WALL FALLS

1996 was a landmark year. It was the year female solo artists out-charted their male counterparts on the Top 20 charts for the first time in history.

[Top 20 charts are compiled from a national sample of retail store and rack sales, and are representative of what the public is buying. Other charts, such as the Top 100 Singles and the Top 40 airplay chart aren't based on sales. They're based on the individual songs that program directors decide to air. Since the vast majority of program directors in the United States are male, the songs they select for airplay are indicative of their individual interests and have very little correlation to what the public is actually purchasing in retail outlets. (I've never put much credence in airplay charts since, historically speaking, they've been the charts most susceptible to payola-minded record companies and unscrupulous managers.) Airplay charts, then, reflect what male program directors are playing, and sales charts reflect what people are buying.]

Not in any year since the modern era began (defined as July 4, 1954, the year Elvis Presley made his first recordings) had more women than men charted on the Top 20. In most years, male solo artists composed about 75 percent of the total. For nearly four decades, female artists had almost been an afterthought for record companies and radio program directors.

The numbers speak for themselves. For example, from 1954 to 1959, women could take credit for only 29 percent of the Top 20 hits. Only three women—Kay Starr, Gogi Grant, and actress Debbie Reynolds—scored Number 1 hits. Actually, that early showing by women during what is today considered an ultraconservative period would remain the strongest for women for more than 20 years. During the next two decades, women would make their worst showing of the modern era despite the reputation of the 1960s and 1970s as liberal, freewheeling, drug-and-sexual experimentation eras of feminist self-fulfillment.

In truth, the 1960s and 1970s were disastrous years for female recording artists. All the talk about advancement for women was just that, talk. From 1960 to 1969, only 71 women made the Top 20, compared to 221 men. That gave the men a 76 percent to 24 percent edge over the women. The next decade was even worse. From 1970 to 1979, 62 women made the Top 20, but so did 208 men, giving them 77 percent of the total. Not until the 1980s did the charts reflect a trend in favor of the women. From 1980 to 1989, 73 women, or 31 percent of the total, made the charts. It was the best decade ever for women, but 31 percent hardly seemed like a victorious number. An analysis of the chart positions from 1954 to 1989, based on gender, leads to only one possible interpretation: American popular music was the sole preserve of male recording artists.

All that changed—forever, some say—in 1996. When the dust had settled on 1996 record sales, chart totals showed that of the 23 solo artists who made the Top 20, 14 were women.* That gave the women a 61 percent to 39 percent margin over their male counterparts. The women who made the 1996 "honor roll" included:

- Tori Amos
- Toni Braxton
- Mariah Carey
- Tracy Chapman
- Sheryl Crow
- Celine Dion
- Janet Jackson
- Madonna
- Natalie Merchant
- Alanis Morissette
- Joan Osborne
- Leann Rimes
- Wynonna

The two women most dominant on the charts for the entire year were Canadians Shania Twain and Alanis Morissette. Their music was similar in that both expressed more aggressive viewpoints toward males than had previously been acceptable for the pop charts. Their music was dissimilar in that Twain was playful, almost teasing, in her approach, while Morissette seemed to struggle to contain her rage toward the opposite sex.

The male list was notable in that of the nine men who made the Top 20, five—Garth Brooks, Vince Gill, Alan Jackson, Tim McGraw, and George Strait—were country artists (considered gender-friendly by female CD buyers) and only one—Sting—came close to fitting the traditional male pop/rocker mold. Simply put, 1996 was the worst showing ever for traditional male pop/rock recording artists. All year, only one male pop/rocker was able to crack the Top 20. For women, this was the musical equivalent of the crumbling of the Berlin Wall. The obvious questions are: What happened? and Why?

WOMEN NEVER WIN

When Kathy Mattea was invited to be a contestant on the television show "Celebrity Jeopardy," she jumped at the chance. How many country singers had been on this successful television show? None that she could think of. Being on the show isn't exactly analogous to winning the Nobel Prize for physics, but it is a popular program, and its question-and-answer format can be intimidating to those unable to think on their feet.

---

* The "solo artist" charts compiled for this book include, as one entry, male groups, such as the Temptations, and female groups, such as the Bangles and the Supremes. Not included as solo artists are such groups as the Beatles and the Rolling Stones. I based my decision to include a group in chart figures on whether all members performed as vocalists and whether the group existed as a backup vehicle for the vocalist. For example, I classify Tom Petty & the Heartbreakers as a solo act, but not Metallica.

Kathy Mattea

Tena Clark

In country music circles, Mattea is known as one of the "smart ones." When she's performing, the Grammy-winning singer doesn't make fun of those parts of her anatomy that are different from those of males. She doesn't sing songs that put women in unflattering or submissive positions. And she doesn't go for the cheap shots. She is a thoughtful, introspective "folkie" who is drawn to music that possesses a semblance of intellectual or legitimate emotional content.

In her own gentle, soft-spoken way, Mattea kicked ass on "Celebrity Jeopardy." "I won my day and at the end of the day I was close to having one of the top three scores for the week and having to come back and do the Friday afternoon show—but I didn't quite make it," says Mattea.

After the show, three women ran up to Mattea in the studio. "We work in the sound booth," they said. "My gosh, we were so excited when you won. Women never win!"

Mattea was stunned. "'Women never win!'" "It was like, 'You made us look good girl,'" she says. "I realized then that no one had told me to bring a change of clothes in case I won because no one in a million years thought I would win because I was female and because I was a country music singer. It never occurred to me that someone would not think I was smart because I was the whiz kid in my family."

THE MUSIC/GENDER CONNECTION

Tena Clark's parents raised her to believe she could do anything she wanted to do. She was never told there were things girls simply didn't do. At an early age, she developed a taste for rhythm and blues, the music that seemed to ooze in plentiful amounts from the red-clay hillsides and bottom-land bayous of her native Mississippi. By the age of 14, she was writing songs and producing them herself in the low-tech studios that would allow her inside. No one told her music was for guys. It just never occurred to her that music had any connection with gender. Not, that is, until she moved to Los Angeles and became one of the most successful female producers and R & B songwriters in the country, scoring hits in the 1980s and 1990s with Patti LaBelle, Dionne Warwick, Vesta Williams, and Gladys Knight.

One day Clark was ushered into a male record executive's office, and the door was shut behind them. The gesture concerned her because in the music business a closed door is never good news. The executive was a vice president in charge of A & R; he was responsible for signing new acts and overseeing production of their records. In addition, he had final approval over the choice of producers and songwriters. Once the door to the office was closed, he got right to the point. "Tena, you are pissing a lot of guys off," he said. "What do you mean?" she answered. "Look, you're white, you're female, and you're from the South," he said. "You're taking their gigs, and it's not sitting real well." Clark couldn't believe what she was hearing. It left her speechless. All she could manage was a lame "What?" It was issued more as a stutter than a question. "You've got to think about it," he said.

Clark was thinking about it. It was a shock to her that being a white, female refugee from Mississippi would piss off anyone. With all the truly bad things happening in the world, was it possible that being a white female from the South would be enough to land someone on an enemies' list? This was 1991, for heaven's sake! "I get a lot of flack for hiring you," the A & R executive continued. Then he paused, a smile inching across his face. "But you know what I think? I think you're the shits, and I don't care what they say."

Joining the Club

In 1990, *Ladies' Home Journal* saluted Frances Preston as one of the 50 most powerful women in America. Nearly a decade earlier, *Esquire* magazine had called her one of the most powerful people in the music business. Today, many consider her to be the most powerful female corporate executive in the country. As president of Broadcast Music, Inc. (BMI), she oversees a vast worldwide empire that is one of the financial bedrocks of the music industry. BMI is one of three licensing organizations—the other two being American Society of Composers, Authors and Publishers (ASCAP) and SESAC—that control hundreds of millions of dollars in royalty payments collected annually for songwriters.

As chief executive officer of the largest of the three agencies, Preston oversees plush offices in New York and Nashville. Although it is possible to become successful in the music business without having your name cross her desk, it isn't very likely. But as influential as she is today, it wasn't always that way.

Once, back in the 1960s, guitarist Chet Atkins invited Preston to attend a meeting at the Nashville Cumberland Club. The meeting was called to discuss ways of raising money for a local charity. The Cumberland Club is what was once known as a "gentleman's club." Today, that phrase conjures up visions of topless dancers and smoke-filled rooms. Back then, it was descriptive of a more genteel, all-male gathering place where executives and power-brokers could meet in private and discuss the problems of the day.

Women were banned from the club in most instances, but when it was necessary for them to enter the building for important meetings, a special room was designated for integrated events. Women were expected to obey two rules.

First, they were to enter the club from the back stairs, where the room set aside for integrated functions was located. Second, they were expected not to walk across the dining room floor under any circumstances.

Preston arrived at the Cumberland Club at the appointed time and dutifully made her way up the back staircase. Unfortunately, Atkins had forgotten to make reservations for the integrated meeting room, and the group was seated in a regular room on the other side of the dining hall. Preston was stopped at the door and forbidden entrance to the dining hall. She ended up missing the entire meeting.

Preston relates the tale, not with a tinge of bitterness, but with a glint in her eye. After she tells the story from behind a massive desk decorated with all the expensive trappings of success in the music business, she smiles. Thirty years have passed. All is forgiven, but not necessarily forgotten. "Yesterday I received an invitation to join the Cumberland Club," she says, sweeping her hand across the top of her desk in the direction of a trash can.

© JAMES DICKERSON

Frances Preston

JUMPING OVER HURDLES

The issues facing women in the music industry today are no different than in any other area of the economy: job discrimination, sexual harassment, creative belittlement, and myriad forms of more subtle intimidation. Not all women run into these hurdles. Many have, though, and despite the successes of the Frances Prestons, Kathy Matteas, Tena Clarks, and others, the struggle for equality is far from over. In some ways, it has just begun.

The music industry has a horrendous track record on gender equity. For decades, women have been asked to trade sex for record contracts, songwriting deals, private secretary jobs, entry-level positions at record labels—you name it, and women have been asked to put out to get it. The familiar line is, "If you don't want to put out to be a star, then you must not want to be a star bad enough to do what it takes." In some instances, women have even instigated the notion of a trade. For some women, the prospect of spending a few nights in the sack with an asthmatic old geezer seems a fair trade for potential stardom and all the financial trappings of success. Those women are in the minority.

It is hard to imagine what the music industry would be like today if the situation had been reversed. Suppose male wannabes had been told that stardom—or even an ordinary career—required them to strip, bend over, spread out, and otherwise "be nice" to certain people in the business. Most men would have a difficult time even imagining a work environment like that, much less submitting to one. They would probably find the suggestion itself laughable.

Not laughing are the many women who have fought back in recent years with sexual-harassment lawsuits and public accusations of wrongdoing in the workplace. Penny Muck, a secretary whose 1991 lawsuit against Geffen Records brought national attention to the issue of sexual harassment in the music industry, received an estimated half million dollars in an out-of-court settlement with the record label. At the time the alleged wrongdoing took place, Geffen Records was an industry leader, with a roster of "bad boy" acts, such as Guns N' Roses and Aerosmith.

In Muck's lawsuit, she alleged that her boss, a high-ranking, male general manager, masturbated in front of her over a two-month period, forced her to touch his penis, fondled her breasts and buttocks, and once jammed her face into his crotch. "I couldn't believe it," Muck told *The Los Angeles Times*. "All of a sudden, he just starts doing it [masturbating in front of her]. He's got this crazy look in his eyes . . . and he's saying, 'Watch me! Watch me!' . . . After he ejaculated, it was so weird. Like something out of *Dr. Jekyll & Mr. Hyde*. He just walks back into his office, and it's like business as usual. As if nothing ever happened. I thought to myself, 'Right, like who's going to believe this?'"

Former Geffen promotions director Christina Anthony believed it. After Muck's allegations became public knowledge, Anthony gave an interview to *The Los Angeles Times* in which she alleged that the same executive who had harassed Muck also had harassed her during her time of employment at Geffen between 1984 and 1990: "I was sexually harassed, intimidated and terrorized. . . . I personally told three top executives under David Geffen of the abuse and nothing was done about it. . . . In order to maintain my self-esteem as a professional, I was forced to resign."

Muck's allegations sent a shock wave through the industry. Boardrooms were suddenly filled with analyses of "The Problem" and proposals to protect the corporate purse. Of course, what had happened at Geffen Records was less a product of corporate management than it was a product of the industry. Wasn't rock 'n' roll supposed to be the voice of repressed, adolescent sexual fantasies? Weren't all rock 'n' roll acts, male and female, selling sex appeal as much as they were selling actual music? Hadn't rock 'n' roll "stars" occasionally masturbated in public during concerts to express their sexuality and their disdain of the uptight, straight "system?" Had rock 'n' roll become its own worst enemy?

Of course, Geffen Records wasn't the only offender, and there was no evidence that the offenses reported by Muck and Anthony were indicative of a corporate policy. On the contrary, one month before Anthony left Geffen, she handpicked her successor. Her choice was Claire Parr, a hotshot promotions person who recently had been given the pink slip from Enigma Records.

"One day I got a call from a friend who said, 'Don't take that job at Geffen until you talk to me,'" recalls Parr. "I said, 'What job at Geffen?' In half an hour I got a phone call from a woman who said she'd like me to come to work tomorrow. Her name was Christina Anthony. I had met her at record conventions, but I didn't really know her very well. She said she had a person on maternity leave in adult contemporary promotions and wanted me to take that position temporarily. I didn't know Christina was leaving Geffen. She brought me into that position as her replacement and so about a month after I came in, she resigned, and I found myself the director of promotions for Geffen without ever going through the normal biting and scratching. Christina was my guardian angel."

Despite Anthony's stated anger over her treatment at Geffen, she apparently didn't blame the company, otherwise she wouldn't have been so conscientious in finding a replacement for herself. Whether because of the negative publicity or because the alleged harassment was due to that one executive, Parr never reported any similar problems at Geffen. By the late 1990s, she'd moved on to Curb Records, where she became a vice president in charge of the pop and Christian divisions.

As word of the Muck case spread, other lawsuits emerged. A secretary at Warner Brothers Records filed a complaint against her male boss. By the mid-1990s, what had once been one of the industry's darkest secrets suddenly became its most widely discussed problem. "I'm afraid to let a woman come into my office alone," confided a high-ranking male executive with Columbia Records. "It's just not worth the risk."

BMI's Frances Preston is among those who worry about a backlash. "There are too many people who sit around reading books on how to sue for sexual harassment and try to create such a situation," says Preston. "It is hard to believe that people do that, but they do, and it ruins it for people who have real cases for sexual harassment. With some people, it's, 'He screamed at me!' or 'He said I was a high school dropout.' They say that to men, too. There are a lot of women who try to sue for harassment, and they do it on the basis of 'He screams at me.' No one should scream at anyone, but sometimes people do lose their cool, and you have to, in a way, say, 'Well, he had a bad day.' And if someone makes the statement, 'Were you a high school dropout?' that could be said to a man, too. When you work with people, you see them more than they see their families sometimes, and sometimes they have bad days. But that doesn't mean they are out to harass you. They didn't say that morning, 'I'm going to harass this woman to death.' Plus, you can create a lot of [problems for] yourself. I've seen some girls in our business who have invited it. If you go to work in a halter top and a skirt that barely covers your panties, I'm sorry—you have invited it. You just don't go to work that way."

Beating the "Big Boy" Network

Debe Fennell is a marketing executive who has had experience in most areas of the music business. She has worked as an editor with *Radio & Records* magazine, a booking agent, an assistant to singer Randy Travis, as well as in the promotions departments of Curb Records, Magnatone, and BNA Records. Sexual harassment is a way of life at some businesses, she says, adding that she was abused physically and verbally at one record label. "[My boss] was always touching people," she says. "I was on the phone talking to a radio station, and he wanted to talk to me and he took the phone out of my hand and slammed it down. Another time, he grabbed my boobs. That only happened twice. The second time, I grabbed him back. It scared the hell out of him. He got the message . . . but I got squeezed out of my job.

"Two weeks after I left, I was at a music seminar, and he walks up and says, 'Well, there's one good thing that came out of this, Debe.' I said, 'What's that?' He said, 'We can see each other socially now.' I said, 'After a bad dream,' and I walked away. I could have sued the record label, but I wanted to continue working in this business."

Fennell thinks progress has been made in recent years, but she feels it has been slow developing. "There are lots of women succeeding," she says. "How they do it is another matter. But you can find that in any walk of life. If you weigh everything out, women are gaining. Does the "good ole boy" network still do the glass ceiling thing? Yes. Do they gang up on women? Yes. Is it inequitable? Yes. Am I going to change it? No. . . . In every situation I have been working in for a record label, the guys in charge have always been looking over their shoulder, going, 'God, she's aggressive.' And I'm saying, 'You'd better watch out. I want your job.' It makes them nervous, and they will do whatever. It is the survival of the fittest. It took me a while to figure that out."

There is no question that unscrupulous men in the music business have preyed on women, but for every woman who has been, there are others who haven't. Is it the luck of the draw, or is it something the women themselves do to forestall potential trouble? Country singer Terri Clark is a tall, willowy woman who wears cowboys hats and T-shirts with the sleeves rolled up to reveal lean, well-defined biceps. As a woman, she has striking facial features and a warm, conversational manner that smacks of big-time femininity. As an entertainer, she has a reputation for aggressive, ass-kicking, foot-stomping performances that smack of no-nonsense in the first degree.

Clark is among those who have never encountered sexual harassment. "I've been lucky in that I never had the casting couch thing happen to me," she says. "I've never had anyone get out of line, not people that I've been professionally involved with—and that's nice to know. They see talent and they hope to cash in on it, and they're not going to screw it up. I think, being a female, you have to be on the lookout for things like that. It is a man's world, and sometimes you have to act like a man to be taken seriously. And I don't mean that in a negative way. I mean it in a confident, aggressive way. You have to come across that way . . . a lot of it is how you carry yourself and your attitude. You've got to come across like you mean business. It's important that you maintain that male attitude in the way you go about it."

The problems women have encountered over the years haven't all been of a sexual nature, nor have they been confined to the creative side of the industry. Liz Gregory owns her own concert-promotions agency that concentrates on large public events, such as county fairs. She started doing that type of work 15 years ago while living in Oregon. "When I started, it was tough," she says. "The men tried to run me out of the business. I've had them tell stories about me and not take me seriously." By the late 1990s, attitudes had changed, she says, but she felt it was still "a man's world."

One way to get around that, says Fennell, is to fight fire with fire. "As you get older, you learn what battles to fight and which ones not to fight," she says. "There is a group of us women who a few years back decided to form a 'good ole girl' network—and we're not the only ones [to do that]. It was very loose. A tacit agreement we wouldn't hurt each other. If you can't beat them, emulate them."

MARKETING STRATEGIES IN THE MUSIC INDUSTRY

A plan was afoot from the beginning of the modern era. Before the mid-1950s, women had enjoyed modest success with blues and jazz, and as frontispieces for big bands of the swing era. Hollywood movies gave women another outlet. But despite the emergence of high-profile women during the first half of the century—Billie Holliday, Alberta Hunter, Judy Garland, and others—their cut of the financial pie was minuscule compared to the generous helping dished out to male competitors.

Gender-based statistics for the first half of the twentieth century are scant, but in 1980 two academic researchers, Peter Hesbacher and Bruce Anderson, did a gender-focused survey, the results of which were published in *Popular Music and Society*. The researchers' analysis of *Billboard*'s popularity charts for the period of 1940 to 1958 found that female solo artists made up 30 percent of the total Number 1 hits during that period. In *All of This Music Belongs to the Nation*, Kenneth J. Bindas looked at the gender breakdowns for the Federal Music Project of the Works Progress Administration (WPA) in the 1930s. He found that the project, which hired musicians, conductors, and composers, never gave women more than 16 percent of the positions available. To summarize attitudes toward women in music for that time period, Bindas chose an article from *Etude* magazine titled "What Great Music Owes to Women." The article concludes that "behind every great male composer a woman contributed to his art by being his lover, friend, cook, and maidservant."

For most of the first half of the twentieth century, music was viewed as a basically female domain. For every male achieving success as a composer or instrumentalist, hundreds of women were teaching music in low paying jobs. Male music teachers often were perceived to be gender confused. Public perceptions about music didn't begin to change until the 1940s. Frank Sinatra and Bing Crosby were, to a large degree, responsible for that; they demonstrated that there was big money in music. Crosby didn't generate the large crowds of enthusiastic females that Sinatra did, but he transformed his stylized crooning into a multimillion-dollar movie career. So did Sinatra, who was probably the first sex symbol associated with popular music.

Watching with great interest was a man who would transform the music industry with his theory of gender-based marketing. Tom Parker, who would later pick up the honorary title of "Colonel" from a Louisiana governor, took the Crosby-Sinatra phenomenon and bumped its threshold up several notches with an unknown, Mississippi-born truck driver named Elvis Presley. No one knows for certain the gender breakdown for record sales before the modern era, but for the nearly half century since Presley topped the charts with "Heartbreak Hotel," women have purchased most of the records, cassettes, and CDs.

The enormously successful marketing theory that Parker and executives at RCA Records developed was based on selling Presley's sex appeal to female record buyers, and selling the music's content to male record buyers. With the exception of such ballads as "Love Me Tender," women couldn't identify anything in the lyrical content of Presley's songs. What they could identify with was the way he looked and the way he moved on stage. It is interesting that a woman, Mae Axton, wrote "Heartbreak Hotel," his first Number 1 hit for RCA. For the most part, male record buyers identified with the aggressive testosterone rhythms of the music and lyrics that often made fun of women or, at the very least, put them in their place.

For 40 years, that philosophy dominated the music industry. Women purchased most of the music, but men pulled the behind-the-scenes strings that determined what they were offered. This formula—good-looking men with songs that offered tough love to women—was never seriously challenged until the 1980s, when Madonna used rebellious sex appeal and strong lyrics to build a predominantly female audience. Even so, Madonna's sex appeal was based on what men wanted to see in women. She was rebellious, but in a way that expressed male sexual fantasies about women.

It was a bold departure, but it wasn't the stuff of which revolutions are made. To actualize the revolution, female artists who could flip the Parker-RCA strategy and use the same marketing dynamics to their advantage were needed. All the pieces didn't fall into place until 1996. By then, there was no shortage of women in executive positions at the record labels. Women had been filling those positions at a steady pace for the past decade.

The Revolution's Leaders

The women who won the battles of 1996 had two things in common: they had sex appeal that was directed at men, and they sang songs that had content with which women could identify. Just take a look at the revolution's chart leaders: Shania Twain, Mariah Carey, Toni Braxton, Sheryl Crow, Janet Jackson, Alanis Morissette, and Madonna. All are Elvis-like in the hormonal appeal they make to men. All connect with women with messages that address ordinary life.

Alanis Morissette

Of the 14 women who made the Top 20 charts in 1996, Morissette probably delivered the deadliest punch to the male dynasty. She seemed like an unlikely sexual warrior. Small, fashionably thin, and soft-spoken in conversation, the 20-year-old downplayed her looks and consciously tried to develop an air of intellectual curiosity. The farther she went down that road, the more interested male record buyers became. The lyrics of her songs are most unflattering to men. Often they bristle with hostility—sometimes with a curious blend of sex and hostility. "I hate to bug you in the middle of dinner," Morissette sings in "You Oughta Know." "It was a slap in the face how quickly I was replaced. Are you thinking of me when you fuck her?" Then in "Right Through You," she sings: "You took me out to wine dine 69 me/But didn't hear a damn word I said."

In 1995, Morissette mentioned to a writer for *Rolling Stone* magazine that she'd been told she didn't look like her songs. "People expect me to have purple hair and a pierced nose and boobs. Then they meet me, and I'm just . . . me. I hate to let anyone down, but I'm not the cleavage sort of aesthetic babe." The more outraged Morissette became in her lyrics, the more women flocked to her. That outrage had a similar effect on men. The tougher she talked, the more they wanted her. Those same men who could never figure out how "nice girls" could take up with gangsters and "bad boys" were being given an insight into that attraction, only in reverse. Men were figuring out something women have known for centuries. Sex with successful people has an added edge. Throughout the 1990s, men were discovering that sex with successful women, even if they were "bad girls," or at least talked like "bad girls," was superior to sex with stay-at-home, submissive sunflowers. Men bought Morissette's CD for the same reason women bought Presley's albums: they wanted to have sex with her. Women bought her album because her message struck a familiar chord.

Unlike Shania Twain, the other flagbearer for the revolution, Morissette didn't have a female manager. She also didn't come under the guidance of a female producer. Males oversaw both her career and her music, thereby opening her up to criticisms that she wasn't a true flagbearer and was merely going through the motions of a career that was the male expression of what was thought to be a feminine identity. What Morissette did have that worked to her advantage was a savvy record company owned and operated by women.

CHAPTER TWO

THE WOMEN BEHIND THE SCENES

The women who captured the charts and hearts of America in 1996 were all media-savvy entertainers who understood that imagery, whether expressed in print photos or on television, was critical to their success. Their images, sometimes haunting, sometimes seductive, sometimes daring, were splashed across the media until they were recognizable by consumers who would get to know them even if they did not get to know their music. Stardom is a measurement of what the public perceives, not what the artist offers. Stardom is always in the eyes of the beholder.

While the public is familiar with the names and faces of the women who made history in 1996—and will, in time, come to define the revolution in terms of the women who made the charts—they are less familiar with the women in the trenches who made the revolution possible. Was it a fluke that women outsold their male competitors in 1996 for the first time in history? Was it some sort of gender-based fate? Was it luck? Or was it something else entirely?

If you examine the bigger picture, you'll find it hard to escape the conclusion that the revolution of 1996 was the inevitable byproduct of a lot of ambitious, goal-directed women who had been working for years behind the scenes of the music industry. For every female recording artist who scored in the Top 20, other invisible, unheralded women were developing strategies and pulling strings, all harmonizing to chants of, "Go, girl, go!"

PIONEERING FEMALE EXECUTIVES

To borrow from President Bill Clinton's 1992 campaign slogan, "It's the song, stupid"—that is where you find the real money in the music business. With that in mind, it is useful to look at the gatekeepers of the song-publishing industry and at the music-licensing organizations that control the collection and distribution of the largest single piece of the economic pie. Two of the largest, most influential publishers are Sony Tree Publishing and Nashville/Screen Gems—EMI. Women head up both companies, Donna Hilley at Sony Tree and Celia Froehlig at Screen Gems.

As the "banks" of the music industry, BMI, ASCAP, and SESAC control hundreds of millions of dollars a year, which gives them concentrated power over the livelihoods of thousands of songwriters who are the foundation of the music industry. All three music-licensing organizations have female division heads: Frances Preston at BMI, Connie Bradley at the Nashville office of ASCAP, and C. Dianne Petty at SESAC.

Of the three, Preston probably exerts the most power; if there is a "godmother" in the music industry, it is she. That power is derived as much from her own accomplishments and personality as from the organization she directs.

Preston is a woman with a past. She began her career in 1950 at radio station WSM in Nashville. WSM was best known for its Saturday broadcasts of the Grand Ole Opry, which had premiered at the station 25 years before Preston started working there as the receptionist. WSM was an NBC affiliate, and despite its reputation as the home of the Opry, the bulk of its programming was popular and classical music. In addition to broadcasting the Opry, WSM fed several programs each week to NBC. One was a big orchestra show called "Sunday Down South" that featured such vocalists as Dinah Shore and Snooky Langston, who later went on to find national success. A morning show featured Nashville Music Row founder Owen Bradley and his orchestra with vocalist Dottie Dillard (Bradley is the father-in-law of Preston's ASCAP competitor, Connie Bradley). Preston's introduction to the music business at WSM was an eye-opener. "Those were days when song pluggers came down from New York to plug their songs, but none of them were women," she says. "The days of radio and no women executives . . . at that time, if you were a woman, you could be a clerk in a department store, you could be a nurse, a telephone operator, a secretary—that's basically it. You were very limited because you were expected to get married and raise a family. When I got married and didn't stop work to rear my children, it was quite controversial."

In 1952, the station decided to celebrate the Opry's birthday by inviting other country music broadcasters to Nashville to participate in a week-long convention; that convention became what is today called "Country Music Week." The following year, BMI decided to use the occasion to give awards to its songwriters. Preston's intelligence and organizational abilities so impressed the New York executives that they offered her a job in 1955 coordinating a BMI branch in Nashville. For two years, she worked out of her home. Then in 1958, BMI opened an office in Nashville and put her in charge. Seven years later, she was promoted to vice president, making her the first female corporate executive in Tennessee. In 1986, Preston was made president of BMI's worldwide operations. "BMI, I must say, was one of the few major music companies that really believed in women.The gentleman who hired me, Judge Robert Burton, was president of BMI for a while and he had more women executives than any company ever dreamed of having in the music industry. He just had a lot of faith in women executives," she says.

Today, Preston looks back over a career that spans nearly five decades with a mixture of awe and pride. "I never felt like a pioneer of any kind; I was never a flag waver," she says, seated behind her desk in the new BMI building in Nashville. Her top-floor office offers a spectacular view of the city's skyline. Preston has an air of authority about her; spend a few minutes talking to her and you realize that she is a woman who knows how to get things done. But

Frances Preston and Gloria Estefan

she is, at the same time, disarmingly gracious and solicitous of others' opinions. If you worked for her, you would have no doubt that she would fire you in a heartbeat if firing was what you needed—but you also would know she would do it with compassion and great style.

"Yes, I am for equal pay," she continues. "Women's rights. But I always felt there were a lot of people who ruined what women's rights stood for because they had the wrong idea about what an executive position was. In other words, they get off on things like 'Don't pour coffee.' . . . I pour coffee for all our meetings. We meet in my office; I get up and pour the coffee. They have the idea that you walk out of the building at 5 o'clock. I never leave the office at 5 o'clock. Usually, I'm the last one to leave. It was that way my whole career. My father taught me to expect not to be treated any differently than a male. When I go into a room for a business, I don't expect every man to stand up."

Throughout the socially turbulent 1960s, Preston was responsible for the entire southern region of the country. Her job required her to travel throughout the South to meet with BMI-affiliated songwriters and to sign up new songwriters. Musically, it was an exciting time. Southern rock, and rhythm and blues were exploding all over the charts. But it was also a troublesome time in that racial integration was still a source of strife. Preston's job was to meet with songwriters, no matter the color of their skin; as a very attractive white woman, she became an easy target for racists who didn't approve of racially mixed conversations.

On one occasion, Preston went to Memphis to meet with Phineas Newborn, one of her newest composers. Newborn was an enormously talented jazz composer and pianist. He was a good catch for BMI. The only problem was that he was an African American. Meeting with him presented a dilemma for Preston. BMI didn't have an office in Memphis, nor did Newborn have an office where they could meet. They couldn't meet in a restaurant or coffee shop because blacks were prohibited from entering public facilities used by whites.

Preston recalls: "I was staying at the Peabody Hotel, so I thought, 'What's wrong with meeting him in the lobby of the hotel?' So we were sitting there, papers were spread out and we were signing contracts, and the manager came over." He said, 'Get that [nigger] out of the hotel.' "I said, 'Excuse me. We're just sitting here signing some papers.' "He said, 'I said get that [nigger] out of this hotel.' Then he looks at Phineas and said, '[Nigger] you know better than to be in this hotel lobby. Get out of here.'" Phineas was embarrassed to death, and I just wanted to die." The hotel manager turned his attention back to Preston, his face reflecting the disdain he felt for what he obviously perceived to be a fallen white woman, a disgrace to his race. "Are you staying in this hotel?" he demanded. "Yes." "Okay, get your bags, and get out. We don't want your kind in this hotel."

As Preston was going out the door, she had the last word. "You'll regret this," she said over her shoulder. When she returned to Nashville, she called that city's most powerful resident, Governor Bob Clement, who happened to be a close friend. Then she called her father, who was a proud Rotarian; he, in turn, called the higher-ups in that organization. Overnight, an ugly racial incident was transformed into a cause for the governor's office and, of all people, the Rotarians. "We got that guy fired," she says proudly. "Not only did I have to go through the 'woman' bit, I had to go through the racial bit. Between the two combined, I was always on a crusade."

The Memphis incident is revealing because it provides insight into why Preston was able to become a top-ranked executive. She isn't an ideological purist. When she encountered the problem at the hotel, she didn't go to the National Association for the Advancement of Colored People (NAACP) or to individuals in the state who had reputations for backing liberal causes. She went to a conservative, white governor and an organization that had a history of racial and sex-based exclusion. Preston knew that if she wanted a problem fixed, she had to appeal to individuals who had the power to bring about change. In this instance, her problem-solving instincts were right on target. The payback to the Rotarians was that she became their first female member once they opened their doors to women. Later, she became the first professional woman to be accepted into the Friars Club; the only other female members were entertainers Liza Minnelli and Nancy Sinatra.

Pioneering Record-Company Executives

Until the 1990s, executive positions for women at the heart and soul of the music industry—the record labels—were a rarity. For nearly 40 years, the only way for a woman to become an executive at a record label was to buy her way into the position. In numerous instances, women have financed independent record labels, but with three notable exceptions those ventures were short-lived.

Estelle Axton, the co-founder of Stax Records, is the most successful female label owner to date, if hit records are used as a measurement of success. During the 1960s and early 1970s, Stax generated some of the most memorable soul music on the market. This small, Memphis-based label was an industry powerhouse, introducing impressive new talents, such as Otis Redding, Sam and Dave, Carla Thomas, and Booker T. & the MGs. The label was financially and creatively successful, primarily because it had the courage to integrate white and black musicians into projects that freed their talents from the restraints of racial segregation. Axton was eventually forced out of the label; not surprisingly, it didn't survive long without her. In 1976, she rebounded with a Number 1 hit, "Disco Duck," recorded by radio personality Rick Dees.

Estelle Axton

Following in Axton's footsteps was Marian Leighton, who in 1970 joined with two male partners, Ken Irwin and Bill Nowlin, to start up Rounder Records, an independent label that focused on bluegrass music. The three Boston-area students ran the label from their communal apartment, using the profits from one record to finance the next project. Eventually, their interests expanded from bluegrass to blues. In 1986, Leighton changed her name to Marian Levy when she married Roomful of Blues producer Ron Levy. Over the years, Rounder has been able to blend artistic success with such artists as Grammy-winning Alison Krauss, and financial success with such gold-record achievers as George Thorogood and the Destroyers. As of late 1997, Rounder remained one of the strongest and most successful independent labels in operation.

More recently, pop recording artist Madonna began a label of her own, Maverick Records. Ronnie Dashev, a female lawyer, runs the label; she is also its chief operating officer (COO) and general counsel. The label's future was cemented in 1995 and 1996 with the success of Alanis Morissette's landmark album, *Jagged Little Pill.* Ironically, Morissette completed the revolution Madonna began in the 1980s. It was as if Madonna ran out of steam or ambition or drive and sought a body double who could pick up where she'd left off. Surprisingly, Madonna has downplayed the success of the label while talking up its product, and Dashev has shunned the media, deliberately avoiding public recognition for her work.

The brightest new star on the horizon is Tracey Edmonds, the 30-year-old president and chief executive officer (CEO) of Yab Yum Entertainment. Her Yab Yum Records label is a joint venture with Sony Music, which has distribution rights to the records the label produces. Edmonds also owns her own music-publishing company and is co-owner, with her husband Kenny "Babyface" Edmonds, of a movie-production company, Edmonds Entertainment. Yab Yum Records came into being in 1994, but it already has an impressive R & B-based roster that includes two-time Grammy winner Jon B., Laurnea, Rotaw, and rapper Berchee.

Tracey Edmonds's entry into the music business was nontraditional to say the least. After graduation from Stanford University at age 20, with a degree in "psycho-biology," (she'd entered the university on scholarship at age of 16), she started up her own mortgage and real-estate company. Not until she met Babyface and they began dating did she develop an interest in the music business. Shortly after they married in 1992, Babyface decided to establish his own music company. As his wife, Tracey found herself fielding telephone calls from producers and A & R executives desperate for songs. Babyface couldn't write songs for everyone who requested them. So to fill that need, she created her own publishing company. That led to an offer from Sony to start up her own record label.

Tracey Edmonds

"Kenny has created opportunities for me in terms of working closely with me on my projects, but he has his own label, LaFace Records, and I have mine," says Edmonds. "I operate very independently of Kenny with my label, although sometimes Kenny might write a song for one of my artists, and some of my writers might write songs for some of his artists on LaFace Records."

This creative partnership led to the creation of Edmonds Entertainment, a movie company that secured production deals with 20th Century Television and Fox 2000, both divisions of 20th Century Fox. "Kenny and I made a deal that we would take turns doing the soundtracks for our movies," says Edmonds. "So we flipped a coin, and he won the first soundtrack." Their first film, *Soul Food,* was released in the fall of 1997; reviewing the soundtrack, *Entertainment Weekly* predicted that "with ingredients that include such platinum powerhouses as Blackstreet, Boyz II Men, Dru Hill, and Sean 'Puffy' Combs, it shouldn't be long before [the soundtrack] can boast 'millions served.'" Edmonds and her production team will do the soundtrack for the next movie, a remake of *The Idolmaker.*

Edmonds feels fortunate to have had Babyface's guidance as she entered the music business, but, even so, it wasn't as easy as it might appear. Sony made her an offer to head up a label, and then put up money to get the venture off the ground. But looking back on it, Edmonds wonders if she was given enough support to beat the odds. "One of the problems I have had has been surviving on the limited overhead budget that was allocated to me when I started the label," she says. "I have had to supplement my overhead money with money out of my own pocket. We had writers and producers who were already signed to our production company who were generating a lot of money for us and money that should have been profit for us on the production side. I had to put money into my record label so I could have proper funding to do what I needed to do."

The biggest problem facing women in the industry according to Edmonds is obtaining funding equal to what male entrepreneurs receive. "I talked to other [women] and that seems to be a persistent problem," she says. "Our funding tends to be a tenth or an eighth of what is given to male-headed record labels, and that makes it difficult because you need to staff it properly and that costs money. So you have to be very creative with nickels and dimes so you can accomplish what your male counterparts accomplish with a much larger budget. . . . It is almost like when I was given this company; it was looked at as a vanity deal. You know, 'Give her a couple of nickels to work with.' I really wasn't, as a female, given a fair chance. Things wouldn't have happened for me if I hadn't taken money out of my own pocket to supplement my budget."

More equitable treatment for females in finance is one area Edmonds thinks requires more work, but it isn't the only area in need of fine-tuning. "Women are sometimes spoken to in a condescending manner—and if a female makes a suggestion, it will go past people, where if a man makes the same suggestion, people will listen to him. Sometimes men get credit for a female's ideas," she says with a laugh. "I've seen that happen—and it's happened to me, where people credit my suggestion to someone who didn't make the suggestion. I think what needs to happen is that women should really stick together and be a support network for each other in this industry. This industry is very competitive. One of the things we need to do is once females get into positions of power, they should create positions for other females and not look at other females as competition."

The women who most influenced Edmonds and served as role models for her entry into the business were Sylvia Rhone, Atlantic Records's first female and African American label head, and Suzanne de Passe, Berry Gordy's right-hand woman at Motown Records and now a successful television producer. "Sylvia Rhone is one of the female black women in the industry who has opened doors for all of us," Edmonds says. "Suzanne de Passe is one of the early pioneers that I always looked up to, and we've had lunch a few times and shared experiences."

Record Label Executives

By late 1997, only two females were heading up major record labels: Sylvia Rhone at Atlantic in New York, and Sheila Shipley Biddy, the senior vice president and general manager of Decca Records in Nashville. They are the only two females ever to head up a major record label. Rhone is now the head of Elektra Entertainment, and her area of expertise is music. She is a behind-the-scenes player who avoids the spotlight and seldom returns calls from reporters. It might be that she is uncomfortable exerting a public persona, or it might be that she feels the corporate stakes are too high, that she has everything to lose and nothing to gain by becoming a more vocal spokesperson for female advancement in the industry.

Not so with Biddy. Accessible, thoughtful, and articulate, she is as comfortable dealing with the public as she is dealing with boardroom strategists. This might be because, like BMI's Frances Preston, Biddy came up through the ranks. At 45 years of age, she has done it all. More important, she has seen it all, good and bad. When she moved to Nashville in 1972 from Kentucky, she was married and had a 2-year-old son, but she had a dream of becoming a television journalist. Without a college degree, her prospects of entering that profession were practically nil; the closest she came was getting a job with a

Sheila Shipley Biddy

local television station tabulating election returns. During this time period, she heard about a receptionist job at Monument Records. She interviewed for the job—seven times. Each time she was turned down. Finally, after about 18 months of rejections, she was hired at 70 dollars a week. The job didn't turn out to be the glamorous introduction to show business she expected. "In those days, you were treated like a servant," she says. "I was told, 'You are nothing but a secretary. How dare you ask for anything this company does?' I was cursed at for pushing too hard when all I wanted was credit for what I did."

After three years at Monument, Biddy moved over to RCA Records in 1979, when the label was at its heyday under the leadership of Joe Galante. "I believe there are crossroads in your life," she says. "I stayed in the music business instead of following the dream I thought I wanted, and each crossroad after that led me in a different direction." Her job at RCA was similar to the one she had at Monument, but she knew she could do more than secretarial work. "I'd get so depressed," she recalls. "When I was driving home, I'd see a truck on the highway, and I would think, 'I can do that.' I'd think, 'I just can't go in there and be beat up again. I wasn't just a secretary. I was making calls to radio stations, and I was taking work home at night. I went in at eight and left at six or seven. I knew in my heart, I was more than just a secretary."

After five years at RCA, Biddy heard that MCA Records, under the direction of Jimmy Bowen, was restructuring and was looking for fresh, new talent. She made a few calls and landed an interview with Bowen himself. "I went in there all prepared to talk about my career, but Bowen did all the talking—his philosophy of music, things like that—and every once in a while he would throw me a question which I would answer, and then he would take off again. I thought, 'Well, I'm probably not going to get this job.' Then he said, 'Is there anything you want to ask me?' I said, 'Don't you want to know about my career, how I've handled certain situations?' He said, 'I've checked you out. I know all about you. You make me feel comfortable, and you'll make my artists feel comfortable.' Then he said, 'If you want this job, you've got it.' I thought, 'Wow!'"

Biddy's first job at MCA was as promotions manager. "All my male counterparts were betting I wouldn't last a year, but I was okay with that," she says. "They had a right to question that. You can't demand respect. You have to earn it." Soon, after piling up a string of Number 1 hits, she was made senior vice president of national promotions. She held this job for 10 years until she took over leadership of MCA-subsidiary Decca Records.

Biddy's experiences have influenced her approach to the music industry as a business, but not the way she views herself as a woman. She wears conservative dresses, which while feminine, don't detract from the authority of her position. She is an attractive woman, and she doesn't attempt to hide her good looks.

She has learned that she can be female and authoritative at the same time. As far as sexual harassment is concerned, she says, "You learn to either laugh it off or walk away." By that, she means she sees it as a game that has its own peculiar set of rules. "For those women better endowed than others, you don't go into work in a turtleneck and no jacket. You're asking for it. I came up [the corporate ladder] at a time when literally there were leers and jokes. It is still the same today. There comes a point where you have to draw the line. You can't help what they're thinking, but you can help how you react and how you encourage them. If a woman goes in as a businessperson with a business attitude and keeps it on the up and up, then no matter what happens, she'll come out unscathed.

"I was blessed in that I never had a bad, bad situation where I was in a corner and couldn't get away. I had a couple when I thought I wouldn't get out, but I did. I've counseled other woman about that. It's hard to be on the road with radio guys, and a lot of times you're taking them back to your car late at night or to your hotel. If you want to be successful, you just swallow your pride and go on. You say 'No thank you' and walk away.

"One time I had three breakers [hit records] at RCA and thought that was quite an accomplishment. It was the first time it had been done there. I had a guy say, 'Why don't you come down to my office tonight, and we'll celebrate and I'll thank you for your hard work?' I said, 'I'm looking for praise, not punishment.'"

A & R Executives

Industry insiders say Renee Bell has the best ear in the business. Since 1995, she has headed up the Arts and Repertoire (A & R) department of RCA Records in Nashville. Before that she held similar jobs at MCA Records and Capitol Records. Since all the female A & R executives at major labels—indeed, all the female A & R executives who have ever worked at the majors—can be counted on two hands, she is a member of a select group, one that has no history of role models for second- or third-generation guidance.

A & R was the next-to-last bastion of male domination in the music business, the last being production and engineering. The reason for A & R's supremacy is simple. While authority at a record label rests with the administrative head, the general manager, or the vice president in charge, the real power rests in the A & R department for that is where the future of the label is determined. A & R executives are the people who sign new artists, monitor the progress of the older artists already on the roster, and oversee what is recorded and by whom. At the beginning of the modern era, the position attracted a certain type of male; typically, he thought of himself as someone who was a little hipper

Renee Bell

than his neighbor, someone who liked to live on the edge. A & R executives were always paid well, but accompanying the paycheck and prestige were certain temptations. For example, if a man had a weakness for sex, dope, or gambling, he could rest assured that unscrupulous promoters and managers would enable him to indulge in these pleasures in plentiful amounts. Added to that were temptations to make money on the side by setting up secret production deals with recording artists who the A & R executive signed, with the executive as a "silent" partner. The long and short of it is that when critics bemoan the sleaze factor of the music business, they're primarily talking about A & R.

The women who have entered A & R in recent years—Renee Bell at RCA, Claire Parr at Curb, Kim Buie at Capitol, Susan Collins at Virgin, Margie Hunt at Sony, Jane Baintel and Laura Hill at Atlantic, Susan Levy at Capitol, Nancy Brennan at SBK Records, and Paige Levy at Warner—have had a significant impact by lowering the sleaze bar on that part of the industry, making it more difficult for the sleazemasters to weasel their way into the companies. It is difficult to know whether that has taken place because women have more integrity than men—and fewer addictive vices—or because women, if they are prone to vices, are accustomed to having them filled by men outside the realm of business. Whatever the reason, these women have injected a sense of professionalism and class into an area sorely in need of an image makeover.

Renee Bell has an energy level that has to be seen to be believed, as well as an incredible talent for hearing what is real in music. Decca's Sheila Shipley Biddy, who worked with Bell at MCA, says of her competitor, "When she said, 'You better hear this,' you would rush to do it; she just has this passion for the song and the songwriter."

If you were to ask the 34-year-old Bell the best way to become an A & R executive, she would probably advise you to work on your good luck. You might say her career began in 1983 when she volunteered to help organize a party in Atlanta for recording artists Steve Wariner and Lee Greenwood. One of the guests was Emory Gordy, an independent producer and A & R executive with MCA Records. "I was more excited about him coming than any of the artists, though I really didn't even know what A & R was at that time—I just loved music," says Bell. "During the party, Emory and I went out to my car and listened to music, and he said I should work for MCA." Within a year, MCA label head Tony Brown hired Bell as a receptionist. Soon she was asked to screen songs, then to dabble in A & R; after she discovered a band named the Mavericks, she was made director of A & R.

"I've been lucky because my superiors haven't been chauvinistic males. I have never felt men were prejudiced against me because I am a woman," she says. "Women are used to working harder than men. We don't play golf, and if we do, we do it on the weekends because we would feel guilty doing it during the week. To get an edge [as a woman], you have to work three times as hard. If you are willing to do that you will get the respect of the men."

Ask Bell to speak in public, and she'll dance around the question, saying, "I'll really have to think about that—I don't like the way I sound." Ask about her success in A & R, and she'll look stunned that you think she is successful. She is as much in awe of the creative process as her peers are of her talent. "I'm still not sure I have an ear for music," she says with honest humility. "I just go with my gut feeling. I never really analyze anything. I never think about a song being rewritten. I either love it or I don't. Same thing with an artist. I would never take an artist and try to change them into something they're not—it's just a gut feeling I get."

Bell's most recent "gut feeling" came from newcomer Sara Evans. Bell asked for a meeting after listening to the singer's demo. They met for breakfast. "I could just see this thing, this sparkle in her eye," recalls Bell. "She gave me this new tape to listen to, and I couldn't wait to hear it. I played the tape [in my car], and by the time I got back to the office I was just dying. I called her manager, and two weeks later she came and played live for us. I swear, I was in tears. To me, the difference in an artist and a great singer is the artist is a great interpreter of the song. You can feel every word they sing. Bonnie Raitt does it. Celine Dion does it. When Sara was singing that day, I was about to cry—and I had never done that before."

Nancy Brennan, an A & R executive with SBK Records, also puts faith in her instincts. In a 1995 interview in *A & R Insider*, she said: "If I go to see a band or a singer, and if I can't take my eyes off of them, then I know that person has star quality." Brennan found her way to A & R by way of CBS Records, where she worked in the publishing division, discovering such talents as Miami Sound Machine, Toto, Jon Secada, Technotronic, and Desmond Child. Like Bell, Brennan finds that her interest in an act begins with a demo tape; if she likes what she hears, she asks for a meeting or goes to a club to hear a live audition. If there is magic afoot, the would-be recording artist gets a contract.

Unlike Bell and Brennan, whose entry into the music business was dictated more by the fickleness of fate and the possession of old-fashioned persistence, Claire Parr had a musical baptism that was more or less genetically determined from the outset. Her father, Jim West, was a well-regarded musician in the 1950s who played bass with such jazz greats such as Dave Brubeck, Count Basey, and Benny Goodman. In 1964, West was attending a broadcasters' convention in Chicago when he received word that his wife had given birth to a baby girl.

"I think I was toasted at dinner that night by all the broadcasters, so I had no escape from the music business," says Parr. By then West had put away his bass to start up a company in Dallas that provided pre-recorded programming to radio. As a child, Parr was treated to a constant stream of jazz musicians who stopped by the house when they performed in Dallas.

Parr was singing jingles for her father's company by the time she was a teenager, but the performance side of the business wasn't what attracted her.

Claire Parr

She really wanted to become a sound engineer. While she was looking for a job interning with an established engineer, a friend asked if she would run sound for his band. She wrote out a proposal for a business loan on manila paper—she was only 17—and talked a bank into advancing her the money to buy a sound system. "I wound up working with Elton John, Genesis, and a lot of jazz people as an engineer. I did that for about four years and burned out on it and decided I wanted to get into radio, so I went to my father and said, 'I see you teach everyone else this stuff. Why don't you teach me?' He said, 'Fine, you can be my receptionist.' Well, that was a tough pill to swallow, but I took the job. Nepotism is not always so great on the inside as it looks to other people."

Parr learned what her father already understood, that working as a receptionist is an excellent way to meet people and learn the ropes of the business. In time, she was able to parlay what she learned working for her father into a successful career, first in radio promotions, then in the record business. Stints at Geffen and Enigma led her to Curb Records in 1994, where as head of the pop and Christian divisions, she is responsible not only for A & R, but also promotion, media relations—everything associated with the artists she signs.

"I've been very lucky in that I've not had to deal with some of the prejudices that some of my cohorts have—but I know they exist," she says. "I don't think it's a man's world. I know it's a man's world, especially from a business standpoint. Still, there are more savvy females than anyone has any idea about. I have had a fantasy of starting a label run by women."

The biggest adjustment she had to make—as a married woman—has been to separate those two parts of her life. "I don't want to take the person I have to be behind this desk home with me," she says. "That's something women struggle with—how to separate the two. You start to live this double life. As an executive, you have to be stronger, tougher than anyone else. As women, we are expected not to be that way at home. That is one reason so many female executives fail to keep their marriages. I don't want to be a man. I want to be a woman.

"But there are certain rules I apply in the boardroom that I don't apply to other parts of my life. . . . I don't lose my cool. I don't start crying. I don't argue emotional issues. I feel an unspoken pressure that I have to work more than my male counterparts. I travel 100,000 miles a year. I work a lot of weekends. I take a lot of work home with me. At times, there are things they ask of me that would never be asked of a male executive—as simple as, 'Fetch me a cup of coffee.' . . . as simple as, 'We are all having dinner. Would you mind making the reservations?' Ten years of those innocent remarks can result in a person becoming bitter and angry."

Managers

Managers are the glue that holds the music industry together. Without them, the people who create the product—the artists—would never be able to sit in a room with the people who manufacture and sell the product—the record companies—long enough to consummate a deal. Being a manager is a hapless job for it means perpetually being in the middle of almost everything that affects an artist's life. Managers approach record companies on their client's behalf for the purpose of securing a recording contract; they help negotiate the contract, with the advice of an attorney; they assist in developing the marketing campaigns that will present the artist's work to the public; they decide who their client will talk to; they relay the record company's suggestions to the artist; they provide the artist's response, translated into more palatable conversation, back to the record company; they break dates with romantic interests and notify spouses that their significant other wants a divorce; they hire and fire the artist's cooks and housekeepers; they investigate why the artist's lawn wasn't mowed to his/her satisfaction; they seldom get credited for the successes the artists enjoy—but they always get blamed for the failures. In short, a manager's job requires unique talents and nerves of steel.

Until the mid-to-late 1980s, there were no successful female managers, other than a handful of wives of country music stars who had managed their husbands' careers from behind the scenes. Lib Hatcher is probably the first successful solo female manager. When she plucked Randy Travis from obscurity and transformed him from an insecure country singer into someone who had potential as a recording artist, she had no female role models to follow. She made it up as she went along, relying primarily on her instincts.

Whether it was that inner voice—or old-fashioned common sense—she felt her best shot at landing a recording contract for Travis was with another woman. Since there were only two female A & R executives in Nashville at that time—Martha Sharp at Warner and Margie Hunt at Columbia—Hatcher didn't have a long shopping list. Fortunately, Sharp liked Travis's demos and offered him a contract with Warner. From the beginning, Travis's career has been the byproduct of female engineering. It is as good an example as you can find of what can happen when women work together for a common goal.

On the heels of Hatcher's success, Columbia Records executive Bonnie Garner formed a partnership with Mark Rothbaum, Willie Nelson's manager. Rothbaum had dealt with Garner at Columbia, Nelson's record label, and when the opportunity arose in the late 1980s to make her a partner of the management team, Rothbaum jumped at the chance. Until 1995, when Garner left the partnership to devote her full efforts to the management of Marty Stuart's career, they managed Nelson's career as Rothbaum and Garner.

Rothbaum has nothing but praise for his former partner—and for the other women entering the profession. "The music industry is a small industry—and a young industry—and the male executives hang on very tightly to their authority. They give up nothing," says Rothbaum, who has been Nelson's manager for a quarter of a century. "For a woman to break in, they have to have extraordinary abilities. Those who do break in are extraordinary people."

Following in the footsteps of Hatcher and Garner was Pam Lewis, who, as Garth Brooks's co-manager until 1996, would have to be considered one of the most successful female managers in music history. Her entry into management

© JAMES DICKERSON

Tiffany (left) and Pam Lewis

came through Bob Doyle, who had signed Brooks to a publishing and recording contract. Doyle knew he couldn't do it alone; he needed a partner, someone who had the creativity and media savvy to make Brooks a star. Lewis already had a successful public relations firm going, representing such clients as singer/songwriter Vern Gosdin and singer/songwriter Townes Van Zandt, who died in 1997, and she agonized over Doyle's offer, pondering the old "bird in a hand" axiom.

Once Lewis decided to take Doyle's offer and become Brooks's co-manager, she proceeded with a dedication and fervor that would have to be witnessed to be believed. At the time Capitol Records released Brooks's first album in the spring of 1988, there was a lot of confusion in the media over who that Brooks fellow was; months earlier Capitol had released an album by a newcomer named Kix Brooks. Was everyone on Capitol named Brooks, or were all that label's new artists named Brooks? All of this wasn't lost on singer Doug Brooks, who changed his name to Stone to avoid the confusion.

Garth Brooks's first album wasn't well received by radio. The print media were slow to take to him because of the way he looked: slightly overweight, bland, and a little too earnest. During the first few months following the release of his first album, it looked hopeless, and Lewis began to wonder if she'd made the right decision.

"Everybody passed on him," she recalls. "I had people I thought I could count on, and they didn't see it right away. They really saw him as sort of a Clint Black clone. . . . Journalists wanted to pit the two together. Clint had won all those awards, and RCA had made him a priority. Everywhere you went, his albums were in the stores. Everywhere we went, there were no albums in the stores. It was ridiculous. Bob and I were going on a wing and a prayer. One time Bob looked at me and said, 'You know, what I feel like? I feel like I'm Mickey Rooney and you're Judy Garland, and it's like, let's do a play.' We were like so stupid that God smiled on us. I'm not saying we were dumb people, but there was a part of us that was so green. It was like us against the world."

Doyle's strength lay within the industry. He did all his fighting on the inside, where his punches were never seen by the outside world. But it was the outside world that was holding up Brooks's career for examination. Doyle won his battle when he and Lewis got Brooks a contract with Capitol. Whether the result of that contract ever saw the light of day was in Lewis's hands—and in her hands alone.

Shortly after the release of Brooks's first album, Lewis called the producer of a syndicated radio program, "Pulsebeat—Voice of the Heartland." It was a small syndication, servicing only about 75 stations, but it offered a back door into the playlists of program directors who had been resistant to Brooks's album.

When you're trying to break a record, every station counts. Lewis pleaded with the producer, assuring him that Brooks was the real thing and was deserving of a chance. Based on Lewis's recommendation, the producer agreed to devote an entire half hour show to Brooks and his debut album. Lewis had been right in the past. There was no reason to doubt her now. Brooks showed up at the studio, which was located in a renovated house on Music Row, looking like anything but a country music star. He had on the hat, but something was out of whack. It was as if Milton Berle had shown up wearing a cowboy hat and carrying a guitar. Brooks looked more like an accountant than a country singer.

The show went well. Brooks was sincere to the nth degree while answering questions asked by the announcer, Kim Spangler, the only female announcer doing country music syndication at that time. The music, all chosen from his only album, fit together into what the producer thought was a good show. Within weeks the show was pressed into vinyl and shipped out to the stations that subscribed to the syndication. Most stations played the program without sending comment back to the producer; but a couple of stations reacted violently and canceled their contracts, saying Brooks had no talent—and if that was the type of music they were going to be sent, the producer could just go to hell.

Lewis overcame that type of resistance by simply refusing to give up. She was absolutely relentless in her determination to get Brooks the break she thought he deserved. She was everywhere, leaving no stone unturned. She became his shadow. "Out on the road, a lot of people thought I was Garth's wife or a fan club president. It used to piss me off a little bit," she says.

Once the dust had cleared—and Brooks's success was assured by a string of Number 1 hits—Ron Baird approached Pam Lewis, Clint Black's longtime booking agent. "Can I ask you a question?" he said. "How'd you do it? We were kicking your butts. How'd you do it?"

"I told him it was a grass-roots thing," says Lewis. "We didn't have any money. We didn't have a label that had the power [of RCA]. I started a 'hearing is believing' campaign. We did bumper stickers. We did advertising. I called all the radio stations every week. Did you add the record? Thanks a lot. Can we have a quote? Oh, they love having their names in print. I sent the press clips out. We sent postcards out before everyone started doing that. If we could get people to listen to the album, then we knew they would get it because he was so good. Garth never had a national radio tour. We set it all up ourselves. When the first single, "If Tomorrow Never Comes," went to Top 40, the label was thrilled to death. We said, 'No, this can be a Top 10 record.' They were going to let it go. They thought that was fine. But we got on the phone and we got it to Number 8."

Lewis's efforts are now legendary in the music business. She is loved, hated, emulated, sought after, avoided, scorned, and worshipped for her pioneering efforts. "I'm not a monster, and I'm not a genius," she says. "It still bothers me that people who don't know me judge me so harshly. I feel really misunderstood, and I get annoyed with myself for thinking that—it's wasted energy. I really want people to like me. I want people to think, 'You know, she's really normal.'"

Despite her own harsh self-criticism, other women have eagerly followed in her footsteps; by early 1998, female managers could claim a solid foothold in the business. They are no longer an absolute rarity. Rolling Stones guitarist Keith Richards has had a female manager for years, Jane Rose, who maintains an office in New York. Jewel has had two women involved in her management: her mother Nedra Carroll, and Inga Vainshtein, both of whom have demonstrated sound judgment and strong leadership.

Publicists

Once, while working as a publicist, Pam Lewis had her job put in perspective by Vern Gosdin, who told her, "You are the only person in my life that I pay, and I don't get anything back from." "What do you mean?" Lewis asked. "Look at it this way," Gosdin answered. "My time is valuable. I either go on a bus and they hand me a check at the end of the night, or I write a song and I either cut it or someone else cuts it and I get a check—but I pay you. You make me talk to people I don't want to talk to—and you keep me away from working, which gives me a paycheck—or writing, which gives me a paycheck."

Lewis thought about what Gosdin said and concluded that it made perfect sense. "He said it kind of funny, but he said it meaning it, too," she says. "He would roll his eyes every time he had to do an interview because it meant he would have to sit there and answer some boring questions from journalists who sometimes didn't do their homework. I can see where it would get old."

The music business has always been dominated by songwriters, publishers—it's the song, she says: "Everything else is ancillary. Only recently have the power of public relations and the power of marketing been taken more seriously. The problem with public relations is that it is not quantitative. You can hire an independent promotion team or you can have your in-house promotions team promoting a record and it is very quantitative, and it either goes to Number 1 or it doesn't and you give bonuses based on that. It would be very interesting to see what happened if PR people were given a piece of an artist. If you are good at what you do, you have more work to do, but you don't get paid any more money. If you are a manager and the phone rings, it brings you money."

No record can become a hit without media support, but publicists often find themselves on the lowest rung of the organizational totem pole. That might be because most publicists are women; it is the only part of the music business that has been female dominated from the beginning. "The way I understand it," says Anita Mandell, who heads up the publicity department at Decca Records, "it evolved from female groupies who headed the fan clubs— and from that, went into publicity."

For that reason, publicity might be the only facet of the music business in which women haven't encountered the level of gender-based hostility found in other departments. Sandy Neese thinks men are just used to dealing with

© JAMES DICKERSON

Anita Mandell

female publicists. She has noticed problems only when female publicists are given titles, such as vice president. The title creates the confusion for some men, especially those who don't have titles, as if they aren't certain if they're supposed to show more respect to a woman who has a title. "When they made me a vice president, I noticed I got spoken to by people who didn't bother with me before," Neese says. "People who I would have had to speak to first were not speaking to me first. So, it was very interesting to me to see how other peoples' perception of me changed.

Once I was at a huge booking agency in Los Angeles with Mary Bailey and Shania—and this was after I had been a vice president maybe six months. We were having a film meeting, and she was being introduced to some of the agents who dealt in films and this and that. I was just kind of sitting there quietly, you know. It wasn't my gig. I didn't really have much to say. So, this guy was acting like I was a piece of the wallpaper. Later, we were down in the lobby and he's standing there talking to Mary Bailey, and I had gone over to use the phone. I saw her talking to him and then I saw him looking at me. Well, all of a sudden he comes flying across the lobby. Can I get you a private phone? Can I get you something to drink? Can I get you this? Can I get you that? He did that because he found out I was a vice president. That's the way of the world, but it offended me."

Before Mandell joined Decca Records, she worked for singer Allan Jackson's management company as a publicist. Working for a record label isn't much different from working for a recording artist—the day-to-day work is pretty much the same—but working for a woman, in this case Sheila Shipley Biddy, does offer contrasts. According to Mandell, "Sheila is a lot more understanding in some respects. She is easier to talk to. When I interviewed for the position, I was able to be frank about my home life—that I have a $2^1/_2$-year-old son. She gives me the flex time I need. Plus, it's different working for someone who can tell stories about when she started out and the way men treated her. I have a lot of respect for her hanging in there and believing enough in herself to continue on despite all the people trying to drag her down because she is a female. She is open to taking risks, and I don't know a lot of men who are open to doing that."

Marilyn Arthur has been in the music business since the late 1960s and has worked as head of publicity for RCA Records in both its Nashville and Los Angeles offices. She hasn't seen many gender-related problems because "most of the media departments are women," except in the area of compensation: "I don't know if women will ever get to where men are with salaries." The women's revolution in music has not surprised Arthur. "Women are doing great and will continue to do greater and greater things," she says, pausing for a laugh, "and take over the world." There isn't a department at a record label, she says, that a woman couldn't walk into and head up.

"The old style of management really doesn't work anymore, not in today's world," says Neese. "Most females are not going to put up with someone being condescending to them. That is an old male mentality that doesn't work anymore. They are liable to wind up with the president of a label being female, so they better be canning all the sex jokes and all the leers."

Neese considers this changing world with a sense of pride and occasional nostalgia. "Without divulging my age, I will tell you that I'm middle aged, and I do have grown children," she says. "I just feel so fortunate that I am in my

© JAMES DICKERSON

Sandy Neese

generation as opposed to my mom's generation, because she never would have been able to do what I have done because in her time no one had come along to really kick doors down in massive numbers like my generation did. Life's just more interesting now for females than it ever was." With that, Neese pauses, smiling at her male interviewer, then breaks out into laughter." Because the world doesn't belong just to ya'll anymore."

As a baby boomer and a product of the turbulent and creatively chaotic 1960s, Neese traces the line of progress of equality over more than three decades of struggle. The enormous success enjoyed in the mid-1990s by women didn't happen overnight. "Until we hit Vietnam, life was just a dadgum (doggone; goddamn) breeze, man, just a breeze. That was the first thing that just really began to rock our world. That was like our defining moment. It was what spawned the flower children and the peace and love and all of that. If all that hadn't happened, who knows, maybe things just would have breezed along like they were. Maybe we'd still be sitting in the suburbs getting sloshed every afternoon playing bridge—and trashing our husbands.

"I really think that the women of today are benefiting from the doors that we had to bang and pry open. Today's young woman is very different because she had us as moms, and we didn't want to bring our daughters up under the restrictions that we had. Get out and do it! Don't depend on a man for anything—for your income, for your happiness! Be capable of doing it on your own. If you have a relationship, have it out of want and not need! When Terri Clark sings, 'If you think I'm gonna be sitting around broken-hearted over you, I've got better things to do,' today's woman can relate to that. That's the way they're thinking. That's the way they've been taught. Now they have music models they can identify with lyrically. Look at Shania's 'Any man of mine had better walk the line.' Could you have had that song recorded 15 years ago? I don't think so. Radio wouldn't have played it, not with lyrics like that. That would have been a man's lyric. You know, 'Shape up or I'm outta here, babe!' Today you have women who were reared like I reared my daughter—and they are going to be singing those kinds of songs."

Record Producers and Engineers: The Last Holdouts

Sometimes it doesn't really hit you until you see it in black and white. In 1984 British writer Bert Muirhead published a directory of rock album producers entitled, *The Record Producers File.* To compile the book, which covers the time period between 1962 and 1984, Muirhead examined the album covers of approximately 75,000 albums. He was able to list 1,016 record producers, along with the titles of the albums they produced. Of those, only three—those by

Emmylou Harris, Suzi Jane Hokom, and Laurie Lathan—could be identified by their names as being female. That's 3 out of 1,016!

The last holdouts of male domination in the music business are production and its first cousin, engineering. No one has to offer up statistics to make that point to women in the industry. They know from experience. By 1998, the number of successful female producers working on major projects could be counted on one hand. Actually, they could be counted on one finger—Tena Clark.

With songwriting and production credits for Cece Winans, Dionne Warwick, Patti LaBelle, Gladys Knight, Olivia Newton-John, Mary Wilson, Rita Coolidge, Angela Bofill, Vesta Williams, and Nicolette Larson—and soundtrack credits on such movies as *My Best Friend's Wedding, French Kiss, Twins,* and *Five Heartbeats,* Tena Clark is easily the most successful female producer/songwriter in the business. Behind the scenes, a number of successful female artists have produced their own projects, though they were always paired with a male for the production credits.

It would probably come as a surprise to a lot of people, but country music singers have worked the hardest to break down the gender barrier in production. One of the first is Reba McEntire. One day she was in the studio working on an album project for MCA Records. While listening to a playback, she suggested to the producer that the song would sound better with a fiddle on the track. She was told to mind her own business and "get back out there and sing." The next day she went to the MCA office to talk to label president Jimmy Bowen. She was distraught and in tears. "This is my album," she said. "I should have input."

Bowen listened to McEntire's story, knowing that what she was asking was sheer heresy. But there was something about her, something about her passion for her music, that made him not want to say no. "You are right—absolutely right," he told her. "From this day on, you will be a co-producer with me on your albums."

McEntire took her new title seriously. She showed up at the studio with a notebook and asked questions about everything that happened in the control room. She made notes and learned it chapter and verse—and never again did she take a backseat on the production of her own albums. Kathy Mattea is another country artist who asked for—and received—co-production credits. By the late 1990s, female recording artists in pop, R & B, and rock were following the lead of their country cousins.

When an artist is in the studio, the producer is the captain of the ship and controls literally everything that happens. The producer also approves the musicians, the songs that are recorded, and how they're recorded, as well as decides whether a track is acceptable. Most male producers are authoritarian by nature, and when they're working with female artists their authoritarian streak tends to be amplified. Any artist, male or female, who isn't co-producing his or her own work is subject to orders from the producer to "get back in there and sing it again." In hundreds of instances, female artists have been "broken" by unethical producers who got pleasure out of seeing stars reduced to tears. Being a co-producer on her own project gives a female artist leverage with her producer in the control room; it gives her the right to say no and not be in violation of her contract.

The fact that Tena Clark is the only woman in the business with a successful "public" track record isn't lost on her. By "public," it is meant she is listed as the sole producer and is given industry recognition for it. "It's sad to me," she says of the obstacles women face in production. "I see so many talented women who want to be producers, and I hate it when I see them with a feeling that, 'Oh, my God, it's so impossible.'" The only reason she was able to get production credits, she concedes, is because she is a songwriter; her songs enabled her to become a producer. One aspect of the record business that baffles her is why it is so far removed from the standards that movies and television set years ago. "When I started working in movies and television, I produced everything I wrote," she says. "The first thing I got hired to do when I moved out to Los Angeles was to produce the title song for 'Police Academy.' From there I went to television and everything I wrote, I produced myself. It was all very unsexist. Then, I got into records and, all of a sudden, it was, 'Oh, no. You're a woman.' It was very frustrating for me."

Clark might never have broken the gender barrier in the record business if it hadn't been for R & B singer Vesta Williams, who had worked with her on several television projects. One day Williams called Clark and asked if she would write and produce three or four cuts on Williams's new record. Clark was flattered but said, "Yeah, that's really going to happen."

"Yes, it will," answered Williams.

Williams went to the A & R executive at her record label, A&M Records, and told him she wanted Clark to produce several cuts on the album. "Won't happen," he said. "We already have someone to produce the entire album."

"Well, then, I guess I will have laryngitis for the next five years," Williams said and walked out of the office. When production on the album began— and Williams was nowhere to be found—the record company executive capitulated. "Okay," he told Williams, "whoever this Tena Clark person is, you've got her . . . whatever."

What Williams did took guts. Clark knows that and appreciates it. "She broke down doors for me," she says. "It's so rare that someone has the balls to stand up for what they believe in, and I will always be indebted to her for that.

When they said, 'Whoever this Tena Clark person is,' it was so patronizing, so we knew our necks were really on the line."

Clark and Williams responded with a song entitled "Congratulations," which went to Number 1 on the R & B charts. It was the biggest hit Williams had ever had, and it resulted in Clark receiving offers to produce other female artists. "There have been a lot of wonderful men in the business who have believed in me and given me breaks, but the person who opened the door for me was a woman," she says. "As a general rule, most men want to see women as artists and writers. They don't want to see them as producers or musicians. I have broken down those barriers and it is an old story to me, but I look at other women and I think, 'Oh, my God, if you only knew —and you will soon find out.'"

CHAPTER 3

I WANNA BE A CONTENDER

1954–1959

TOP 20 HONOR ROLL
1954–1959

Annette	Georgia Gibbs	Jane Powell
Lavern Baker	Gogi Grant	Della Reese
The Bobbettes	Bonnie Guitar	Debbie Reynolds
Teresa Brewer	Joni James	Jody Reynolds
Cathy Carr	Kitty Kallen	Jo Stafford
The Chordettes	Eartha Kitt	Kay Starr
Rosemary Clooney	Peggy Lee	Dodie Stevens
Jill Corey	Kathy Linden	Gale Storm
Doris Day	Laurie London	Caterina Valente
The DeCastro Sisters	Denise Lor	June Valli
The DeJohn Sisters	Giselle Mackenzie	Sarah Vaughan
Toni Fisher	The McGuire Sisters	Dinah Washington
The Fontane Sisters	Jaye P. Morgan	Joan Weber
Connie Francis	Patti Page	
Ronnie Gaylord	The Playmates	

For the first half of the nineteenth century, women dominated American music, at least as far as vocalists were concerned. They weren't dominant financially: social convention or unscrupulous male managers and handlers usually restricted their compensation. But when it came to star power, women shined bright. Women, including Billie Holiday, Bessie Smith, and Dinah Shore, fronted most of the successful bands and orchestras, and a healthy portion of the recordings issued each year featured female vocalists. The perception that music was a profession for male vocalists didn't start changing in a significant way until the 1940s. During that decade, male crooners, such as Bing Crosby and Frank Sinatra, and "singing cowboys," such as Roy Rogers and Gene Autry, gave gender respectability to male vocalists.

In the early 1950s, male singers like Nat King Cole, Perry Como, Tony Bennett, and Eddie Fisher bumped record sales up a notch industry-wide, primarily by appealing to female record buyers. But female artists were still going strong, led by the Andrew Sisters, Teresa Brewer, Eileen Barton, Patti Page, Rosemary Clooney, Kay Starr, Vera Lynn, and Doris Day. All that would change in 1954, however, with Elvis Presley's first recordings at Sun Studios in Memphis—and it would stay changed almost until the end of the century. Still, women remained strong contenders throughout the 1950s. In fact, the decade would give them their best showing until the 1980s.

From the beginning of 1954 through 1959, 45 female solo artists made the Top 20, compared to 108 male solo artists, giving women 29 percent of the total. The biggest female hitmakers between 1954 and the end of 1959 were Jo Stafford, Kay Starr, Gogi Grant, Patti Page, and Debbie Reynolds, women who directed their efforts toward melodic pop songs. That percentage would drop during the 1960s and 1970s, making a lie of the myth that the 1950s was a stifling period for women. In truth, the freewheeling 1960s and 1970s proved to be disastrous decades for women, giving them their lowest numbers of the century.

Female songwriters also did relatively well during the 1950s, though most of their hits were as co-writers with male partners. There is no way to know how many of the male co-writer credits were authentic and how many were "add ons" provided to give the women credibility. "Heartbreak Hotel" was Elvis Presley's first release for RCA and his first Number 1 single. Although songwriter credits list Presley, Tommy Durden, and Mae Axton, Presley had nothing to do with writing the song (Colonel Parker simply added Presley's name as a songwriter to all of his songs as a means of increasing their income). Durden gave Axton the idea for the song when he showed her a newspaper story about a suicide victim who left a note saying, "I walk a lonely street." How much of the song Durden actually wrote might never be known.

Other hit songs co-written by women include Carole Joyner's "Young Love" (1957), recorded by Tab Hunter; Felice Bryant's "Wake Up Little Susie" (1957), recorded by the Everly Brothers; Rose Marie McCoy's "I Beg of You" (1958), recorded by Elvis Presley; Barbara Ellis and Gretchen Christopher's "Come Softly to Me" (1959), recorded by a trio, The Fleetwoods (Ellis and Christopher were two of the vocalists); and Ann Farina's "Sleepwalk" (1959), an instrumental recorded by her two brothers.

The first woman to be the sole author of a Number 1 record was Sharon Sheeley, whose "Poor Little Fool" provided Ricky Nelson with his sixth hit in August 1958. Sheeley was a prolific songwriter and a major influence on the music of the 1950s. Professionally, her life was gilded, and she could do no wrong; by comparison, her private life was chaotic and marred by tragedy. In 1960, she went to Europe to tour with her boyfriend, singer Eddie Cochran ("Summertime Blues"). Midway through the tour, Sheeley and Cochran decided to return to America to get married. As they were riding in a taxi to the London airport, one of the tires blew out, sending the taxi crashing into a lamppost. Both Sheeley and Cochran were seriously injured in the accident; Sheeley recovered, but Cochran later died of head injuries.

Within the music industry itself, women were nonexistent in positions other than secretary or receptionist. BMI's Frances Preston, who was in the first stages of her career, found the early days rough and demoralizing. "I was young and fairly attractive and people thought, 'Oh, look what BMI sent to me,'" she says. "You really had to be the 'ice woman' to let them know that you were there for business. When you started talking, they knew you knew about the business, but you had to be a little bit smarter. Your homework had to be done. The least they knew to talk about was performing rights, so I spent quite a bit of time going to seminars to learn every aspect of the business so that I could converse about whatever they wanted to talk about. There were instances when people would remind you that you were a woman."

MARION KEISKER: THE WOMAN BEHIND ELVIS

By the time Marion Keisker started working with Sam Phillips at his 706 Union Avenue recording studio, Memphis Recording Service, she was in her mid-thirties and the divorced mother of a young son. Her title at the studio was secretary, but she was much more than that. Keisker first met Phillips in 1946, four years before he opened the studio. They both worked at radio station WREC. Phillips was an engineer; Keisker was an on-air personality, the host of a popular talk show, "Meet Kitty Kelly." She'd made her debut on the station in 1929 at the age of 12, appearing on a weekly children's show,

"Wynken, Blynken, and Nod," and she'd remained a presence at the station until she joined the staff in 1946 and became Kitty Kelly.

By post-World War II standards, Keisker was light years ahead of her time in her professional aspirations. She was intelligent, ambitious, energetic, and, most important of all, aggressive in her pursuit of a career. In addition to playing the role of Kitty Kelly, she was on the air five days a week pulling duty on various shows; after hours, she worked on a nightly show, "Treasury Bandstand," which was broadcast from the top floor of the Peabody Hotel, a landmark gathering place for mid-Southerners. In later years, she recalled, perhaps to her own amazement, that she'd written, directed, or produced several shows at a time for the radio station.

By the time Phillips rented a building for his studio down the street from the hotel (WREC's offices were located in the basement of the Peabody Hotel), he and Keisker had been working closely together at the radio station for four years. In the book *Last Train to Memphis,* Peter Guralnick says that Keisker had fallen "hopelessly in love with Sam," though the exact nature of her relationship with Phillips, who was married at the time, has never been established. At first, Phillips tried to operate the studio while holding down his job at WREC. He worked at the station in the mornings and early afternoons, then left to open the studio for a few hours, then returned to his job at the radio station that evening, then went back again to the studio later that night. This wasn't an unreasonable time schedule for the studio since musicians are by nature nocturnal creatures. Besides, there were no full-time musicians in Memphis; they all had to have day jobs of one kind or another.

For the most part, Memphis Recording Service operated as a vanity studio. Phillips recorded bar mitzvahs, weddings, and birthday greetings; transferred tapes to records, and made off-air checks for radio stations. A separate enterprise was a record label he named Sun Records. For that, he recorded musical groups and pressed the recordings into records; if he got lucky, a radio station somewhere would play the record. Phillips didn't get lucky often. There wasn't a long line of musicians waiting to get into the studio to work with him. That first year, he learned that the most commercial recordings he could make were of black musicians performing the music native to the region, the blues. He took those recordings and sold them to record labels that specialized in African American music.

Creatively, Phillips was quite successful, discovering talented black musicians who later went on to considerable fame. Howlin' Wolf, Joe Hill Louis, and Walter Horton were all graduates of the Sam Phillips school of music. Financially, Phillips was always on shaky ground. After he burned the candle at both ends for a year and a half, the pressure of working long days got to Phillips. In addition, his boss at the radio station was criticizing him at every opportunity, the studio was bringing in very little money, and he had a wife and two sons to support. Emotionally, he fell apart. Twice he was admitted to Gartly-Ramsay Hospital to undergo electroshock treatments.

Abruptly, in June 1951, Phillips handed in his resignation at WREC to devote his full efforts to Memphis Recording Service. He printed up cards that read: "We record anything—anywhere—anytime." To Keisker, he must have resembled a wounded bird. In the early 1950s, quite a stigma was attached to anyone who was admitted to a mental hospital for electroshock treatments. The only rung lower on the social scale of that era was reserved for racial transgressions. By working with black musicians, Phillips had violated that social convention as well. Besides being a two-time loser in those areas, his employment itself was, by definition, the lowest on the radio station pecking order. At the top was the general manager, then the on-air personalities, then the sales staff—and, at the very bottom the lowly engineers.

In contrast, Keisker was a real somebody in Memphis. Newspaper articles called her "Miss Radio of Memphis." It was her voice that people heard interviewing the celebrities who came to town for performances or special events. It was her voice that made Memphians feel good about themselves. And it was her vibrant personality that helped two generations of Memphis women define themselves. If Keisker was in love with Phillips, as author Guralnick alleges in his book, it would explain why she gave up everything she'd accomplished at WREC to work with Phillips at the studio.

Although she was identified as the secretary, she was his partner in every sense of the word. She was the public persona of the company and greeted the customers, she did the bookkeeping and the billing, she was the business manager and made the arrangements for the distribution of the records, and she wrote up all the contracts and sent out the letters. Thinking the front door made a bad impression, she bought a new one with her own money. Years later, in an interview with author Jerry Hopkins, Keisker put the early days in perspective. "I threw over the whole thing [the radio career] for the record company," she said. "The only sleep I got in those days was at the desk."

For the first three years of that arrangement, Phillips was able to generate interest in his work with African American recording artists, but that success didn't translate into financial success. Whatever promises he'd made to Keisker, it was becoming clear they weren't going to come true—at least not without her help. Three years is a long time to watch a company flounder, especially under the leadership of a man whose greatest claim to fame was his association with African Americans at a time when it was against the law for people of color to eat in white-owned restaurants or enter public facilities.

Keisker became more aggressive as a talent scout. After three years, it had become clear to her that Sun Records was never going to be successful promoting black artists. What Keisker needed was a white artist, someone the community she'd represented so well as "Miss Radio of Memphis" would embrace. If she could find a white singer who could sing like the black singers she worked with, she would have something. Since there was no line of white singers queued outside the studio, she paid particular attention to the people who came into the studio to make vanity recordings. In these situations, would-be singers who wanted to make a birthday or holiday greeting for someone special would come into the studio, pay $4, and speak or sing into a microphone that went directly into a machine that recorded the message onto an acetate disk, which resembled the records sold in the stores. If Keisker felt the client was someone who had talent and would be a possibility for the record label, she would turn on the tape machine and record the brief session so that she would have a copy to play for Phillips.

That was how Keisker discovered Elvis Presley. "I first saw Elvis on a Saturday afternoon. It was a busy, busy afternoon, and for some reason I happened to be alone at the time," she said in her interview with Hopkins. "The office was full of people wanting to make personal records. It was a 'stand and wait your turn' sort of thing. [Elvis] came and said he wanted to make a record. He sat down [with his guitar] . . . and while he was waiting his turn, we had a conversation. . . . He said he was a singer. I said, 'What kind of singer are you?' "'I sing all kinds,' he said. "Who do you sound like?" "'I don't sound like nobody.'" "I thought, 'Oh, yeah, one of those.'"

Keisker took Presley into the back room to record the acetate. When he was about a third of the way through the first song, she turned on the tape player and got a partial copy of the first song and the entire second song on tape. Later, she said she thought Presley was unaware he was being taped. When Phillips returned to the studio, Keisker played the tape for him. He told her he was impressed, but felt that Presley needed a lot of work. He asked if she had the singer's name. She showed him a piece of paper that said: "Elvis Presley—good ballad singer—hold." Phillips told her to do just that—hold it.

The entire world knows the story from this point: how Keisker kept asking Phillips about Presley and how Phillips kept putting her off. Then one day while they were having coffee at Taylor's Restaurant next door to the studio she brought up Presley's name again, this time in front of guitarist Scotty Moore, who had been coming at Phillips from a different direction, urging him to explain what kind of talent he was looking for.

Phillips figured he would kill two birds with one stone. He suggested that Moore get in touch with Presley and arrange an audition at his house. If Presley were any good, then Moore could bring him in for a taped audition. Keisker didn't win the way she wanted to—on the merits of her good judgment—but she did win. Later, she would tell the story of Presley's discovery, first with pride, then with some bitterness as the years wore on.

Once Presley's career took off, Keisker worked the media on his behalf. On the morning of July 27, 1954, she took him into the newsroom of the *Memphis Press-Scimitar* to do his first interview. Edwin Howard, the reporter, agreed to do the interview on her recommendation. Later, he wrote: "The boy's hair looked as if it had been cut by a lawn mower, but the trademarks were already there—flat top, duck tail and sideburns. He was shy and, except, for 'Yes sir' and 'No sir,' let Marion do all the talking."

When Keisker saw how people reacted to Presley, she gave Sun Records everything she had. In fact, from that point on everything—even her family— took a backseat. Long days became long nights. Early one morning, at about 3 A.M., she fell asleep at her desk while doing the bookkeeping. Suddenly, she was awakened by the sound of her name.

"Marion—Marion—Marion," the voice said.

Keisker lifted her head up off the desk, and standing before her was Presley, looking as white as a ghost. "I thought you were dead," he said. He explained that he'd driven by the studio on his motorcycle and spotted her through the open blinds.

That first year, Keisker worked tirelessly on Presley's behalf. She called radio stations, worked the press, and attended the recording sessions, doing what she could to help. During one session, when they were recording a cover of "I Don't Care If the Sun Don't Shine"—first recorded by Patti Page in 1950—everything came to a screeching halt. Presley knew only one verse. Keisker told the boys not to worry and to take a break. While they were on break, she wrote a second verse for the song. It began, "I don't care if it's rain or snow / drivin's cozy when the lights are low / and I'm with my baby. . . ." Presley finished the recording with her lyrics, and a few days later Phillips took their only copy to a record convention in Nashville. He played the song for several people at the convention, then called Keisker and told her to go ahead and master the record. He said everyone liked it, and he was taking orders like mad.

Some time later, Keisker received a telephone call from the song's publisher, who told her that the original writer, Mack David, would have to approve any changes made to the song. She sent her only copy to New York via air mail and awaited the verdict. To her surprise, the publisher called back and said that David loved the new lyrics. Phillips could release the record, but there was a catch. Keisker would have to sign a disclaimer, relinquishing any rights she might have acquired to the song with the new lyrics. She gladly signed the papers, but for years afterward felt a tinge of anger whenever she heard the song on the radio with her lyrics.

Shortly before Phillips sold Presley's contract to RCA Records in November 1955, he purchased a radio station with money he'd received from Holiday Inns developer Kemmons Wilson. The station was located in a Holiday Inn on Third Street and given the call letters WHER. It would be the first all-female radio station in the nation. For the station's general manager, Phillips chose Dotty Abbott, well-known locally as an actress and broadcaster. He also hired his wife, Becky, and a staff of female salespersons and announcers, including Keisker, who was removed from her position at the recording studio and hired as an announcer/news reporter for the station.

The partnership that Keisker and Phillips had forged was effectively over. On her last visit to the recording studio, she took down the door she'd purchased and installed herself. She wasn't happy about moving over to WHER, but she didn't allow anyone to know how unhappy she was. In an article for a book published by the Memphis Brooks Museum of Art in 1986, she wrote with pride of her involvement with WHER. "As it happened, mine was the first voice to be heard on WHER," she wrote. "When the time came to run the required pre-opening engineering tests, I went on the air after midnight with a prepared text giving the station's call letters, assigned frequency, and location and asked listeners to call the station to help establish range and transmission quality. One caller, sounding very puzzled, commented: 'You sound like a lady!' I replied, 'I thank you, and my mother thanks you.'"

Keisker lasted less than two years at WHER. In the fall of 1955, she and Phillips had a big fight—their last big fight—and she stormed out of the radio station and joined the Air Force. She'd made the mistake women have made throughout history: she'd given her talents in the name of love—a trade that always ends poorly for the woman. Keisker never made a dime off of Presley's career, and she received little credit for her contributions at Sun Records. As the years went by, she remained loyal to Phillips, but she became less and less supportive of the role he played in Presley's career. At times, she openly disputed Phillips's version of events. The only recognition she ever received came from the person who most mattered, Presley himself. While she was in the Air Force and stationed in West Germany—and Presley was in the Army in the same country—she was allowed to attend an event he was scheduled to perform at. He was shocked to see her there, especially showing the rank of captain. He gave her a big hug, but not before asking, "Do I kiss you or salute you?"

The Army captain in charge was outraged to see an Air Force captain there—and a female one to boot. He ordered Keisker to leave. She refused. At that point, Presley stopped and addressed his superior officer. "Captain, you don't understand," he said. "You wouldn't be having this thing today if it wasn't for this lady!"

"You mean, this WAF captain?" he asked.

"Well, it's a long story," Presley responded, "but she wasn't always a WAF captain." He went on to explain who she was, all the while reaching behind his back where Keisker was standing to make sure she was still there. That was thanks enough for her.

COUNTRY MUSIC PIONEERS

In the 1950s the women of country music were matching the success women were having on the pop charts. While the general perception among record executives on Nashville's Music Row was that "girls don't sell," there was a string of female recording artists whose success defied conventional wisdom. Patsy Cline, Minnie Pearl, Kitty Wells, the Carter Family—all were breaking new ground for women. Of all the women emerging during that time, it was probably Kitty Wells, whose real name was Muriel Deason, who made the greatest impact. By the time Decca Records issued her single "It Wasn't God Who Made Honky Tonk Angels" in 1952, she was discouraged about her career—discouraged that any woman could have a career in music. To her surprise, the record went to Number 1 on the country charts and stayed there for weeks, selling more than 800,000 copies, a huge number back then. This was the first time a woman had ever topped the country charts.

Wells never thought the song would be a hit because it went against the flow. It was a gutsy, pro-feminist ballad that tore into lying, cheating husbands. Women loved the song, and they bought it and played it for their husbands. Male record executives—and in those days all record executives were male—thought it was just a fluke. Wells quickly took the title "Queen of Country Music" (a title she wore until the end of the decade), and while she was no feminist—and the women who adored her would never have considered themselves feminists—she became an underground hero among the women of her generation. Wells followed up her early success with a series of hits, including "I Can't Stop Loving You" and "Love Makes the World Go 'Round," but none of them had the strong, pro-woman perspective of "It Wasn't God Who Made Honky Tonk Angels." She eventually lost the momentum initially gained from the hit.

Minnie Pearl, whose real name was Sarah Cannon, made an impact on the music industry, not with her musical talents but with her humor. As a member of the Grand Ole Opry, she was a familiar figure to country music fans for more than five decades. From the moment she stepped out on stage wearing an old-fashioned dress and a flowered straw hat with a price tag dangling in full view and yelled out, "How-Dee! I'm just so proud to be here!" she connected with music fans in ways that transcended the simplicity of her homespun comic routines.

One of Pearl's favorite routines went like this: "I was coming out of the back of the auditorium—and it was dark—and this fellah comes up, and he has a gun in his hand. He says, 'Give me your money.' And I say, 'I don't have any money.' And then he looks me up and down and says, 'You really don't have any money, do you?' And I say, 'No, but if you'll do that again, I'll write you a check!'"

Technically, Pearl's talents lay beyond the realm of music, but she was so much a part of everything that was—and is—the music business, most observers would be hard-pressed to exclude her on a technicality. "I think the star among all was Minnie Pearl," says BMI's Frances Preston. "She was a genuine person who cared for other people and gave back to her industry."

No discussion of the women of country music in the 1950s would be complete without a mention of Mother Maybelle and the Carter Sisters. In the 1920s, the Carter Family— composed of A. P. "Doc" Carter; his wife, Sara; and his sister-in-law, Maybelle—had been among the first to record and popularize country music. By the 1950s, the Carter Family had broken up. and Maybelle had formed a new group with her three daughters, Anita, Helen, and June, who later married Johnny Cash. They quickly became a featured group on the Grand Ole Opry, along with their guitar player, Chet Atkins, and had a number of successful records, including "Amazing Grace," "Wildwood Flower," and "Wabash Cannonball." Mother Maybelle and her daughters continued performing up until her death in 1978, but by the mid-to-late 1950s the girls had branched out to pursue other interests. For a time, June was an opening act for Elvis Presley, with whom she shared the same manager, Colonel Tom Parker, before she went to New York to study acting.

Patsy Cline didn't enter the picture until late in the decade, but her influence was so great she seemed to overshadow everyone else. Cline, whose real name was Virginia Hensley, was a product of a new medium, television. Since the age of 16, she'd tried to break into country music. No one was interested, and she ended up making a living as a dancer. Then in 1957, at the age of 25, she was given an opportunity to appear on "Arthur Godfrey's Talent Scouts," one of the most popular nationally televised shows of its time. She sang "Walkin' After Midnight" and won first prize and a recording contract with Decca Records. For 10 years, male record executives in Nashville had failed to spot Cline's talent. The television audience cinched it for her. Female viewers identified with her immediately. They could see themselves in her face, and they could hear the long-suffering hurt in her emotion-drenched voice. They responded by buying "Walkin' After Midnight" in large numbers, making it an instant hit.

Record executives followed up with a series of songs they thought women wanted to hear. They were wrong, and Cline's career stalled. She didn't rebound until 1961 with a song titled "Crazy." She followed up with "I Fall to Pieces." By 1963, Cline was one of the most popular female singers in the country. Her career ended abruptly on March 6, 1963, when the twin-engine Comanche she was riding in crashed during a thunderstorm, killing all aboard.

Because Cline died when she was still young and her career hadn't peaked yet, she has a mystique. Even in death, her powerful voice and her face tug at heartstrings. This is as much a result of the influence of television as it is her music. She was the first to go over the heads of male record executives and appeal directly to a female audience. The music industry was slow to grasp the importance of that strategy, but, once it did, it embraced television with a passion and never looked back. Once again, a woman had led the way.

THE FIRST QUEENS OF ROCK 'N' ROLL

Kay Starr was living with her family in Memphis when at age 15 she was offered a job singing with jazz violinist Joe Venuti's dance band. While fronting for Venuti, the teenager was asked to fill in for Marion Hutton, Glenn Miller's vocalist, when she was hospitalized briefly for an illness. Starr, whose real name was Katherine Starks, recorded two songs with Miller, "Love With a Capital U" and "Baby Me."

Mesmerized by the glamour and excitement of the music business, Starr left her family behind in Memphis, where her father worked for a sprinkler company and her mother raised chickens, and moved to California, where she lived with Venuti and his wife. During World War II, while traveling extensively on unheated transport planes to entertain American troops, she contracted pneumonia and lost the use of her voice. She didn't regain her voice for a year and a half, but when it returned it was more mature and a husky resonance that she put to good use. In 1948, she signed a recording contract with Capitol Records, turning out a string of hits, including "Side By Side" and a Number 1 single, "Wheel of Fortune."

In 1956, after signing a contract with RCA Records, Starr prepared for her first session with her new label. From the beginning, nothing went right for her. The RCA studio had a large floor area and a high ceiling, and she felt intimidated by the studio's vastness; she simply didn't feel comfortable singing in that setting. By the time she adjusted to the room itself, she was

Kay Starr

given another surprise, a string section. Starr had never recorded with strings, and the thought terrified her. But if she thought RCA was through with its surprises, she was wrong. The label had one more card up its sleeve.

A little over two months before the session began, RCA had signed Elvis Presley to a recording contract. A&R executives at RCA felt they'd stumbled upon something with this new music called rock 'n' roll. For Starr's first session, they gave her a tune titled "Rock and Roll Waltz." Who better to usher in the new music from Memphis than a woman from Memphis who had connections to the big band era? Starr might have heard of Presley by then, but it is doubtful since his success at that time was confined to a handful of southern states. Starr was offended by the song. In fact, she suspected it was a joke that the executives were playing on her. She'd built a reputation for singing serious songs that expressed serious emotions, and "Rock and Roll Waltz" sounded like a nursery rhyme. When she found out they were serious about the song, she did her best with it, although she later confided that her heart really wasn't in it.

By February 1956, "Rock and Roll Waltz" was the Number 1 single on the pop charts with sales of more than 1 million. Starr was stunned. The song she thought was a joke became the first Number 1 single RCA ever charted. But there was more: it was the first song to ever have the words "rock 'n' roll" in the title—and, most importantly, it secured Starr a place in history as the first woman in the modern era to score a Number 1 hit. The bewildered Starr had become the queen of rock 'n' roll.

Two months later, Starr found out what all the fuss was about when Presley bumped her out of the Top 20 with the Number 1 hit "Heartbreak Hotel." For the next several months—and into the start of the new decade—American music underwent a spirited, gender-based tug-of-war as rock 'n' roll struggled to define itself as a male medium. The women refused to go quietly.

About six weeks after "Heartbreak Hotel" made Presley a household name, Gogi Grant, a striking, 32-year-old brunette from Philadelphia, knocked him out of the Number 1 spot with "The Wayward Wind." In retrospect, it is obvious American music was undergoing radical change, with the battle lines drawn along traditional gender-related themes of aggressive exploration versus nurturing self-assessment. But at the time it seemed more like a cultural change than one related to gender. Rock 'n' roll was an invention of the South. Many critics considered it crude, sexual, and devoid of redeeming social value. The South had already given the world the blues, jazz, bluegrass, and country music. Would the South, once again, dictate American musical tastes?

Unlike Starr, Grant didn't have a string of hits to pave the way for her. RCA Records initially signed her, but when none of her releases—all recorded

Gogi Grant

under the name Audrey Brown—made the charts, the label dumped her. Grant's career looked bleak until Dave Knapp, a former RCA executive, started up an independent label named Era Records. Knapp signed her to his new label and changed her name from Audrey Brown to Gogi Grant. A song was selected for her first session, but when she met with the writers and they played her some of their other material, she expressed an interest in "Suddenly There's a Valley." The songwriters, both males, looked at each a little strangely. When Grant asked why, they confessed they thought that a man should sing the song. Perhaps challenged by their comment, Grant recorded "Suddenly There's a Valley" instead of the song the men had chosen for her. It went to Number 9 on the charts and made her an overnight sensation.

After completing a 28-city promotional tour, Grant returned to the studio to record a follow-up to her hit. "Who Are We" took less than three hours to record. With the time remaining, they looked for another song. Herb Newman, the executive in charge of Era Records, asked Grant to come into his office. He showed her the dog-eared manuscript of a song he'd written with Stan Lebouysky while they were students at UCLA. The song was titled "The Wayward Wind." Like those of her previous hit, the lyrics were written for a man. Grant said she liked the song and would like to record it if he would allow her to rewrite the lyrics. That was fine with Newman, so Grant changed the lyrics to reflect a woman's point of view. In the remaining 15 minutes of the session, they recorded the song and prepared for the release of "Who Are We." When "Who Are We" peaked at Number 62, Newman decided to release "The Wayward Wind." It took the song only five weeks to move into the Number 1 slot.

From June 1956, when Grant went to Number 1 with "The Wayward Wind," until August 1957, males dominated the top of the charts, with hits by Presley, Pat Boone, Guy Mitchell, Perro Como, Buddy Knox, and Tab Hunter. In August, actress Debbie Reynolds knocked Presley out of the Number 1 position with a song entitled "Tammy," a syrupy ballad that rode the soundtrack of the movie *Tammy and the Bachelor*.

At the time, Reynolds was married to singer Eddie Fisher, who until Presley's arrival, was RCA Records' top artist. The more success Presley had, the less Fisher had. Reynolds hadn't put much thought into her recording of "Tammy." She sang it accompanied only by a piano. Later, when movie executives decided to release the song as a single to promote the movie, strings were added to the track to give it a fuller sound. Reynolds was surprised at the success of the record, as was everyone else, but her biggest surprise came from her husband. "From Eddie, there wasn't a word of congratulations or joy; not a momentary kick that his wife was on the charts," Reynolds wrote in her autobiography entitled *Debbie: My Life.* "I was surprised by the record's success. I could be happy, but I couldn't be glad. I had offended my husband without even trying."

It is ironic that an actress—and not a committed singer—was able to make Presley topple off the top of the charts. But the event is significant in that the success that accompanied "Tammy" created tensions in Reynolds's marriage, and was indicative of the professional and intergender tensions that would develop between men and women in the years ahead. Reynolds's 1957 success would be the last Number 1 hit scored by a solo female artist until the dawn of the new decade.

SUCCESSFUL RHYTHM AND BLUES PIONEERS

African American female artists recording for R & B labels were unaffected by the raging gender and cultural battles taking place on the pop charts. Almost from the beginning, female R & B singers were given equal status with men—creatively if not financially. Over the years they seemed immune to the ups and downs that women striving for slots on the pop and country charts experienced.

Among the most successful of this era was Etta James, who had a Number 1 R & B hit in 1955 with "The Wallflower," which she followed up that with a Number 6 hit, "Good Rockin' Daddy." A few years later, she scored as a backup singer on Chuck Berry's "Back in the U.S.A." and "Almost Grown." Sadly, she never made the Top 20 on the pop charts and didn't receive her due until the 1990s when she was awarded a Grammy for *Mystery Lady,* an album that saluted Billie Holiday.

Like Etta James, Big Maybelle Smith and Ruth Brown recorded singles that did well on R & B charts. But most of the female R & B singers worked the club circuit, and while their influence was significant on a year-to-year basis, their fame was transitory and confined to local venues.

BRENDA LEE, THE ROCKABILLY/POP MUSIC PRODIGY

Brenda Mae Tarpley started singing in 1949 at the age of 5. Her version of "Take Me Out to the Ball Game," which she sang at a fair in Conyers, Georgia, won first prize—and, as of late 1997, she was still going strong, averaging more than 200 performances a year. Musically, she was a child prodigy with a prodigious memory; her mother was proud of telling people that even as a very young child Tarpley could hear a song twice and then sing it back without missing a word.

In the beginning, Tarpley's musical talents were as much a novelty as anything else for her family. Her father was a construction worker, and her mother worked in a cotton mill; together they eked out a hardscrabble living in rural Georgia for their family of three daughters and a son. The Tarpley family didn't own a record player, so the only music she was exposed to came over the airwaves or was heard first-hand from street-corner and front-porch musicians. Most of what Tarpley heard was R & B and gospel—Ray Charles, Fats Domino, and Mahalia Jackson—because that was the music that her neighbors enjoyed.

Tarpley might have remained a neighborhood novelty but for a freak accident that turned her world upside down. In May 1953, just seven months short of her eighth birthday, her father was killed at a construction site when a hammer fell on his head. The accident left the Tarpley family destitute. It was then that Mama Grace Tarpley, seeing all the attention that Brenda was getting with her singing, investigated the possibilities of a music career for her daughter. Brenda Tarpley became Brenda Lee.

During the week, Lee attended school, and on weekends she boarded a bus to travel to the bookings around the state that her mother had arranged for her. In no time at all, she became the family's principal breadwinner. When Lee returned to school on Mondays, she was so tired that she put her head down on her desk and slept past noon. Her teacher, knowing how desperate Lee's family was for money, allowed her to sleep in class.

This routine continued for three years.

In 1956, Lee got the big break that she and her family had hoped for. She was invited to appear on an Augusta, Georgia, television show with country star Red Foley. He was so impressed that he invited her to perform on his popular television program, "Ozark Jubilee." Equally impressed was Foley's manager, Dub Allbritten, who took her on as a client. Instead of focusing on getting Lee a recording contract—females of any age were a hard sell with record executives, but a little girl, forget it!—Allbritten targeted television. As savvy managers were quickly learning, this was the best way to go over the heads of record executives and make their case directly to the public. Television was still in its infancy, but it was known to be an especially effective vehicle for reaching a female audience. In short order, Allbritten got bookings for Lee on "The Perry Como Show," then followed that up with appearances on "The Ed Sullivan Show" and "The Steve Allen Show."

Almost overnight, Lee became a national singing star, yet she'd never made a record. Decca corrected that before the year was out and signed the 12-year-old to a recording contract. The label's most immediate problem was how to package her. Since she wasn't a country singer per se, record executives, along with Allbritten, decided to fit her into the rockabilly mold Presley exploited so well.

Brenda Lee

Legendary producer Owen Bradley supervised Lee's first session. "Jambalaya," her first single, didn't chart, but it did garner a favorable review in *Billboard,* which predicted that she had the talent to skyrocket "to great heights, not only in the country field but in the pop field as well." The flip side, "Bigelow 6-200," was successful, but wasn't a big hit. Lee didn't make the charts until the following year with a song entitled "One Step at a Time." The song is probably most notable for a line that offers an indirect reference to Elvis Presley: "Every old hound dog once was a pup." By the fall of 1957, Allbritten and Decca were getting concerned about their child prodigy. She was 13 when Allbritten, a close friend of Colonel Tom Parker, learned that Presley was going to visit the Grand Ole Opry. It was a spur-of-the-moment decision by Presley (he'd driven to Nashville to give Parker an early Christmas present), and before going to the Opry he had to stop by a Nashville clothing store to buy something to wear.

To Allbritten's delight, Lee, looking much younger than 13, was photographed backstage with Presley at the Opry. He put his arm around her and clasped her hand, leaving her positively beaming as she looked up at him with admiration and something akin to child-lust. It was a great photograph, and Allbritten used it for all it was worth to promote Lee's career in the months ahead. She performed that day at the Opry—it was her first time—but neither the performance nor the publicity shot with Presley boosted her career.

Lee recorded a string of bop songs in 1958 and 1959, including "Rock the Bop," "One Teenager to Another," and "Dynamite," the song that earned her the nickname "Little Miss Dynamite," but nothing really clicked. Allbritten decided to book Lee in Europe, with the hope that overseas publicity would generate greater interest in the States. Everything was going smoothly until the promoter of a show at the Olympia Music Hall in Paris learned that Lee was a child—not an adult as he'd been told. The offended promoter canceled her appearance.

Allbritten, taking a cue from his friend Colonel Parker, then planted a story that Lee was actually a 32-year-old midget. The press ran with the story. Once it was published, Allbritten denied that she was a midget, and then he denied that he'd ever planted the story that she was. The resulting controversy forced the promoter to reinstate Lee as the opening act. She was such a hit that the show was held over for five weeks, and she was then asked to tour Italy, Germany, and England. When she returned home, she was an international star—and poised to zoom to the top of the pop charts with her first Number 1 single, "I'm Sorry."

Lee's experiences as a female in the music industry are unique for several reasons. Her young age, the fact that she always looked even younger than she was, and her status as a fatherless child elicited protective feelings from most of the male authority figures she encountered in the business. "My experience is probably different than most [women], in that I started out so young," Lee says. "I was looked over so closely by my mother, and then when I acquired my first manager, he was like more of a father figure than a manager, and he cared about me as a person, not just as a product. All the people around me really cared about me and didn't take advantage of me. I didn't encounter any of the things [other women have faced], but then I didn't live in California or New York. I lived in Tennessee, where I had a legal guardian who saw to it that no one could spend my money without me knowing where it was going."

By the time "I'm Sorry" went to Number 1 in July 1960, money—or the lack of it—was no longer a problem in the Tarpley household. Lee was a genuine star, the first female pop star of the modern era. Although she was still a teenager, there was nothing girlish about her powerful voice, and there was nothing childish about the sensual overtones of her music. These were two reasons why her Nashville record label was hesitant to allow her to release "I'm Sorry." Male executives thought she was too young to be singing about unrequited love. They were so concerned that they held the record up for several months out of fear of a backlash.

Lee's ability to be something she wasn't amazed people. Was she a grown woman in disguise? Was she a child in disguise? Or was she something else entirely—something so exotic it didn't yet have a name? They flocked to auditoriums and concert halls by the thousands to see the little girl who sounded liked a sex kitten. They thought if they could only see her, they would know the truth.

Technically, Lee was a pop star by virtue of the fact that her songs were topping the pop charts, but her music was closer to rock 'n' roll, and she was viewed as more of a rock artist by the teenagers who bought the records. For five consecutive years, both *Billboard* and *Cashbox* named her the most programmed female vocalist on radio. During a 1962 tour in England with Gene Vincent, they were billed as the "King and Queen of Rock." She was embraced as a female rock 'n' roller not just by the fans, but also by the performers—most of them males—who were defining the new genre. Jerry Lee Lewis wanted Lee to tour with him, but Mama Tarpley, perhaps mindful of the negative publicity Lewis got for marrying his 13-year-old cousin, put her foot down and refused to allow her daughter to tour with a man she called a barbarian.

Later that year, Lee followed up "I'm Sorry" with her second Number 1 hit, "I Want to Be Wanted," knocking off the charts the dominate males of the decade—Elvis Presley, Chubby Checker, and the Drifters. More Top 10 hits followed: "Dum Dum," "Emotions," "Break It to Me Gently," "All Alone Am I," and "Losing You." When she opened at the Copacabana, New York City's most popular nightclub at the time, a *Billboard* reviewer wrote that she had the "fire" to be a "teenage Sophie Tucker."

Decca signed Lee to a 20-year contract, guaranteeing her a fixed income for the duration of the contract, but she never saw the contract through to the end of the term. In 1977, she asked to be released from the contract so that she could pursue other musical interests. She recorded one single with Electra Records, then later returned to MCA Records, which had absorbed Decca into its operations.

Despite Lee's many pop hits in the early 1960s, she was a product of the 1950s and was an early casualty of the clampdown on women that took place later in the 1960s. Part of the problem was the rapidly changing music scene. The other was probably her 1963 marriage to Charles Shacklett, the son of a Nashville politician. Her mother was opposed to the marriage, so they eloped; two years later, at age 21, she had her first child. While the marriage was a good personal move for Lee and seemed to ground her and give her a sense of reality, it also went a long way in removing the mystique that had surrounded her age and sexuality. In an instant, she became a 19-year-old married woman. No longer was there anything exotic about her sexuality. She was now like everyone else. The mystery was gone.

As of the late 1990s, Lee was still a performing dynamo, doing daily performances at Branson, Missouri. She marvels at the progress women have made during her musical lifetime. "Women have pretty much come into their own, haven't they?" she said in a 1997 interview. "When I started out, we were not starring in our own road shows. It was always a male star. We were on the bill, but we were not the stars—and there were no women executives then that I knew of. Now you have women heading up publishing companies. Women in top jobs in every facet of the music industry. Being a woman, I always want to see women do well. Right now women are at the creative edge of everything they are doing. I think women are doing fabulously."

In early 1997, Lee performed with LeAnn Rimes, the newest teenage sensation on the pop and country charts, whose hit, "Blue," had made the 14-year-old an overnight superstar. If anyone had "been there, done that," it was Brenda Lee. She used the occasion to talk to both Rimes and her parents about success at a young age. "I told LeAnn I think it is important to have a life apart from [the music]," says Lee. "You have to be a child. I think it's important to go to school with children your own age, and she's not having those experiences. When you have a hit record, you have to get out there and be seen—and when you do that you are missing out on precious time you could be spending with people you love. That's one of my big regrets. If I had it to do all over again, I would spend more time with my brother and sisters, the people who are precious

LeAnn Rimes

to me, because I can't bring those times back. I look back and wish I hadn't done it the way I did. But LeAnn seems to be happy. She's such a talented person, and I think she will have longevity in this business. I think she should just pace herself. I know she's under a lot of pressure, but I think she is the one who wants it. I don't feel she is being pushed by her parents to do it."

In September 1997, Lee was inducted into the Country Music Hall of Fame. That same night, Rimes was awarded the association's Horizon award. Lee thanked the audience and all the people who had supported her throughout her nearly 40-year career. Rimes thanked the same audience and her mother and father for "being behind me 100 percent."

Backstage, Lee and Rimes stood side by side for a joint television interview. Rimes smiled and was gracious, especially toward Lee, but she seemed subdued and had a look of sadness in her eyes. Earlier that day, it had been announced that her parents had filed for divorce. The young singer's personal life was about to undergo radical change. Throughout the television interview, Lee glanced at Rimes, her face sympathetically reflecting the pain she sensed the teenager was feeling. If anyone could understand the lonesome sigh of the moment—and the ultimate price of the long, hard road ahead—it was Lee.

CHAPTER 4

THE COUNTER-REVOLUTION

THE 1960s

TOP 20 HONOR ROLL
1960–1969

Jewel Akens	Gale Garnett	Della Reese
The Angels	Bobbie Gentry	Jeannie C. Riley
Annette	Barbara George	Diane Renay
Shirley Bassey	Gladys Knight & the Pips	Julie Rogers
Jeanne Black	Lesley Gore	Rosie & the Originals
Marcie Blane	Eydie Gorme	Merrilee Rush
Jan Bradley	Brenda Holloway	Linda Scott
Anita Bryant	Mary Hopkins	The Shirelles
Vikki Carr	Janis Ian	Nancy Sinatra
Cathy Jean & Roommates	Brenda Lee	The Singing Nun
Cher	Barbara Lewis	Millie Small
Claudine Clark	Little Eva	Joanie Sommers
Dee Clark	Lolita	Dusty Springfield
Petula Clark	Barbara Lynn	Connie Stevens
Patsy Cline	Little Peggy March	Barbra Streisand
Judy Collins	Miriam Makeba	The Supremes
Skeeter Davis	Mama Cass	Carla Thomas
The Dixiebelles	Martha & the Vandellas	Sue Thompson
Patty Duke	Barbara Mason	Doris Troy
Shirley Ellis	Hayley Mills	Dionne Warwick
Shelley Fabares	Patti Page	Mary Wells
Toni Fisher	The Paris Sisters	Nancy Wilson
Inez Foxx	Ester Phillips	Kathy Young
Connie Francis	Sandy Posey	

By the mid-1960s, rock 'n' roll had been around for a decade. It wasn't so much that rock 'n' roll displaced women on the pop charts (it had 10 years to do that), as it was that the music was becoming something else, a genre that didn't really see a place for women. The reasons for this could be argued until doomsday. The changing role of women in society. The emergence of the feminist movement.

Arguments could also be made that *women* themselves were changing the music simply by virtue of changing the rules of the game. This is a valid argument, but a more convincing one is the influence of the growing rage that men of the 1960s were feeling toward society in general. Eighteen-year-old American men were being asked to fight in Vietnam in a war that was not only illegal and immoral, but made no sense to growing numbers of people, including scores of male recording artists who were treated with disdain by their conservative elders within the industry. The result was an understandable rage that was characterized by angry lyrics and driving, hard-edged rhythms that went out as a clarion call to a new generation of record buyers. Male recording artists expressed anger not just at society, but also at those who had been excluded from the demands of a society that spoke of equal rights with one voice and then, with a separate voice, excluded women from the same societal demands imposed on males. Women became the targets of this misdirected rage, both on stage and off.

The response from women is surprising in retrospect. They provided "free love" to the men expressing the rage, and they proclaimed to the world that they were now free from the shackles of society. At the time, such expressions of individuality seemed revolutionary, a vehicle for dramatic social change. Today, that revolution wasn't so much that as an invitation for abuse. Women went from being the "stars" of the recording industry to being backup singers and groupies. They swore to God that they were "free at last, godamighty, free at last," but, in truth, they'd sold themselves into even deeper bondage. They could damned well fuck any man they wanted—or more to the point, any man who asked them for it, if that was what they wanted—but they could damn well forget about competing with men on the charts.

If men were exerting such domination over women, why would female record buyers—still the majority—purchase records that reflected that attitude? Why would they buy such records as Leslie Gore's "You Don't Own Me" one minute, then turn around and buy Dion's "Runaround Sue" or Elvis Presley's "You're the Devil in Disguise"?

Women were of two minds. When they wanted meaningful lyrics, they turned to female artists. But when they wanted to dance, when they wanted to tap into that inner male rage that skewed their hormonal balance and set their toes tapping, they flocked to the male artists who weren't ashamed to give it to them. For those women who exchanged sex for the right to dance, the dancing apparently had the most meaning in their lives because it gave them the freedom they'd been promised in sex but never received.

For a decade that began with the chart domination of Brenda Lee and Connie Francis and ended as the second worst decade of the modern era for female recording artists, the 1960s has a mystique—richly undeserved when you consider the facts—for unbridled political liberalism and unlimited sexual freedom for women. The 1960s has been called the decade of "free love." Doesn't that, at the very least, imply sexual freedom for women? Most people thought so at the time.

Female singers were in abundance in the 1960s, though not in as great a supply as male singers. In fact, for every three men who made the Top 20, only one woman did. Petula Clark, Dusty Springfield, Gladys Knight and the Pips, and Dionne Warwick were all major players on the charts in the 1960s, but of that group only Clark made it to the top, first with "Downtown" in 1965, and with "My Love" the following year. Clark also made history by becoming the first British female artist of the rock era to top the charts.

© MCA RECORDS

Gladys Knight and the Pips

Petula Clark

Women showed flashes of solidarity in the 1960s, but the decade wasn't without its strife, particularly between the races. One source of discord was the way white female rock singers dressed. They wore faded and well-worn jeans, cheap pullover shirts, and sandals. Their hair was long and unbrushed. They seldom used makeup. And if they were like Janis Joplin, they didn't bother to bathe, wearing body odor as a badge of honor.

For many white kids of the 1960s, this was the "cool" look of that generation, but for blacks it was a constant source of discomfort. Black girl groups and solo singers would show up for a performance, even at outdoor concerts, dressed to the nines—elegant gowns, jewelry, high-heel shoes, lots of makeup, and well-coiffed. To them, the jeans and T-shirts worn by the white women who shared the stage with them were uniforms of slavery. They regarded this antiestablishment dress code as a sign of disrespect, not just to the music they were dedicated heart and soul to, but to them as African Americans. It was common to hear black singers, beneath their breath, bitterly refer to the "white trash" who shared the stage with them. This conflicting view of the way performers should dress was never openly addressed, and it continued, to a lesser degree, well into the 1990s.

CONNIE FRANCIS: A MULTIMEDIA CELEBRITY

As the decade began, Connie Francis, whose birth name was Concetta Rosa Maria Franconero, knocked Elvis Presley and the Everly Brothers off the top of the charts with her 1960 hit "Everybody's Somebody's Fool." Two years earlier, the 22-year-old Italian American thought her career was over. She'd recorded 10 songs for MGM Records, but none of them had made the charts. She was preparing for the final session with MGM when she played the song list for her father, a roofing contractor who had taken an interest in his daughter's career. When he heard the songs, he grimaced and told her they weren't any good. He gave her a 1923 song, "Who's Sorry Now," with the admonition, "Now there's a song."

Francis went to the session with the songs that her producer had chosen. During the last 15 minutes, she asked to record "Who's Sorry Now" out of respect for her father. Actually, she thought the song was much too old-fashioned to be a hit. Her thoughts probably weren't even on music that day: MGM had made it clear it had lost interest in her. Francis had applied for a scholarship at New York University and had every intention of getting out of the music business.

"Who's Sorry Now" lingered for months after its release and showed no indication it would chart. Francis wasn't surprised. Late one afternoon as she was sitting down to a big Italian dinner with her family, she turned on the television; she'd grown accustomed to watching Dick Clark's "American Bandstand." She heard Clark say something about a new girl singer who was going straight to the top. "Well, good luck to her," said Francis, thinking her own career was finished. Suddenly, she heard the song—her song—and started screaming: "Dad! Dad!" After Dick Clark mentioned "Who's Sorry Now," it peaked in the Top 10 and opened the door for a second hit, "My Happiness," which peaked at Number 2 in 1959.

Francis's first Number 1 hit, "Everybody's Somebody's Fool" bumped Elvis Presley off the top of the charts. Her second Number 1 hit, "My Heart Has a Mind of Its Own" displaced Chubby Checker, who had become a national sensation with "The Twist." She was the first woman to have two consecutive singles at the top of the charts. In between Francis's two hits, Brenda Lee scored with her Number 1 hit, "I'm Sorry." With Presley's movies doing so well at the box office, Francis was asked to do a film of her own. She asked Howard Greenfield and Neil Sedaka, two New York songwriters, to write the title song for the movie, *Where the Boys Are*. The result made her a multimedia celebrity and opened the door for Sedaka to have a career of his own.

Francis starred in three more MGM films: *Follow the Boys, Looking for Love,* and *When the Boys Meet the Girls.* A year and a half later, she scored with "Don't Break the Heart That Loves You," another song that her father had recommended. The intervening months had enabled Lee to have another Number 1 hit, "I Want to Be Wanted," and two black "girl" groups—The Shirelles with "Will You Still Love Me Tomorrow?" and The Marvelettes with "Please Mr. Postman"— to make history by becoming the first black girl groups to top the charts.

Knocking Francis out of Number 1 was actress Shelley Fabares, a co-star on the popular television sitcom, "The Donna Reed Show." Tony Owen, the show's producer, asked Fabares to record a song for the show. She wasn't a singer and was reluctant to do the song, but Owens convinced her it was necessary for an upcoming episode. To everyone's surprise, "Johnny Angel" was an instant hit, peaking at Number 1 in April 1962. Two years later, Fabares left "The Donna Reed Show" to pursue a recording and movie career. None of her subsequent recordings made it into the Top 20. She was right the first time; she wasn't really a singer—but she co-starred in three movies with Presley and in one movie with Fabian, who emerged as a major recording star later in the decade.

"Don't Break the Heart That Loves You" was prophetic for Francis. Later that year, she recorded two songs that made it into the Top 20, "Second Hand Love" and "Vacation," but by 1963 she was history as a hitmaker. She continued to perform in nightclubs until 1974 when she was brutally raped in a Howard Johnson's Motel in suburban New York. Emotionally devastated, she was unable to perform for six years. Then no sooner had she recovered from that trauma than she learned that her brother had been murdered gangland style at his New Jersey home.

"THERE'S NO PLACE TO GO BUT DOWN"

For the first two or three years of the decade, estrogen levels ran high on the charts as women stood toe-to-toe with their male competitors. Besides Connie Francis, Brenda Lee, and the emerging girls groups, solo performers like Peggy Lee and Nancy Wilson made a significant impact. Reviewing Wilson's 1964 album, *How Glad I Am,* a *Playboy* magazine critic wrote that the singer was "ultrafancy throughout." In the same issue, the magazine gave a good review to Peggy Lee's new albums and a bad review to Barbra Streisand's new album, *People:* "Color us disenchanted . . . the latest LP from the hottest female property in show business goes over with a whimper, not a bang." That review aside, *Playboy* was one of the few magazines that consistently gave good reviews to female recording artists.

By mid-decade, female recording artists were in deep trouble, and by the end of the decade, they'd been displaced almost entirely by male artists. Figures for the decade show that of the 292 solo recording artists to make the Top 20 during the decade, only 71—or 24 percent—were women. Since the 1950s, women had lost five percentage points, and the numbers were destined to get even worse. By mid-decade, women were experiencing a backlash. A 1962 article in *Time* magazine about the newly emerging folk movement is indicative of the tone the media used toward female recording artists: "It is not absolutely essential to have hair hanging to the waist—but it helps. Other aids: no lipstick, flat shoes, a guitar. So equipped, almost any enterprising girl can begin a career as a folk singer."

BREAKING DOWN DOORS

Nothing about Estelle Axton smacked of the music business. She was a former schoolteacher, 40 years of age, married with two children, and working as a bookkeeper at Union Planters Bank in Memphis. She didn't stand out in a crowd except for her red hair, which in the South of the 1950s was a rarity. Redheads were so uncommon that whenever someone encountered one, it was always good for a comment or two. Whether it was a case of the egg begetting the chicken or the other way around, Axton fit the redhead stereotype: shy but surprisingly outspoken when challenged, temperamental over small details, ambitious, and eager to prove herself.

When Jim Stewart, Axton's younger brother, approached her in 1958 with a business proposal to start up a record label, it came as a surprise. Stewart worked in the bonds department of a rival bank. After serving for two years in the army, earning a degree in business from what is now the University of Memphis, he'd settled into a button-down-collar career as a banker. Everyone in his family knew he had an interest in music. He'd played fiddle in several swing bands and occasionally performed on country music segments aired on radio station WDIA, which normally adhered to a black music format. But his musical excursions were viewed more as a hobby, something akin to a grown man playing with a Lionel train set.

Stewart's proposal was simple. He wanted to start up a record label, but didn't have the money to buy a recording machine. If Axton would provide the $2,500 for the machine, she could be his partner. She said she didn't have $2,500. "But you have a house, and you have several years paid into it," Stewart replied.

When Axton talked to her husband, his response was, "No way!" But the more Axton thought about it, the more she liked the idea. Finally, she talked her husband into mortgaging their house and investing the money in her brother's proposed record label. Axton and Stewart bought a one-track Ampex recorder and set up shop in a vacant grocery in a small community a few miles from Memphis. The building was owned by Stewart's barber, who told them they could have it rent-free if they would work with his 16-year-old daughter. The biggest item in the news at the time was Sputnik, the Russian satellite that had become the first manmade object in space, so they named their company Satellite Productions.

After more than a year of experimenting in the former grocery with the barber's daughter—and without the slightest hint of success—Axton and Stewart decided that they would have to move their studio to Memphis if they were to ever have any hope of recovering her investment. With the help of Chips Moman, a guitarist who had been working with Stewart, they located a vacant movie theater. "The guy that owned it rented it to us for $100 a month," says Axton. "Can you image a whole theater for $100? We ripped out all the seats and put a partition down the middle to compact the sound. The screen was up on the stage and that was where we put the recording machine that I had paid $2,500 for."

Once Axton and Stewart had the studio set up, they opened a record shop next door in the space that the barber shop had occupied. They kept their day jobs, but after work they put in time at the site of their new venture, with Stewart working in the studio and Axton operating the record shop. Like the recording studio, the record shop was put together piecemeal. Axton took orders for records from the people she worked with at the bank, then she went to Poplar Tunes, the largest record store in town, bought the records for 65 cents, and then re-sold them for $1 at the bank. With the profit, she bought stock for her own store.

For the longest time, the record shop kept the studio afloat. None of the early records Satellite Productions issued were successful. One day, Rufus Thomas, a popular black disk jockey on WDIA, came by the studio to pitch some ideas. He brought his 16-year-old daughter, Carla, and they sang together on "Cause I Love You," a song he'd written. Axton and Stewart thought it was

Rufus and Carla Thomas

good enough to release as a record. It did well enough locally—about 15,000 copies sold—so Atlantic Records head Jerry Wexler offered Axton and Stewart $1,000 for the right to distribute it nationally. "Cause I Love You" ended up selling about 35,000 copies, which wasn't a huge number, but was impressive enough to give the brother-and-sister team exposure as record executives.

One day, Axton and Stewart were sitting around the studio with Rufus and Carla, trying to come up with another idea, when Carla said, "I've got a song." Axton remembers, "As soon as Jim and I heard that song, we knew it was a hit. It's funny, when you hear a song you know if it's got something in it that will sell." With the $1,000 Axton and Stewart had received from Wexler, they took Carla Thomas to Nashville to record her song, "Gee Whiz," in a state-of-the-art studio. They played the recording for Wexler, who promptly signed Carla to a five-year contract and released the song on Atlantic. "Gee Whiz" peaked at Number 13 on the pop charts in March, 1961, making Thomas a teenage singing sensation. All of this came as quite a shock to the teenager. Those were the days of segregation in Memphis. The law prohibited blacks from using public libraries and swimming pools. It was also illegal for them to request service in white-operated restaurants and hotels. You can only imagine Thomas's feelings as she was ushered into a brave new world where she was treated even better than the white people back home. No other black teenager in Memphis had ever had such an experience.

At the time, Thomas really didn't grasp the significance of what was happening. "I'm going to be honest—no, I didn't," she says. "I was young. Being young and black in the Sixties, it was a thrill just to record. The kids are so sophisticated now. It took me a while to see the significance of what I was getting into. What I thought was fun, was a business. . . . There were so many things on the business end that I didn't know."

Over the next few years, Thomas outgrew her label as a "teen queen" and went on to record a series of solid R & B records, one of them a duet with Otis Redding ("Tramp"). When she went to Europe as part of the Stax/Volt Revue (Satellite Productions had become Stax Records after a California company named Satellite threatened a lawsuit), everyone enthusiastically received her, including Beatle Paul McCartney, who went to the Bag of Nails to hear her perform in a club setting. "There's an old saying that what comes from the soul, reaches the soul," she says. "From the blues came soul music, and it reached out and grabbed people, and I don't think people have been the same since." When interest in soul music tapered off in the 1970s, so did interest in Thomas's career. She eventually found a new career in the public school system, but she continued performing into the late 1990s at special events and soul music revivals.

RITA COOLIDGE: ADDICTED TO MUSIC

Carla Thomas opened doors, not just for other black entertainers, but for women in general, especially white women who felt rebellious over the race issue. One of those was Rita Coolidge, who had become addicted to Memphis soul while attending college at Florida State University. A native of Nashville, where her father was a minister, she'd performed in church from a early age, using the money she saved over the years to pay her tuition at Florida State. While she was in college, her parents moved to Memphis; upon graduation, she went there to spend the summer with her parents before returning to college to pursue a Master's degree in art. To earn extra money that summer, Coolidge sang radio jingles for a local company. That led to some studio work—and, before she knew what had happened—she was hooked on the record business, especially the soul music recorded by female singers, such as Carla Thomas.

By 1968, Axton and Stewart had built Stax Records up into the premier soul music independent in the country. Otis Redding. Booker T. & the MGs. Sam and Dave. The Mar-Keys. There seemed no end to the hits turned out of that old movie theater. In addition to Stax, hits were flowing like crazy from American Recording Studio, which Chips Moman had opened, and from Hi Records, which black producer Willie Mitchell operated. Coolidge was never able to gain entry into Stax, but she was a frequent visitor at American and Hi.

To Mitchell, Coolidge was a novelty. He recalls that she used to come to his studio, which was located in a black neighborhood, and sit there until all hours of the night, quietly watching, listening, and soaking up the music like a sponge. That amused Mitchell because at that time white girls in Memphis simply didn't do this. "I knew she was a singer, but we never did anything she wanted to sing on," he says. "Anytime we had a gig in Memphis, she came and observed what we were doing. She liked the rhythm section. She liked the feel of Memphis music."

After spending a year—instead of just a summer—in Memphis, Coolidge returned to Florida State to pursue her education. Then it hit her. Music was what she wanted, not an academic education. "If I hadn't spent that year in Memphis, I don't think I would have ended up in the music business," she says. "I went back and realized that I was hooked on the music business and didn't want to further my education. I wanted to further my musical career." Coolidge returned to Memphis and began singing in nightclubs with her sister, Priscilla. Coolidge also continued doing radio jingles, sometimes with her friend Donna Weiss, who was perfecting her talents as a songwriter. Coolidge recorded one of her friend's songs, "Turn Around and Love," at American, but before the record was released, she got an offer to tour as a backup singer

Kris Kristofferson and Rita Coolidge

with the Los Angeles-based Delaney and Bonnie. Coolidge moved to the West Coast and discovered shortly after getting there that "Turn Around Love" was a Top 10 hit on Los Angeles radio stations.

Coolidge went on to establish herself as a recording artist with A&M Records and to work with some of the leading male vocalists of her generation, Eric Clapton, Joe Cocker, and Graham Nash. While out promoting her first album, she met Kris Kristofferson in an airport; they became traveling companions and then got married and had a daughter. Weiss also moved to Los Angeles, where she co-authored "Bette Davis Eyes," once of the biggest hits of the 1980s. Priscilla Coolidge shocked polite Memphis society, first by dating Booker T. Jones, the leader of Booker T. & the MGs, and then by marrying him. Such things simply weren't done in Memphis—at least not in those days.

ESTELLE AXTON: GETTING THE LAST LAUGH

By the time Rita Coolidge was finding a new life in California, Estelle Axton was being squeezed out of Stax Records by business interests in California. Over the years, Stax had grown too large for a brother-and-sister operation. When they got word that Warner Brothers was acquiring Atlantic Records, they learned Stax would have to renegotiate its distribution agreement with Atlantic. By then, tensions between Atlantic head Jerry Wexler, and Axton and Stewart were well established.

Axton's relationship with Wexler had deteriorated early on, with the 1961 success of the Mar-Key's instrumental, "Last Night." When she first heard the song, she just knew it was a hit, and she pressured her brother to release it as a single. He didn't like the song. Neither did the song's producer, Chips Moman. Neither thought it would sell. But Axton continued to argue for the song's release. Stewart and Moman thought she wanted the song released because Packy, her son, played saxophone on it, but that wasn't the case. She'd been studying the records in her shop, and she just knew "Last Night" was a hit.

Finally, Stewart agreed to release the record. It was an instant hit in Memphis, but when Atlantic released it to national buyers, sales stalled. Axton blamed it on Atlantic and told Wexler he wasn't doing a very good job. "He wasn't promoting it," she says. "He didn't believe in it. He didn't believe it was a hit, but I knew from experience that it was. I was arguing with Jim about it, and he said for me to get on the phone and talk to Wexler about it. I did. I told him that it had been a hit in Memphis, and a record that could be a hit in Memphis could be a hit anywhere. Well, he didn't like my attitude at all. He called Jim back. He said, 'Don't let your sister get on the phone anymore to me. I don't want to talk to her.'" Axton laughed when she told the story years later, but that is because she got the last word when "Last Night" zoomed to Number 2 on the pop charts, making it the most successful record in Memphis recording history. "Well, I proved [Wexler] wrong," she says. "I didn't want to lose that record. I knew it was a hit."

When Stax Records was sold to Gulf & Western, Axton was offered 4,000 shares of Gulf & Western stock, along with a yearly salary of $25,000 for five years. There was one added condition. She had to agree not to re-enter the music business for five years. She agreed to those terms—and laughed all the way to the bank. About the time her five-year term was up, Stax went into bankruptcy, with Stewart and the others losing everything they'd invested in the company.

Axton had 4,000 shares of valuable stock, and she still had an ear for music. With her son-in-law as a partner, she started up a new label named Fretone. One of the songs she recorded for her new label was "Disco Duck," a tune disk jockey Rick Dees recorded. As the doors to Stax Records were being permanently shut in 1976, "Disco Duck" went to the top of the charts. Again, Axton had proved that she was more than just another "girl" executive. "Disco Duck" was the first Number 1 a female record executive ever ushered onto the charts and—as of 1998—still stands as the last Number 1 record out of Memphis.

Axton never received the recognition she deserved for her efforts at Stax. She received even fewer platitudes for her success with "Disco Duck," which initially sold more than 2 million copies. Yet, by any yardstick, she is the most successful—and influential—female executive in recording history. "Estelle never got credit for it," says BMI's Frances Preston. "She ran the place [Stax]. She was the groove that kept it together. That's what so many women have been: the glue that holds things together. Behind so many of the big names are women who have held things together."

BREAKING THE COLOR BARRIER

Carla Thomas was one of the first black female solo artists of the modern era to make the Top 20, but she wasn't the first black woman. Two girl groups, the Chantels and the Chordettes, already had cracked the Top 20. Three months before "Gee Whiz" peaked, the Shirelles, a black girls group from New Jersey, became the first to have a Number 1 single when "Will You Still Love Me Tomorrow?" knocked Elvis Presley off the top in January 1961. "Will You Still Love Me Tomorrow?" was released by Sceptor Records, a tiny New Jersey label owned by Florence Greenberg, whose daughter, Mary Jane, was a classmate of the four students who sang under the name, the Poquellos. Mary Jane urged her mother to listen to the group; she did and signed them to a contract. Not surprisingly, Florence Greenberg suggested they change their name. They chose the Shirelles, although afterward no one could remember the reason why.

Greenberg released their first single, "I Met Him on a Sunday," on her own label, then named Tiara Records. When the record charted at Number 49, Greenberg thought they would be better off if she leased the next two records to Decca Records. Neither record charted. Not ready to give up on the Shirelles, Greenberg decided to release their next single, "Dedicated to the One I Love," on her own label, which she renamed Sceptor. The record barely made it into the Top 100. The next song, "Tonight's the Night," made it just inside the Top 50. By that time, Greenberg had hired Luther Dixon, a former member of the Four Buddies, to produce the group. When time came to chose a followup song to "Tonight's the Night," Dixon told Greenberg and the Shirelles that he wanted to use a tune by Gerry Goffin and Carole King, two new songwriters.

When the Shirelles listened to the demo of "Will You Still Love Me Tomorrow?" they hated it. They thought it sounded too white for a black girls group. Not until they got into the studio and started recording the song did they change their minds. During production, Dixon added his own special R & B touch, and Carole King came into the studio to help out, playing kettle drums when needed.

"Will You Still Love Me Tomorrow?" scored a number of "firsts." The first record by a girls group to go to Number 1. The first to be released by a label that a woman owned. The first chart-topper for Carole King, who went on to become one of the most influential songwriters of the 1960s and 1970s. A decade later, King would score a Number 1 hit—as an artist—with "It's Too Late/I Feel the Earth Move."

Female label owner, female songwriter, female singers—it was a new experience for women in the music business. The gate had been opened. But more was at stake than new opportunities for women. Coupled with that were new opportunities for African Americans. Florence Greenberg in New Jersey—and Estelle Axton in Memphis—did more than simply flex their newly discovered female muscle; they pricked the conscience of white America and paved the way for black entertainers to enter the mainstream. The African-American/white-female coalition would prove to be unbeatable.

In between "Will You Still Love Me Tomorrow?" and the Shirelles' second Number 1 hit, "Soldier Boy," emerged yet another Number 1 hit from a black girls group, "Please Mr. Postman." The song was recorded by the Marvelettes, a Detroit high school quartet that auditioned for Berry Gordy, Jr.'s record label, Tamla Records. Gordy was a former boxer and Ford Motors mechanic who had a knack for music. He'd launched Tamla Records in 1959. He'd wanted to name the label Tammy, after the Debbie Reynolds hit of the same name, but trademark restrictions forced him to use Tamla. He'd found some success with a girls group named the Miracles, but the Number 1 slot eluded him.

When "Please Mr. Postman" was first offered to the Marvelettes, group member Georgia Dobbins liked the melody but hated the lyrics, so she asked the three male songwriters if she could change them. She completely rewrote the song, keeping only the title. Meanwhile, she learned that her mother was seriously ill. Dobbins taught the other group members how to sing the song, then dropped out of the group to take care of her ailing mother. "Please Mr. Postman," with 22-year-old unknown Marvin Gaye on drums, went to Number 1 in December 1961, providing Gordy with his first hit.

WOMEN: MOTOWN'S CLAIM TO FAME

Encouraged by this success, Gordy formed a new label, Motown (short for motor town) and sought new talent. He was immensely successful with several of his male acts: the Temptations, Marvin Gaye, Eddie Holland, the Miracles, and Little Stevie Wonder. But Motown's biggest claim to fame would come from its female acts. More so than any other male record executive in America, Gordy had become a believer in the musical power of the female. He was unable to get another Number 1 with the Marvelettes, but they scored with two hits in 1962, "Playboy" and "Beechwood 4-5789." He was, however, able to find success with three female acts that became legendary in the 1960s and 1970s: the Supremes, Martha & the Vandellas, and Mary Wells.

Detroit-born Wells proved that Gordy's faith in women was well placed when her song, "My Guy," went to Number 1 in May 1964. Before that, she'd recorded a number of singles that made the charts: "The One Who Really Loves You," "You Beat Me to the Punch," and "You Lost the Sweetest Boy." Wells was the first person signed to the Motown label, and she was the first to have a Number 1 hit. "My Guy" went on to become a classic, but, unfortunately, it was her last single to make the Top 20. Wells was also the first major artist to leave the Motown fold, and she was unable to carry her earlier success into the 1970s. In 1990, she was diagnosed with throat cancer and died shortly thereafter.

Martha Reeves, later of Martha & the Vandellas, was working for Gordy as a secretary when he pulled her out of the office and into the studio to sing background with two other women on a Marvin Gaye session. Two of the songs, "Stubborn Kind of Fellow" and "Hitch Hike," were two big hits for Gaye and convinced Gordy that the women had a future as a recording act. As Martha & the Vandellas, they scored with four Top 10 hits: "Heat Wave," "Nowhere to Run," "Jimmy Mack," and "Dancing in the Street," which peaked at Number 2 in October 1964. After the group ran out of steam in the 1960s, Reeves continued to record as a solo artist in the 1970s, although without ever achieving the commercial success of the group.

Motown's biggest selling and most enduring group was the Supremes, a trio made up of Diana Ross, Mary Wilson, and Florence Ballard. The group provided Motown with its third Number 1 in August 1964, when "Where Did Our Love Go?" topped the charts. The Supremes weren't an instant success; they'd released eight singles, all of which had failed to make the Top 20. Gordy continued to release the group's records because he believed in them, particularly in Diana Ross. The Supremes followed up the success of "Where Did Our Love Go?" two months later with their second Number 1, "Baby Love." For the next five years, they gave Motown some of the most memorable hits of the decade: "Come See About Me," "Stop! In the Name of Love," "My World Is Empty Without You," and "You Can't Hurry Love." In 1969, Ross broke away from the group to pursue a solo career, but not before contributing to "Someday We'll Be Together," the group's twelfth Number 1 hit.

Other girl groups, such as the Dixie Cups with their Number 1 "Chapel of Love" (1964), the Shangri-Las with their Number 1 "Leader of the Pack" (1964), and the Angels with "My Boyfriend's Back" (1963), were competitive. But only the Supremes survived as chart-toppers from 1964 until the end of the decade.

THE METEORIC RISE OF TWO COUNTRY MUSIC STARS

The 1960s was an interesting decade for female country singers. The explosion of rock music and the British invasion cut deeply into country music sales; sales of records by female artists were especially affected. In spite of those limitations, the decade produced Loretta Lynn and Tammy Wynette, two of the strongest female voices in country music history.

Other female country singers of the 1960s include: Skeeter Davis, whose 1962 hit, "The End of the World," did well on the pop charts; Jessi Colter, whose album *A Country Star Is Born* received critical acclaim; Barbara Mandrell, whose first hits emerged toward the end of the decade; Melba Montgomery, who is best known for her duets with George Jones; Sandy Posey, who turned to country music after her first hits, "Born a Woman" and "Single Girl," scored on the pop charts; Jeannie C. Riley, whose "Harper Valley P.T.A." was one of the biggest single hits of the 1960s; Jeanne Seely, who liked to be called "Miss Country Soul"; Jean Shepherd, known for her yodeling; and Connie Smith, who was Music Row's "insider" favorite of the 1960s.

Diana Ross

Loretta Lynn: A Legend's Slow Rise to Fame

Loretta Lynn's rise to fame is legendary by now. Most people have heard the story of the "coal miner's daughter," as told in the movie and autobiography of the same name. From humble origins in Butcher Hollow, Kentucky, she became—almost by grit alone—a household name at a time when American society was undergoing its most convulsive upheaval since the Civil War. Her success didn't come overnight, but it almost did. From 1961 to 1962, she went from being a wannabe with a record out on a small label no one had ever heard of, to a regular on the Grand Ole Opry with a Top 10 hit, appropriately entitled "Success." That year *Cashbox* magazine identified her as the most programmed woman in country music.

If Lynn's contributions began and ended with her output of passionate, heartfelt songs, that in itself would be enough to justify her career. But there is more to her story than great music. Just as important were her efforts to obtain equality for women. Minnie Pearl once said that Lynn was the person who battered down the barriers for other women in the music business—and there is truth to that.

Lynn knew about breaking down barriers because she had to do it just to survive. To her, it had nothing to do with gender. After a Vancouver lumberman financed and released "I'm a Honky-Tonk Girl," her first record, on a label named Zero Records, she and her husband, Mooney, struck out in their old Mercury on a promotional tour, with a goal of visiting as many radio stations as they could in three months. Radio DJs were so shocked to see her breeze into the studio that they played her record. No one told Lynn that recording artists—especially female recording artists—didn't dare call on radio stations for fear of offending someone, so she followed her instincts. How was she going to get her record played, she reasoned, if she didn't get out and ask those radio people to give it a listen? Lynn's common sense forever changed the way records were promoted. It also lifted the hearts of other women who dreamed of being brave and creative and free at heart.

The first years of Lynn's career coincided with the birth of the women's liberation movement. Betty Friedan's *The Feminine Mystique* found a growing readership during that time, and the National Organization of Women (NOW) was formed. Lynn was never what most women would call a feminist, but if an educated woman without a rural Southern accent had acted that way and uttered the public statements she'd made, the woman would probably have been branded a flaming feminist. Lynn was never shy about expressing her opinions to interviewers or to anyone in the audience who had questions about the role of women in American society. But her strongest statements were issued in her music. That was her most eloquent voice on the issue of women's rights.

Loretta Lynn

Lynn's most recurring theme was that women should have control over their lives. Her belief that the birth-control pill was an important advancement for women was expressed in her 1975 song, "The Pill." She caught hell for that song. Some radio programmers refused to play it, and arch-conservative preachers held her up as an example of how women were going to hell in a handbasket— but she never apologized for the song.

Some of Lynn's best songs in the 1960s and 1970s reflected women's issues. Sometimes the titles are enough to explain the content: "We've Come a Long Way Baby," "I Wanna Be Free," "You Wanna Give Me a Lift (But This Gal Ain't A-Goin' That Far)," and "When the Tingle Becomes a Chill." In her 1973 hit, "Hey Loretta," Lynn sings about a runaway housewife who calls for women's liberation to begin in her life "right now." Says Lynn in her autobiography, *Coal Miner's Daughter:* "Sure, I've heard people say men are bound to run around a little bit. It's their nature. Well, shoot, I don't believe in double standards, where men can get away with things that women can't. In God's eyes, there's no double standard. That's one of the things I've been trying to say in my songs. . . . There's plenty of songs about how women should stand by their men and give them plenty of loving when they walk through the door, and that's fine. But what about the man's responsibility? . . . No woman likes to be told, 'Here's the deal.'"

Tammy Wynette: A Legend's Fast Rise to Fame
Of course, it was Tammy Wynette who wrote the book on "Stand By Your Man." Literally. It is the title of her 1969 Number 1 country hit and her autobiography. "Stand By Your Man" resurfaced in the early 1990s as a topic of national debate when Hillary Clinton told a television interviewer that she didn't intend to be a "Stand By Your Man" type of First Lady. The remark offended Wynette, as well as many of the singer's fans. If Clinton had done a little more research— and perhaps had been a fan of country music—she undoubtedly would have had a greater appreciation of the contributions Wynette had made to women's rights. Even before Clinton's comments, the women's movement had criticized Wynette. "I don't see anything in that song that implies a woman is supposed to sit home and raise babies while a man goes out and raises hell," she wrote in her 1979 autobiography. "But that's what women's lib members thought it said."

In an August 1971 *Newsweek* magazine article, under the headline "Songs of Non-Liberation," reporter Eleanor Clift described Wynette as a "platinum-haired divorcee," then went on to explain that "the way she sings, almost manfully, about how tough it is to be a woman, accounts for her edge over her rivals." The article is interesting because although Clift berated Wynette for her country ways—observing the required political correctness of the times—would she have dared describe city slicker Jane Fonda as a "platinum-haired divorcee?"

Tammy Wynette

Clift was obviously impressed by the singer's accomplishments. Unless Clift's article was rewritten by a male editor, it serves as a reminder that sexism wasn't reserved solely for males. Although *Newsweek* poked fun at Wynette for not being attuned to women's liberation, the masthead of that issue indicates that only one of the magazine's 45 top editors was female.

Wynette's beginnings were like Loretta Lynn's. Born in a tar-paper shack near Tupelo, Mississippi, Wynette had to overcome a series of obstacles, including a very bad marriage and health problems, to find success as a recording artist. She didn't sign her first contract until 1966, by which time Lynn was already the reigning queen of country music. But Wynette's success came quickly, first with "Apartment #9" in 1967, and then later that year with "Your Girl's Gonna Go Bad." She became even more popular than Lynn on the concert circuit, and by the late 1960s Wynette had entered the "legend" category with such classics as "D-I-V-O-R-C-E" and "Take Me To Your World."

Wynette followed in Lynn's footsteps by recording songs that presented a strong female perspective. "Unwed Fathers" offered a criticism of men who abandoned women when they got pregnant. "Another Chance" tells the story of a victim who survives. By the time Wynette found success on the charts, male vocalists still accounted for the great majority of sales. "Because of this the producers would always sign a man before a woman," Wynette wrote in her autobiography. "The labels were convinced that women, who buy most of the records anyway, would spend money to hear a male singer quicker than they would to hear another woman." A series of failed marriages, including one to country star George Jones, kept her in the news throughout the 1960s and 1970s. But throughout it all, she displayed the same survivor's instincts that Lynn possessed. Wynette was able to move past her personal problems and focus on her career, turning out one hit after another well into the 1980s. She was still a popular concert draw in the late 1990s and continued with her recording career.

Tracy Nelson: Folk-Blues-Rock Maverick

About the same time Loretta Lynn and Tammy Wynette were making inroads for women in country music, West Coast blues mama Tracy Nelson moved to Nashville. Some say the city still hasn't recovered. Nelson was a student at the University of Wisconsin in 1965 when she released her debut album, *Deep Are the Roots*. It was a folk-blues collection, a genre that was popular on college campuses. Reaction to the album was good, so Nelson packed up and moved to San Francisco, where she thought she would find an even greater acceptance of her music. This was during the height of the hippie free-love and cheap-beads era, and she was appalled at what she saw. She formed a rock band named

Mother Earth, recorded an album in 1968 that brought comparisons to Janis Joplin, and then hit the road with the band to promote the album.

The last date on the tour was Nashville. While there, Nelson got word from her record label that it wanted a new album. She decided to stay in Nashville and record there. She and the band rented a farm west of the city and settled into a recording routine at a studio named Bradley's Barn. One day, after the album was finished and the band had returned to California, Pete Drake, Nelson's producer, took her by Music City Recorders, a studio owned and operated by Scotty Moore, who had achieved fame in the 1950s and 1960s as Elvis Presley's first guitarist and manager. The meeting with Moore resulted in a decision to record a second album, a collection of country songs with Nashville session musicians and Moore as engineer. It was an educational experience for all involved.

Although Nelson had been every bit as offended by the San Francisco hippie scene as most country session players would have been had they witnessed it for themselves, she was like nothing any of them had ever seen. In their eyes, she was the epitome of the West Coast hippiedom they'd read about and seen on television. She cussed a blue streak. She flashed an occasional marijuana stash in the studio. She dressed like a man, wearing jeans and pullover shirts. She showed no reverence for anything traditional. She was absolutely fearless. Rose Drake, Pete's widow, laughed when she talked about it years later. "We had never heard women say four letter words before," she says—and Nelson threw them out like there was no tomorrow. If she saw that her language was embarrassing the men, she would escalate the tempo of her profanity. "It was unbelievable what she came out with. They were afraid to bring people into the studio because they didn't know what Tracy was going to do next," says Drake.

Make a Joyous Noise, the Nashville album, was released as a two-disk set, one disk country, the other a rock collection they called "city" music. Nelson ended up buying a farm west of Nashville. Although she mellowed considerably in the 1980s, she continued recording her special blend of blues-rock.

JANIS JOPLIN: A SHOOTING STAR

Janis Joplin escaped the San Francisco music scene via another route, heroin. She'd grown up in Port Arthur, Texas, a conservative oil refinery town where men were men and women were women—and the twain never met except on Saturday night. She had a very hurtful and confused childhood, primarily because she felt different from the other girls and didn't seem to fit their concept of what a little girl was supposed to act like. She was so despised that other students actually threw things at her. Adolescence amplified her childhood hurt a hundredfold.

Joplin's solution to her adolescent pain was to run away from home at age 17. She enrolled in a school to learn to become a keypunch operator, but that didn't last for long. All she could do really well was sing, so in 1966 she gravitated toward the Haight-Ashbury district in San Francisco, where she hoped to connect with a band. Her reaction to the hippie scene was every bit as negative as Tracy Nelson's, and she returned to Texas. The following year, Big Brother and the Holding Company, a San Francisco band, contacted her and asked if she would be interested in returning to the West Coast. Joplin jumped at the offer. Big Brother and the Holding Company was the house band at the well-known Avalon Ballroom, and singing for them would mean steady work.

Joplin and the band recorded an album for a small label; a single from the album, "Down On Me," attracted a lot of attention but didn't make the Top 20. She didn't attract the attention of a major label until the following year, when she gave an electrifying performance at the Monterey Pop Festival; Columbia Records signed her to a recording contract and released an album, *Cheap Thrills,* followed by a single, "Piece of My Heart," that made it onto the charts in 1968. Buoyed by the success of the album, Joplin left the band and recorded a solo album, *I Got Dem Ol' Kozmic Blues Again.* When that album failed to sell as expected, she stopped performing for a while, then reemerged with the Full Tilt Boogie Band to work on what would be her final album. Songwriter Kris Kristofferson stayed with her for a short time during this period; when he moved on, he left a song, "Me and Bobby McGee."

Joplin had been an alcoholic for years, but by 1970 she'd become a full-blown heroin addict. She died of an overdose on October 4, 1979, in a hotel room littered with empty whiskey bottles, before work on her album was completed. When it was released posthumously in 1971, "Me and Bobby McGee" went to Number 1 on the pop charts. Like soul singer Otis Redding, Joplin died without knowing her work would ever receive widespread acceptance. It probably wouldn't have mattered to Joplin. Her voice was powerful—filled with gut-wrenching angst—but not especially melodic. She was a sexual creature, on and off stage, but not what you would call physically attractive, except when she sang and then everyone agreed she was absolutely beautiful. Music to Joplin was a lifestyle, not an art form; it was who she was, not what she did.

With Joplin's untimely death evolved a mystique that has continued to the present day. With the passing of time, it has become apparent that her popularity was due as much to the intensity of her performances as to her recordings. Her pain made her different—the fact that she seemed to be dying, spiritually and emotionally, each time she stepped out on stage. People seemed mesmerized by the sight of her. Their faces showed the same awe and titillation reflected in the faces of people watching a public execution, or a train wreck. Joplin was giving her life for her fans right there on stage, and it was riveting to those who witnessed it. "Have you ever been loved?" she once asked a friend. "I haven't. I only feel it on stage."

TURNING THE TABLES ON MEN

Janis Joplin stood alone in the 1960s in her efforts to adopt the male persona. Most women wanted success, but as women. The first woman to turn the tables on men by using the same technique perfected by Elvis Presley was Nancy Sinatra, Frank's daughter. In 1961, Frank started up his own record label, Reprise. Nancy was one of the first artists signed. Her first single, "Cufflinks and a Tie Clip," died a quick death, but no one at the label was about to give up on Frank's daughter. For five years, she released single after single, with none of them making the Top 20. Finally, after 15 successive failures, Reprise turned to successful writer/producer Lee Hazlewood and asked him to help. "You're not the virgin next door," Hazlewood told Nancy Sinatra, according to *Time* magazine. "You've been married and divorced. You're a grown woman. I know there's garbage in there somewhere."

Hazlewood wrote a song he thought would do the trick. "These Boots Are Made For Walkin'" was a brassy, no-nonsense anthem to female liberation. It went to Number 1 in February 1966, giving Sinatra the first chart-topper by a woman since Connie Francis's 1958 hit, "Stupid Cupid." Hazlewood, who also produced the record, was savvy enough to take the Presley formula and use it for Sinatra. The lyrics were designed to appeal to women, and her appearance—short skirts and hot pants that showed off her toned thighs, coupled with a striking girl-next-door face and a Playmate of the Month body—was designed to appeal to male record buyers.

That same formula had worked for Leslie Gore two years earlier, though the sex appeal aspect wasn't consciously stressed because of the singer's young age. In June 1963, her first release, "It's My Party," went to the top of the charts. Gore was only 17 at the time and attending a New Jersey high school. The record was produced by Quincy Jones and gave him his first Number 1 hit. Female record buyers, who identified with the song's stand-up lyrics, devoured it. It also caught the attention of males, who thought Gore was cute but sexy.

If it appears unseemly to equate sex appeal to an underage teen, you must keep in mind that in the early years of the rock era, teenagers purchased the vast majority of records. Over the years, the median age increased, stretching into the fifties and sixties, as many of the early rock stars, such as the Rolling Stones, approached their sixties. But, in the beginning, it was a teenage thing—and it is a documented fact that teenage boys are attracted to teenage girls. Gore followed her first hit with a string of Top 10 hits: "Judy's Turn To Cry," "She's a Fool," and "You Don't Own Me," whose lyrics advocated the radical concept that men had no right to tell women what to do or what to say. This was strong stuff for its time and ultimately cost Gore her male audience and her supremacy on the charts.

THROWBACKS

The decade saw the emergence of a number of singers who preferred to remain in the pop field that female artists in the 1950s had defined. Nancy Wilson was able to crack the Top 20 with only one song, "(You Don't Know) How Glad I Am" (1964), but she maintained a strong nightclub base and received positive reviews from pop-oriented magazines, such as *Playboy,* which described her as "the girl with the golden voice" and "ultrafancy throughout." In that same category was Barbra Streisand, who *Playboy* recognized as the "hottest female property in show business" in 1964. Although that assessment was based primarily on her theatrical work—she appeared on Broadway in *I Can Get It For You Wholesale* and *Funny Girl*— she had a Top 20 hit in 1964 with "People," a song taken from *Funny Girl.* Streisand was a chart contender throughout the 1960s, but her best work was yet to come.

One of the strongest voices of the decade belonged to Aretha Franklin, a Memphis-born soul singer who zoomed to the top of the charts in 1967 with "Respect." The song had been written by Otis Redding, who had released it earlier only to watch it founder on the charts. The success of Franklin's version shocked Redding. Why would a woman have a hit with a song he'd tried—and failed—to score with? Same melody. Same lyrics. Opposite results.

Obviously, the success lay with a female audience. It was one thing for a black male to sing to a largely female audience about respect—and another thing for a black woman to deal with the same issue. Gender trumps race. At least in the Top 20 it does. With her powerful, gospel-laced voice, Franklin became a symbolic expression of the feminist movement. There is no indication she ever sought that role, but there is plenty of evidence that she didn't back away from it. She followed up the success of "Respect" with a string of hits in the 1960s, including "Chain of Fools," "Think," and her own version of Carole King's "(You Make Me Feel Like) A Natural Woman."

Aretha Franklin

BOBBIE GENTRY: A SURPRISE SUCCESS

Roberta Lee Streeter was inquisitive from an early age. In the early 1950s, when her family was living in a multi-unit house in a pleasant neighborhood in Greenwood, Mississippi, she sometimes played outside in the fenced-in backyard with a 6-year-old boy who sometimes dropped by to visit his cousins, who also lived in the house. Sometimes Streeter and the boy would squirt the water hose at each other. Other times they would poke around, peering into storage sheds and behind vine-covered trees.

One hot summer day, Streeter said, "Wanta' see something?" The little boy said, "Sure." Streeter, who was about 7 years old, led the little boy inside, moving quietly through the dark shadows of the house. Without saying a word, the two of them made their way past a gauntlet of oscillating electric fans that purred with quiet efficiency, sending currents of cool air through the house. When they entered the back bedroom where Streeter's mother was lying on the bed, she glanced up at her daughter. "Hi, honey," she said; then she looked at the little boy, surprised to see him in the room.

Streeter then swept her arm out toward her mother, saying proudly, "See!" The little boy looked at the mother, who was cradling an infant to her breast. He'd seen infants before, but he'd never seen a female breast. He stared at the woman's breast, seemingly paralyzed, then heard his playmate say, "Let's go back outside." He slowly backed out of the room as Streeter broke into a skipping gait that little girls are so fond of.

Eventually, Streeter moved away from Greenwood, first to Houston, Mississippi, then to Palm Springs, California, where she attended high school. After studying music at the Los Angeles Conservatory of Music and philosophy at UCLA, she did secretarial work for a while, then put together a song-and-dance team and struck out for Las Vegas in 1966.

By then, Streeter had changed her name to Bobbie Gentry. Within a year, she'd built up a successful nightclub act. She wrote all of the group's material and performed with them as a singer and hoofer. Clearly, the display of bare breasts that permeated the Vegas nightclub scene didn't intimidated her. Because men threw together most Vegas acts, Gentry's success was unique for the times. She was aggressive, but she had a charming, sultry way about her—part of that Southern upbringing, no doubt—that enabled her to effectively deal with men and get what she wanted. Vegas was a tough town, but the city's reputation didn't threaten her in the least.

One day, Gentry made a demo of "Mississippi Delta," a song she'd written. She took it to a song publisher, who played it for Kelly Gordon at Capitol Records. Gordon took one look at this darkly exotic woman with a striking face and long, waist-length black hair, and signed her as an artist. Capitol agreed to release "Mississippi Delta" as a single. Since the label needed something for the flip side, she went into the Capitol Records studio on Vine Street in Hollywood to record "Ode to Billie Joe," another song she'd written. It took less than an hour to record the song. It was just Gentry accompanying herself on guitar. Later, Gordon went in and added strings to the track and listed himself as producer.

Capitol wasn't all that excited about "Ode to Billie Joe." It was too long. It couldn't be categorized, and it couldn't be aimed at a specific audience. Capitol reminded Gentry that she was entering the market as a solo female singer, a category that wasn't doing very well on the charts. In July, 1967, "Mississippi Delta" was released. It was a good song, but not one that was likely to break out of the pack. For some reason, disk jockeys all over the country flipped it over and started playing "Ode to Billie Joe." On August 5, 1967, the song debuted on the Hot 100; three weeks later, it bumped the Beatles' "All You Need Is Love" out of Number 1 and prevented Diana Ross and the Supremes' "Reflections" from moving up. The record's success stunned both Gentry and Capitol Records.

In September, accompanied by Gordon, Gentry returned to Houston, Mississippi, for a town-sponsored homecoming celebration. By that time, everyone in the country wanted to know about Gentry. "Ode to Billie Joe," with its mysterious reference to something being flung from a river bridge, had intrigued the record buying public. A media contingent befitting a presidential candidate descended upon tiny Houston. Gordon was inundated with requests for interviews. *Newsweek* was there. So was *Time*. The wire services. "Who is this Bobbie Gentry?" they demanded to know—and "What's the deal with that song?"

Gordon turned down all the media requests, saying that Gentry just wanted to enjoy the homecoming celebration. Among those requesting an interview was a student reporter from the University of Mississippi, who had been sent to cover the homecoming for *Mississippi* magazine. He was among those Gordon had turned down. Later in the day, when everyone, including Gentry, was seated in a banquet hall, the reporter approached the singer and asked for an interview. Neither Gentry nor the reporter knew it at the time, but the reporter was the little boy she'd escorted into her mother's bedroom that hot summer day nearly 20 years earlier. Gentry looked over the reporter for the longest time. She'd heard the question, clearly, but something was preventing her from giving the answer Gordon had instructed her to give. The reporter couldn't take his eyes off the singer. There was a connection that neither understood. Finally, Gentry nodded, the words following at a slower pace. "Okay," she said. "Meet me after the reception and we'll talk then." "Bobbie!" Gordon said, shaking his head. "You don't have time."

Gentry did the interview—it was the only one she granted—but the reporter didn't understand why until years later when he learned that Bobbie Gentry and Roberta Streeter were one in the same. Gentry herself didn't know why. During the interview, the reporter asked her if "Ode to Billie Joe" was meant as a veiled protest of some kind. Opposition to the war in Vietnam was at its zenith, and the national media analyzed every book, record, and movie that the under-30 generation created with suspicion. There was talk among the reporters at the banquet that Gentry might be a subversive of some kind, so asking her if she was a protest singer seemed appropriate. She laughed at the question. "No, I am not a protest writer," she said. "My theme is indifference. I am not protesting. I am trying to call attention to the indifference that individuals possess even while discussing a boy who has jumped from a bridge."

After the interview, the reporter offered to give Gentry a ride back to the Memphis airport in his Mustang convertible. As they were walking toward the car, Gordon came running up, clearly agitated. "What are you doing?" he demanded. Gentry told him. "No, no," he said, taking her by the hand. "Sorry," Gentry said, looking like a woman who didn't enjoy taking orders from a man, even if he was her producer and a big-shot record executive.

Years later, Gentry would complain about her treatment as a woman: "I originally produced 'Ode to Billie Joe,' and most of the others, but a woman doesn't stand much chance in a recording studio." No matter what a woman did in the studio, the record always contained a man's name as producer when it was released.

"Ode to Billie Joe" sold more than 3 million copies and won three Grammys. Gentry continued writing and recording songs that focused on women. "Fancy" was about a prostitute, "Belinda" was about a stripper, and "The Girl from Cincinnati" was about a movie star who had been forced to earn stardom in the backseat of a thousand different cars. None of Gentry's subsequent efforts, however, ever achieved the level of success of "Ode to Billie Joe." In 1969, she married Bill Harrah, president of the Desert Inn Hotel in Las Vegas. They divorced soon thereafter, and she married singer Jim Stafford. That marriage lasted less than a year, and she divorced him shortly after giving birth to their baby.

When "Ode to Billie Joe" was made into a major movie in 1976, Gentry returned to Mississippi for a visit. Interviewed by a reporter for *The Delta Democrat-Times,* she said she thought the song had been successful because people were tired of male-dominated psychedelic rock groups. "There were no songs on the charts by female recording artists then. But all the drawbacks turned into advantages," she said.

Gentry wrote and recorded more than 70 songs in the 1970s, and starred in her own television series on BBC-TV in London. But she was unable to recreate her earlier success and eventually dropped out of sight. In 1991, Reba McEntire had a major hit with a remake of Gentry's song "Fancy."

JEANNIE C. RILEY: THE DREAM BECOMES A NIGHTMARE

Following in Bobbie Gentry's footsteps was Jeanne C. Riley, a Kentucky-born singer who moved to Nashville from Texas in 1966 in hopes of landing a recording contract. She recorded demo after demo, but none of them caught anyone's attention. She was working as a secretary when Shelby Singleton, Jr., asked her if she would come into Sun Records to sing on a record titled "Harper Valley P.T.A." Singleton had purchased Sun Records from Sam Phillips in Memphis and had relocated the label to Nashville. The song had come his way from songwriter Tom T. Hall, who had recorded the demo with a female singer whose voice Singleton felt was too soft to sell the song.

"Harper Valley P.T.A." tells the story of a widowed mother who the P.T.A. attacks for what it considers loose morals. It is an angry song, one that lashes out at hypocrisy and promotes the right of women to follow their destiny. Singleton sensed that the song was right for the times. Everyone, it seemed, was on edge in 1968. The Vietnam War was raging. Martin Luther King, Jr., and Robert Kennedy had both been shot to death.

Riley was no different. She was angry about the anger. When she stepped up to the microphone, all those pent-up feelings—anger at the way society was falling apart, anger at the way her music career was going nowhere—came bellowing out in "Harper Valley P.T.A." Singleton had records pressed within 24 hours of the session and sold nearly 2 million copies within two weeks.

On September 21, 1968, "Harper Valley P.T.A." was the Number 1 record in America, out-selling the Rascals' "People Got To Be Free" and the Beatles' "Hey Jude." If Riley had once lain awake at night dreaming of a hit record, those dreams turned into nightmares as she struggled to adopt the "fallen woman" image depicted in the song. That fall she attended the Country Music Association Awards to accept an honor for having the "Single of the Year." She showed up at the nationally televised event wearing a floor-length gown. When Singleton learned this, he ordered the gown cut off into a mini-dress, and he provided Riley with silver boots to wear with the dress. The incident humiliated her, but it was just one of many in which she was forced to be someone she wasn't.

The success of "Harper Valley P.T.A." came close to destroying Riley. She pulled herself out of that morass in 1972 by becoming a born-again Christian, but she never again had a major hit.

This was becoming a common theme in pop music. When male artists had hit records in the 1960s, they seemed to thrive on the success, using it as a stepping stone to even bigger things. Invariably, when female artists had hits, it unleashed a barrage of professional and personal hurdles that few women were able to overcome.

In July 1969, six months before the end of the decade, *Newsweek* magazine recognized what was happening to women in the music business and expressed hope that the situation would improve. "For all its individuality, the rock-music scene has lacked the personal touch," wrote Hubert Saal. "Largely, it has been a world of male groups, of pounding, thunderous music that drowns out the words, which are rarely of moment. It needed the feminine touch and now it has got it."

As proof, the magazine offered profiles of five women—Joni Mitchell, Elyse Weinberg, Lotti Golden, Laura Nyro, and Melanie—that Saal predicted would turn things around with their "feminine touch." Weinberg, a Canadian, is best known for the bleak picture she paints of society in "Here Is My Heart" and "Band of Thieves." In the beginning, most of her work was in the protest vein, and she often named Bob Dylan as the songwriter who influenced her the most. Golden belonged to New York City's East Village hippie scene. Atlantic Records released her first album, *Motor-Cycle,* which she recorded when she was 19. Saal showed impeccable taste in his selection—but he wasn't a soothsayer.

CHAPTER 5

AN UNMITIGATED DISASTER

THE 1970s

TOP 20 HONOR ROLL
1970–1979

Lynn Anderson

Joan Baez

Blondie

Debby Boone

Beverly Bremmers

Alicia Bridges

Cher

Natalie Cole

Judy Collins

Jessi Colter

Rita Coolidge

Kiki Dee

Carol Douglas

Yvonne Elliman

Donna Fargo

Roberta Flack

Aretha Franklin

Crystal Gayle

Gloria Gaynor

Heart

Thelma Houston

Janis Ian

Rickie Lee Jones

Janis Joplin

Carole King

Evelyn King

Gladys Knight & the Pips

Jean Knight

Nicolette Larson

Vicki Lawrence

Cheryl Lynn

Mary MacGregor

Melissa Manchester

Maureen McGovern

Sister Janet Mead

Melanie

Bette Midler

Joni Mitchell

Dorothy Moore

Maria Muldaur

Anne Murray

Olivia Newton-John

Maxine Nightingale

Marie Osmond

Dolly Parton

Freda Payne

Pointer Sisters

Helen Reddy

Minnie Riperton

Vicki Sue Robinson

Linda Ronstadt

Diana Ross & Supremes

Sylvia

Carly Simon

Phoebe Snow

Barbra Streisand

Donna Summer

Bonnie Tyler

Anita Ward

Jennifer Warnes

Dionne Warwick

Betty Wright

Hey, I want the big 'un!" The anonymous voice shot out of the audience like a lightning bolt. Up on the stage were four women and a man. One of the women—the terrified object of the catcall—was an attractive, rather buxom, musician. From the demeanor of the all-male audience, it would be reasonable to conclude that the musicians were part of an adult entertainment revue, that type of show that would traditionally include strippers, drag queens, and bawdy comedians. In reality, the group was a folk and bluegrass band named the Good Ole Persons.

They were performing at a trade show in a small town in northern California. The 1970s had brought hope to small towns in that part of the state. The economy was showing signs of expanding, and real estate sales were booming. To accentuate the positive, the movers and shakers in the town held a huge trade show, inviting representatives from all the major businesses of the region.

In between serious-minded presentations from real estate firms and chambers of commerce from surrounding communities, the 400-plus men in the audience were treated to slide presentations of nude women. Bare breasts and protruding buttocks were projected onto the huge screen amid thunderous applause and screams of approval. Taking all that in were the Good Ole Persons, who stood backstage patiently awaiting their cue to take the stage. They couldn't believe their eyes and ears. They were folkies, for God's sake—the Good Ole Persons!

Once they took the stage, it quickly became apparent their audience wasn't there to hear music. "We were all very young—sweet things," says Laurie Lewis, a vocalist and fiddle player with the group. "We were terrified. They were screaming and yelling, and we were doing our sweet little songs. We lasted for about three songs, then got off stage."

Lewis went on to become one of the top female bluegrass fiddle players in the country. She can laugh about the situation today, but at the time it was difficult to see any humor in it. The trade show audience was indicative of how attitudes toward women had changed. By the time the decade ended, it would prove to be the worst in modern history for female recording artists. From 1970 through 1979, 270 solo artists would chart hits in the Top 20. Of those, only 62, or 23 percent of the total, were women. Individual recording artists, such as Cher, Diana Ross, and Carly Simon, scored sizable hits, but for women as a whole the decade was an unmitigated disaster.

The situation on the business end was even worse. When the decade began, only one female top executive was in place—BMI's Frances Preston—and when the decade ended, there was still only one female executive in place—Preston.

The War Between the Sexes

If you had to chose one word to describe the war between the sexes in the 1970s, it would have to be strident. Feminist Kate Millett's scorched-earth policy toward men in *Sexual Politics* drew an equally bellicose response from Norman Mailer, who wrote an article for *Harper's* magazine, "The Prisoner of Sex," that offered the male perspective. In 1972, *Time* magazine wrote a cover story about the raging war, noting that, "The most lordly male chauvinist and all but the staunchest advocate of Women's Liberation agree that women's place is different from men's. But for the increasingly uncomfortable American woman, it is easier to say what that place is not than what it is." The magazine focused on the disparity in music, noting that an all-female rock group in Chicago was belting out verbal attacks against the male domination of music. "Rock is Mick Jagger singing 'Under my thumb,' it's all right," sang the women, their identity cloaked in anonymity. "No Mick Jagger, it's not all right."

Music itself reflected the conflict, with lyrics from male songwriters and artists who often alternated between indifference at one extreme, and outright hostility toward women at the other. That, of course, created problems since the first requirement for a hit record is the ability to attract a healthy mix of male and female buyers. It is one reason why so many "sensitive guy" ballads were thrown into the mix. Al Green's "Let's Stay Together." Stevie Wonder's "You Are the Sunshine of My Life." Charlie Rich's "The Most Beautiful Girl." The biggest exception was Chuck Berry's "My Ding-a-Ling," a song that went to Number 1 despite being about the singer's penis (female record buyers must have had their reasons for helping it become a hit).

Sexual imagery in music reached a crescendo in the 1970s with the addition of a new word to the lexicon: groupie. Male rock stars accumulated large gatherings of women in their teens and early twenties who followed their heroes from city to city, offering sexual favors to the entertainers and to their roadies. They would do anything to get backstage to meet their heroes.

Typical was the young teen who begged and pleaded with the stage crew of one male artist to get backstage to meet him. "What's it worth to you?" she was asked. "Anything—everything," she answered. The young girl was allowed to meet the rock star, but not before stripping naked and masturbating with a long-necked beer bottle in front of several dozen men, who yelled and stomped their feet as the victim writhed on the dirty floor. "Damn," one of the men said, "I love the music bidness!"

At the high end of the groupie spectrum were those women, invariably glamorous model-types, who pursued rock musicians as potential mates. One of the most famous is Bebe Buell, whose union with Aerosmith's Steven Tyler produced a daughter, Liv Tyler, who achieved fame of her own as an ingenue actress in the 1990s. Buell, a former *Playboy* playmate, who in addition to dating Tyler was linked to Todd Rundgren, Elvis Costello, and Rod Stewart, told the magazine in 1997 that she hated to be called a groupie. "I think it's sexist," she said. "Nobody calls males groupies."

The Impact of Payola

In addition to the war between the sexes, the other variable in the 1970s was the introduction of payola. Scores of grand jury and FBI investigations rocked the industry, resulting in executive shakeups at several major record labels. The investigations began after federal officials linked a CBS Records official to a heroin ring operating between New Jersey and Canada; the trail led investigators from illegal drug operations to industry payoffs, all channeled through company promotions departments. Then, to make matters worse, organized crime entered the picture, giving the industry an image as an arena in which the only game was hardball. Payola affected women in music because it involved record companies paying off radio programmers to play certain records. Invariably, those chosen records were by male artists, unless on rare occasion the record companies—displaying the "my nigra is better than your nigra" mentality pervasive in college athletics—decided they wanted "their bitch" to do battle with a competitor's "bitch."

Once the payola was exposed, it brought attention to another inequity in the system for female recording artists. All of the radio program directors of that era were males. They chose the records that received air time—and they, as a group, decided which records would make the charts that reflected airplay. For that reason, the charts that listed hits based on airplay and the charts that listed hits based on sales weren't always in sync. Sales charts reflected female buying habits. Airplay charts reflected the opinions of male program directors. Guess which charts showed women in the most favorable light?

THE CHILD/WOMAN MYSTIQUE

Early in the decade, sex was the key to success for many women. Melanie Safka, who performed and recorded simply as "Melanie," had a Number 1 hit in 1971 with "Brand New Key." Ostensibly, the song—delivered with the playful resonance of a child's voice—was about a little girl who needed a key that would fit her skates. Almost from the instant it was played on radio, it created a firestorm of protest from people who interpreted the song in terms of sexual imagery. Some radio stations banned it.

Melanie was stunned. She'd composed the song in about 15 minutes to use as an uptempo, change-of-pace tune during her concerts. Two years earlier, in an interview with *Newsweek,* she'd confessed discontent as an entertainer: "There's no one to share my experiences with, and I get very low sometimes. . . . I feel like a product, a machine. It's as if I'm wearing a nun's habit. I feel there are things I can't say and that people coming up to me don't know how to talk to me."

The success of "Brand New Key" only amplified her alienation. She'd spent three years building a reputation as a serious artist who had serious things to say. Then, in the blink of an eye, everyone wanted her to continue with the cutesy, little girl image portrayed in "Brand New Key." That kind of success wasn't what Melanie had in mind when she started out. So she quit performing and returned to her South Jersey home, where she devoted the next four years to the more traditional female role of raising a family. In 1975, she attempted a comeback—falsely concluding that America had gotten over its obsession with sex—but by then it was too late to recapture her audience.

Country singer Tanya Tucker had the same kind of experience after her hit, "Delta Dawn." But there was a major difference: Tucker really was a little girl. She was roundly booed by a Grand Ole Opry audience during a performance in which she flaunted her blossoming sexuality and sang several rock-oriented songs that ran counter—at least in the opinion of the audience—to her image as country music's "darlin' little girl."

Tucker was 12 years old when she and her father traveled to Nashville from their home in Las Vegas for her first recording session. Dolores Fuller, a female songwriter, discovered Tucker and pitched her to Billy Sherrill, the artists and repertoire (A & R) director at Columbia Epic Records. Sherrill liked what he heard and wasted no time setting up a session. The first single was "Delta Dawn," a gutsy song written with a much older woman in mind. Before the year was out, "Delta Dawn" was a Top 10 hit and Tucker was a country music star.

"I thank the lucky stars and the Good Lord for that song. If I cut it now for the first time, I think it would be a hit. I was fortunate to have latched onto that one, and that was all Sherrill's doing. If it hadn't been for Sherrill, I probably would have been a rodeo queen or something. Any other producer would have stuck me with some puppy dog song. I wasn't used to singing those songs. I had sung mature songs all my life. I was singing, 'You Ain't Woman Enough to Take My Man' when I was 8 years old," says Tucker. She recorded a number of hits for Epic in 1973 and 1974, including "Would You Lay With Me (in a Field of Stone)" and "The Man Who Turned My Mother On," but then moved to MCA Records on the advice of her father, who had become her manager.

Looking back, it is difficult to understand how people could have missed Tucker's woman-child message. But they did. She sang adult songs that dealt with adult themes, and she did so in an adult voice, and she wore mini-skirts and Nancy Sinatra-style boots. In a 1973 feature about country music, *Newsweek*

Tanya Tucker

published a photograph of Tucker with the caption: "Teenage mythmaker." Did the magazine know she was only 13? Probably not. She looked much older than 19 in the photograph.

In 1978, fed up with being criticized for what she'd done all along—be herself—Tucker went to Los Angeles to record a rock-influenced album titled *TNT.* It was one of the top-selling country albums of 1979 and proved, once and for all, that Tucker was at her best when she was being herself. By then, being Tanya Tucker meant traveling in the fast lane. Drugs. Alcohol. A failed marriage to Glen Campbell. By the 1980s, Tucker had become fodder for the tabloids, as she seemed to drift from one misfortune to another.

In an interview with *Newsweek,* Tucker blamed some of her troubles on her being a woman. Bemoaning the fact that American women weren't allowed to vote until the 1920s, she says: "I can't imagine that. Probably one hundred years from now they're going to be saying that about us. 'Wow! You mean they couldn't get drunk and screw anybody they wanted? God! Poor girls!'" Tucker has received more criticism for the excesses in her personal life than praise for her leadership on women's issues, but surely the latter is more appropriate for over the years she has been a tireless, if not always politically correct, advocate for women's rights.

HELEN REDDY: PROJECTING A POSITIVE IMAGE

Following in Tanya Tucker's footsteps, both musically and in the arena of gender politics, was Helen Reddy, an Australian who recorded a remake of "Delta Dawn" that became a Number 1 pop hit in 1973. Women embraced "Delta Dawn," which was written by two men, Alex Harvey and L. Collins, long before it ever became a hit. Harvey recorded it first on an album he did for Capitol. One of the backup singers at the session was Tracy Nelson, who sang the song at the Bottom Line in New York City. In the audience that night was Bette Midler, who decided to use the song in her nightclub act. The response was so good she included the song in her album, *The Divine Miss M.* While out promoting the album, she performed the song on "The Tonight Show with Johnny Carson," thus giving it its first national exposure. Watching television that night was Billy Sherrill, who thought the song would be perfect for Tanya Tucker. The lesson was obvious: If women like it, it is probably a hit.

"Delta Dawn" was Reddy's second Number 1 in less than 12 months. In December 1972, she'd topped the charts with "I Am Woman," a song that unabashedly celebrated the female gender. Her record label hated the song and didn't really want to include it on her album. Her producer thought that it would make people think that she was a lesbian. Her friends told her it would ruin her career. But the song struck a chord with Reddy, who had experienced difficult times after moving to America from Australia in 1966. When time came for her to choose songs for her first album, she deliberately looked for material that would project a positive image for women.

Reddy was vindicated when the song went to Number 1, but it wasn't until the following year, when she was awarded a Grammy for top female vocalist, that she expressed her sentiments about the women's movement to a national television audience. After accepting the award, she said, "I want to thank everyone concerned at Capitol Records; my husband and manager, Jeff Wald, because he makes my success possible; and God because She makes everything possible."

Reddy received an outpouring of approval from feminists and was subjected to hostility from right-wing zealots and religious fundamentalists who considered the song and her remarks about a female God blasphemous. "I Am Woman" quickly became the theme song for the women's liberation movement, and Reddy encouraged those associations at every opportunity. She had another Number 1 hit with "Angie Baby" in 1974, but by mid-decade her career as a hit-maker was over. She continued to perform, and even starred in her own television variety show. By 1982, however, her professional problems had spilled over into her personal life as her divorce from Wald elicited headlines about his cocaine use and their unfriendly battle over custody of their son. The following year she married Milton Ruth, a drummer. When that marriage ended in divorce, she told *People* magazine she had no interest in ever again getting married: "What can any man give me that I can't give myself?"

By the mid-1990s, Reddy had focused on a career as an actress. She appeared on Broadway in the musical *Blood Brothers,* and she went out on the road to tour with Willy Russell's comedy, *Shirley Valentine.* After one performance, she told a reporter for *The Arizona Republic* that she sometimes thought people were disappointed not to hear her sing. "For some people, it's a nice break to come to see me and not have me sing 'Delta Dawn' and the rest of it," she said. "But there's the inevitable person who walks out upset because I didn't do 'I Am Woman.'"

In 1995, talk-show host David Letterman did a spoof on the women's liberation movement by asking Reddy to repeatedly pop out onstage to sing lines from "I Am Woman." The comedy bit called for Letterman to shoo her off stage each time she appeared. It was all in good fun, and Reddy wasn't adverse to poking fun at herself. It was also a commentary on the fragile link that always exists between music and politics, no matter how noble the intent: A song is a song is a song.

"SMALL-TOWN GIRLS AT HEART"

One of the most reluctant hitmakers of the 1970s was Canadian singer Anne Murray, who went from high school teacher to international star in one giant step. Her first single, "Snowbird," made the Top 20 and earned her the first American gold record ever awarded to a Canadian singer. Murray, a product of laidback rural Nova Scotia, found success a distraction from her feminine instincts. Not all female singers of the decade were hellions like Tanya Tucker or outspoken women libbers like Helen Reddy. After a couple of years of one-night stands and a constant stream of offers to "Please, just do this one show," Murray put her foot down and told her manager and record label that she'd had enough. The music business wasn't really her cup of tea. She was a small-town girl at heart and intended to stay that way. After Murray married, she stayed at home for two years and raised her two children. "I've always dreamed of a family," she told United Press International (UPI). "It's nicer than I ever thought it would be."

In 1978, Murray decided to resume her career and record a new album titled *Let's Keep It That Way*. The first single sputtered, failing to even make the Top 100. The second single, "You Needed Me," went to the top and gave the singer her first Number 1 hit. Murray told reporters she knew it would be a hit the first time she heard it because it left her "all choked up." She had another Top 20 hit with "Daydream Believer" in 1980, but then her career stalled and she was never again able to recapture the magic of her early work.

Linda Ronstadt was a product of the 1960s, when she recorded her first songs with a folk-rock trio, The Stone Poneys. But success didn't come her way until 1975, when her recording of "You're No Good" went to Number 1. For the 10 years prior to that, she'd jumped around quite a bit musically in an effort to find herself. Her greatest liability was also her greatest asset: she could sing just about anything and do it justice. For that reason, no one quite knew what to do with her. If you do everything well, nothing you do stands out. What did stand out was Ronstadt herself. She was petite and attractive, and she had a shy way about her that endeared her to everyone who met her or watched her perform. She was small-townish and worldly at the same time. Every small town in America has a girl singer everyone just knows is good enough for the big time. Ronstadt was America's singer everyone knew was good enough for the big time.

When "You're No Good" struck gold, *Rolling Stone* magazine did a cover story on her titled "Linda Ronstadt: Heartbreak on Wheels." This piece was an acknowledgment that she'd made it into the inner sanctum of rock 'n' roll. The article pointed out that at age 28, she still looked and talked like a little girl. If the magazine writer was struggling to define his subject, Ronstadt was struggling to fit herself into an ever-widening universe. "I'm very dissatisfied with everything," she said. "I'm hard to please and very restless, so it's always a battle between that and my real deep desire to have a home and roots."

Success brought Ronstadt new problems, but it was always the old problems—true love and the stress of putting together and keeping a band—that kept her on the ropes. Relationships were always a hassle for her. Like most women, she tried to please. She had a hard time standing up for herself. "I was so unsure of myself," she told writer Mark Bego. "I have a tendency to let other people shape me. If I'm going with someone, and he gets at all critical of my music, the bottom falls out for me."

In 1970, Ronstadt traveled to Nashville to appear on the Grand Ole Opry and to record an album called *Silk Purse*. She hated the album, primarily because she was never able to get into a comfortable groove with the Nashville musicians. The experience convinced her that her future as a recording artist lay in country-rock, even if it was a Los Angeles variation. When she returned to Los Angeles, she put together a first-rate group of musicians who would eventually rename themselves the Eagles and have a few hits of their own; she found them easy to work with, but knew they were too talented to remain her backup band.

Finding and keeping a band would always be a problem for Ronstadt. Male musicians didn't want to work for a woman—at least never for long. Frankly, she didn't know how to talk to them, how to give orders to men. She knew they felt working for a woman wasn't cool, and a secret part of her agreed with them.

By 1970s standards, rock 'n' roll was a guy thing; it was one of the reasons she kept flirting with country music. It was the only place she could find comfort with kindred spirits like Emmylou Harris. Ronstadt first went to hear Harris perform after friends told her that Harris was doing the same type of music. Ronstadt became an instant fan and friend. Harris was indeed doing her style of music—only better, she confessed to friends. Ronstadt asked Harris to sing on her albums, and she sang harmony with her on "I Can't Help It," which won a Grammy. During this same period, Ronstadt was drawn to the music—and uncritical persona—of Dolly Parton, who then was a successful country artist but not yet a pop star. The three of them—Ronstadt, Harris, and Parton—began recording together as a trio at this point in time, but it would be a decade before they would be able to complete enough material for an album.

Ronstadt's friendships with other female performers kept her sane. "In the old days we couldn't afford psychiatrists," she told Bego. "Maria Muldair, Bonnie Raitt, Wendy Waldman, and I kept each other from having nervous breakdowns for years. And my attitude towards anyone who is new on the horizon is that if they're good, and it's honest, then it has to be helped; those people have to be brought in. My feeling about girls that are better than I am

© ALAN L. MAYOR

From left to right: Linda Ronstadt, Emmylou Harris, and Dolly Parton

is that we need 'em because they'll make the music better, and I can learn from them. There's always somebody who's better than you."

Ronstadt's success from mid-decade on caught her off guard. She really wasn't prepared for all the attention she received from the media and from the increasing numbers of people in the industry who wanted something from her. She charted eight Top 20 singles in the 1970s, including "Blue Bayou," "That'll Be the Day," and "It's So Easy." Her success made it even more impossible, or so it seemed to her, to have a decent relationship with a man. For a time, she swore off being anyone's "girlfriend." She told a reporter from *People* magazine that what she wanted was a relationship with someone who was an equal. "I'm so disorganized," she joked, "what I really need is a good wife."

BONNIE RAITT: A SLOW ROAD TO SUPERSTARDOM

Bonnie Raitt has changed over the years, and so has her audience. Blues was her first love, and by the age of 12, she'd taught herself to play guitar. Growing up in Los Angeles, where John Raitt, her father, was discovering himself as an actor, she didn't come into personal contact with many blues musicians, as she would have done had she grown up in the South. But she compensated by listening to all the blues records she could find. Memphis Minnie was her favorite. To hear her play blues guitar was more than a musical experience; it was a religious epiphany. The very idea that a woman could play guitar like that inspired the budding musician and convinced her that she, too, could follow that road. Her aspirations take on added significance when you consider that Raitt's parents were Quakers, a religion that doesn't stress female self-reliance, and she spent her summers attending Quaker camps. By the time she was 18, her father was finding steady work as a Broadway singer, and she moved east to attend college.

In the late 1960s, Raitt enrolled at Radcliffe College in Cambridge, Massachusetts, where she spent several years as a student, working in local coffeehouses. Her audience, for the most part, was an eclectic mix of educated white kids her own age who grooved on the straightforward blues rhythms and soulful intonations she'd mastered. There was something alluring about the diminutive redhead using her delicate, ivory-toned fingers to connect with her guitar, exploring the dark and mysterious recesses of the bottomland blues that had originated in the Mississippi Delta.

Eventually, Raitt had to choose between getting a formal education at Radcliffe or a more worldly education in music. She chose the latter, trading the certainties of college for the chaos of one-nighters in nightclubs in New York, Boston, and Philadelphia. She also headed South, taking a plane to Memphis, then renting a car to drive down into Mississippi, where she sought out bluesman Fred McDowell in his hometown of Como. McDowell taught her to play slide guitar, and Sippie Wallace gave her lessons on how to phrase the songs so they would sound authentic.

Raitt wasn't making up her music as she went along. She wanted it to be real. She wanted to carry on a tradition, not adapt old music to something new. In the early years, she surprised more than one down-and-out bluesman with words of praise and questions about his guitar technique. "I'm always sad because I was lucky enough to know a lot of the great blues people, the traditional blues artists as well as the ones from Chicago—and a lot of them have passed on, and unfortunately that music heritage has been relegated to some kind of cult," said Raitt in a 1985 interview.

With a college following that was itself almost cult-like, Raitt moved to Los Angeles in 1971 and signed a recording contract with Warner Brothers. Her self-titled debut album, recorded at an abandoned lakefront summer camp in rural Minnesota and released that same year, contained many traditional blues songs. While it didn't make a dent on the charts, it did solidify her fan base. There was a politics to music in those days. The Vietnam War was in its final throes, and Raitt's generation viewed music as an expression of solidarity. There was no protest in her music, but she performed a type of music that was more or less forbidden in polite, white society. Her considerable musical talents aside, she belonged to the hip crowd of her generation. Everyone liked her, especially other female performers, such as Linda Ronstadt. Raitt was accessible, both to her fans and to the music media, which by the early 1970s found her a refreshing change of pace from the uptight male hitmakers of the day.

Even conservative, mainstream publications like *Newsweek* were finding themselves infatuated with Raitt. In 1972, less than a year after the release of her first album, Hubert Saal, the magazine's music writer, stopped by a New York rock club to sample her music. He was more accustomed to writing about the ballet and symphonies, but he left the club that night with the feeling that he'd witnessed something special. "[Some might feel] it's kind of freaky for a girl who looks like Bonnie to be singing and playing the country blues of the black man," he wrote, describing her as a "beautiful redhead." "But she draws gasps from the crowd when she lets herself go on the guitar." Raitt told Saal that she didn't want to be a star. She wanted people to enjoy her music the way they would a visit with their friends. She needed the feedback, she said—and the love.

Between 1971 and 1987, Raitt recorded nine albums for Warner Brothers, none of which were commercial successes. At a time when Donny Osmond, the Bee Gees, and America were sugaring up the charts in a decade that was disco bound, Raitt stayed true to her musical roots, tipping her hat whenever possible to the traditional blues. Sometimes she would do more than tip her hat, as when she recorded a live duet with her hero Sippie Wallace on "Woman Be Wise." It is impossible to listen to the song without hearing Wallace's pleasure and pride in exchanging gut-wrenching vocals with the redheaded white girl who provided her with a new definition of sisterhood.

As Raitt entered the 1980s, and her thirties, she found that her audience was changing. Her fan base was no longer young and no longer spending Saturday afternoons in the record store. Mortgage payments displaced rebellion as a topic of conversation. Middle age loomed on the horizon. The music business itself was changing. Radio was solidifying and specializing on specific formats. It was a rough decade for Raitt. She wondered if her recording career was over.

In a 1986 interview, she expressed frustration at the way radio was segregating musical styles. "I, for one, am happy to see black music played more on the radio in the crossover sense, but I wish there was a way to obliterate those categories. . . . When I was growing up, there was no black or white radio. Everyone just played good music. You could hear the Temptations, the Supremes, Sam and Dave, and the Beatles on the same radio station. I would like to see that situation come back because I think there are a lot of black musicians who have always

Bonnie Raitt

Bette Midler

been ignored, especially in the financial sense, considering the number of white artists who are making a lot of money have been influenced by what they do," says Raitt.

Despite Raitt's misgivings—and her pessimism about the future—she ended the decade with a bang. After leaving Warner Brothers and signing with Capitol Records, she found renewed success, though not on the charts. In 1989, she was awarded four Grammys. Two years later she would release her most successful album, *Luck of the Draw.* The first single, "Something to Talk About," gave her the first Top 20 hit of her career. It also gave her a new audience as women in their late teens and early twenties discovered her for the first time. The song was a defiant declaration of independence and became a particular favorite among liberation-minded strippers who requested the song at gentlemen's clubs across the country.

By then, Raitt's relationship with her audience was changing. Now approaching 50, she is no longer described as a young, beautiful redhead; instead, she is regarded as one of the founding mothers of blues-rock, an elder in the church of get-down boogie. Raitt has responded by making herself less accessible to her fans and to the media. She no longer mingles with fans after concerts or returns calls from reporters. She has become the star she said she never wanted to be.

BETTE MIDLER: A THEATRICAL APPROACH TO MUSIC

Bette Midler was an anachronism, even by 1970s standards. With a big, polished voice and a saucy stage presence—once, at the height of President Richard Nixon's difficulties, she dedicated "Daytime Hustler" to the "divine Dick"—the 5-foot veteran of *Fiddler on the Roof* played out the role of the unrepentant feminist. Critics were brutal, not in their criticism of her voice, which everyone seemed to agree was spectacular, but in their descriptions of the singer herself. Her body was described as "absurdly inadequate" and her mouth as "toothy"; her nose was compared to a "ski jump."

Such comments must have hurt Midler, but if they did she never let on. Her first ambition, she told reporters, was to be a comedienne. She didn't decide that she wanted a career in music until she heard an Aretha Franklin record. It was a good choice, though comedy would always be a part of Midler's nightclub act. After signing with Atlantic Records in 1972, she released an album, *The Divine Miss M,* that in addition to winning her a Grammy gave her a new identity as the "Divine Miss M."

Midler had a Top 20 hit in 1973 with "Boogie Woogie Bugle Boy," but despite a series of releases throughout the decade, she didn't have another hit until 1980, when "The Rose" peaked at Number 3. Nearly another decade would pass before she would have a hit again, this time with "Wind Beneath My Wings" (1989).

By the 1990s, Midler would devote most of her efforts to a movie career. This isn't surprising since her approach to music was always theatrical. She competed with rock divas for space on the pop charts, but she had an entirely different outlook from that of such contemporaries as Bonnie Raitt and Linda Ronstadt. Midler was more at home on television, wearing a glitzy gown, than she was in jeans and T-shirt traveling across country in the back of a psychedelic rock 'n' roll van. Her 18-month stint as a regular on "The Tonight Show with Johnny Carson" launched her recording career. An argument could be made that she is one of the first pop stars to be shaped and influenced by television.

OLIVIA NEWTON-JOHN: AN IDENTITY STRUGGLE

One of the few solo, white female artists to have a Number 1 hit in the 1970s was Olivia Newton-John, who scored with "I Honestly Love You" in 1974. Sandwiched between Eric Clapton's "I Shot the Sheriff," Barry White's "Can't Get Enough of Your Love, Babe," and Billy Preston's "Nothing From Nothing," Olivia's heartfelt ballad resembled a solitary flower on a football field in the midst of a rough and tumble game.

Actually, the song had been written for a man. Jeff Barry and Peter Allen were writing songs for an album that would feature Allen as the vocalist and Barry as the producer when they came up with the idea for "I Honestly Love You." After they recorded a demo and handed it over to their publisher, it found its way into Newton-John's hands. The British-born singer had a single that charted in 1971, a remake of Bob Dylan's "If Not For You." But it wasn't until she won a Grammy for "Let Me Be There" in 1974 that she was taken seriously as a recording artist.

The following year, Newton-John followed up with "Have You Ever Been Mellow," her second Number 1 hit. The song was written by guitarist John Farrar, who doubled as her producer; it was considered a country song by the industry and by the awards committee of the Country Music Association (CMA), which honored her as the 1974 Female Vocalist of the Year. All of this created a strange situation for Newton-John, who really didn't consider her music to be country. She said as much to reporters. Her comments angered the country music establishment and led to a number of association members resigning in order to establish a competing organization, the Association of Country Entertainers.

The protest both confused and hurt Newton-John. She tried to mend fences by opening for Charlie Rich and playing rodeos and livestock fairs;

Olivia Newton-John

however, she wasn't able to feel accepted until she decided to record an album in Nashville, *Don't Stop Believin'*. Once that was done, she focused her attentions on a television and film career. Her next Number 1 hit was "You're the One That I Want," a song from the 1978 movie *Grease,* which she co-starred in with John Travolta. Two years later, she was starring opposite Gene Kelly in the musical, *Xanadu.* The movie bombed, but a song from the soundtrack, "Magic," gave her yet another Number 1 hit.

Newton-John's biggest hit was "Physical," an upbeat song that went to Number 1 in November 1981. The song was controversial because of lyrics that suggested a physical relationship. Some radio stations banned the record. The controversy amused Newton-John, but she protested that people were taking it entirely too seriously. She continued to place songs in the Top 20— "Make a Move on Me" and "Heart Attack." She also undertook a cinematic reunion with John Travolta in *Two of a Kind* and did a number of television specials. Another chart topper eluded her, though, and by the 1990s, her recording career had practically disappeared. In 1997, she signed with a country label and made plans for a comeback.

Throughout her career, Newton-John seemed to struggle with her identity. She didn't think she was a country singer, yet that is how she found her initial success. She didn't think she was an actress, yet the public said she was. Her movies, and not her heartfelt recordings, made her a pop music star. She was one of the most successful female solo artists of the decade, but she never seemed to connect with other female performers. If she showed leadership, which she did by becoming a role model for a generation of little girls who, taking a cue from "Physical," learned to use double entendres, she accomplished this via her actions, not her statements, for she never became a spokesperson for women's issues.

GRACE SLICK: THE QUINTESSENTIAL BAD GIRL

Grace Slick was the first female artist to breastfeed her baby on the pages of a national news magazine. Somehow it seemed appropriate in the 1970s for the acid queen of the 1960s to display a sense of radicalism on the subject of motherhood. During the heyday of Jefferson Airplane, she was a hard-driving rocker who dared to go where other women had never ventured. Usually, she was stone-cold drunk on Dom Perignon champagne by the time she walked out on stage, but her audience, which was itself usually stoned on LSD, seldom seemed to notice Slick's condition.

By the mid-1970s, when the group was transformed into Jefferson Starship— and motherhood had put new demands on her—Slick was preaching the evils of drugs, although she did confess to reporters that she still had a deep, abiding appreciation for a good bottle of wine. Jefferson Airplane had two Top 20 hits in the 1960s, but was more successful in the 1970s, scoring five hits, including "Runaway," "Count On Me," and "Miracles." The group didn't survive the 1970s, though technically it had a Top 20 hit in 1980 with "Jane."

Slick wasn't a solo artist, but she had a strong influence on other women who respected her independence and rebelliousness. She was living out the rock 'n' roll lifestyle because she chose to, not because she didn't have other options. She was the rich girl gone bad. Her parents were well-to-do and had sent her to Finch College, the same girls' school that President Nixon's daughter, Tricia, attended. Slick, a former model, performed at gritty outdoor festivals, and wasn't afraid of the mud and slime or her admirers' boisterous overtures. Once she was invited to a tea at the White House; she arrived with 600 micromilligrams of LSD with the intention of lacing the tea, but something came up and she got distracted. In a 1976 interview, Slick told a reporter that she had no intention of ever growing up. Her goal was to still be hanging out at bars when she was 75, though she conceded she didn't expect to be picked up as much.

BARBRA STREISAND: THE PLAYBOY CONNECTION

When the October 1977 issue of *Playboy* magazine hit the newsstands, it featured Barbra Streisand on the cover, reclining blissfully in a gigantic, Freudian-inspired circle. She wore white shorts and a white T-shirt with the *Playboy* emblem. During the photo session, she had taken off her shoes and socks and stretched out in a pose calculated to show off her toned and well-oiled legs.

"Hey, guys, now you can say I took it off for *Playboy*," Streisand said. The magazine's editors were ecstatic: this was the first time a female celebrity had ever posed for the cover. The headline writer posed the question: "What's a nice Jewish girl like me doing on the cover of *Playboy*?" The editors addressed the headline to themselves as much as to the readers. Actually, it was a very good question. The answer could be found in the fact that Streisand had completed *A Star Is Born*, a controversial film she co-starred in with Kris Kristofferson. Making the movie had been an nightmare. No one seemed to get along, and the principals spent more time arguing and doing midnight rewrites on the script than they did before the cameras.

Professionally, this was a very insecure time for Streisand. She hadn't had a Number 1 record for three years, and she'd gone out on a limb and co-written a song for *A Star Is Born*. The movie took a roasting from the critics and was snubbed by the Academy of Motion Pictures Arts and Sciences, with the exception of the soundtrack song, "Evergreen," which she'd co-written. About the time she did the *Playboy* interview, she learned "Evergreen" had become her second Number 1 hit. In an interview with record executive Joe Smith for his book, *Off the Record,* Streisand offered some advice to new artists: "Don't be afraid of the establishment. There are always those who are going to say, 'No, you can't, no, you shouldn't. . . . You've got to do your own thing.'"

In 1977, Streisand felt fenced in creatively. She wanted to make hit records. She wanted to star in hit motion pictures. For more than a decade, *Playboy* had been among her staunchest supporters, reviewing each and every record she released, often in glowing terms, such as the 1966 review of *My Name Is Barbra, Two,* in which the critic referred to the "epic success of the miraculous Miss Streisand." It wasn't popular at the time to say so—and among feminists it still isn't a popular notion to suggest—but the magazine did as much to promote the careers of female performers as any major-circulation publication of its day. The "Big Bunny" adored female singers and wasn't ashamed to admit it. Streisand knew that and found it hard to say no to being on the cover.

The interview itself was the best Streisand had given to date. There were questions about her career and about her nose, but the best questions—and answers—revolved around issues specific to her gender. She was asked about the women's movement, as well as her own experiences as a woman in the business. She was asked if she considered herself a feminist. "It's funny, I never thought about the women's movement while I was moving as a woman. I didn't even realize that I was fighting this battle all the time. I just took it very personally; I didn't even separate it from the fact that I was a woman having a hard time in a male society. Then they started to burn the bras, and I thought it was ridiculous, although I now understand it in the whole picture of revolution—one has to go to these crazy extremes to come back to the middle. Actually, I believe women are superior to men. I don't even think we're equal," she replied.

CARLY SIMON: ELEVATING SEX TO AN ART FORM

Barbra Streisand never said publicly that she thought Carly Simon was her biggest competitor, but she did admit to reporters that she co-wrote "Evergreen" because other female recording stars were writing their own songs. Carly Simon and Carole King were the two most successful singer-songwriters of the decade, and of the two, it was Simon who was dazzling the world with her toothy smile and sexy album covers. The front cover of her 1972 *No Secrets* album, which contained the Number 1 single "You're So Vain," showed her nipples outlined against a thin blue pullover shirt. On the back cover was a closeup of her face, her sensual mouth, with lips parted, measuring a good 5 inches across.

Barbra Streisand

Sex was a big part of the record business—always had been—but Simon elevated it to an art form. She swore up and down that the sexy images were all unintentional. She explained to reporters that as a child she'd mugged for her father (publisher Richard Simon, co-founder of Simon & Schuster) whenever he took her photo; it was a means of getting his attention, and if it was a habit she had been unable to outgrow . . . well, she wasn't going to apologize for it.

Simon was arguably the best lyricist of her generation. The songs not only expressed complicated emotions, they revolved around mysteries, such as the identity of the person she was writing about in "You're So Vain." If her success had been confined solely to music, more specifically to her songwriting, her place in American music history would be secure. But to her generation, Simon was more than a singer or songwriter. Her marriage to singer James Taylor (the prototype of the sensitive male of the 1980s). Her friendships with such male rockers as Rolling Stone Mick Jagger, who sang backup for her on "You're So Vain." Her ability to travel in social circles only dreamed about by her fans. It was the extra-musical associations that made her an icon to other women. In the eyes of many women, Simon was the epitome of what a woman could do once she was freed of the constraints of society.

In songs like "Anticipation," "The Right Thing to Do," or "Haven't Got Time For the Pain," Simon reached out to other women on a consistent basis with sympathy, attitude, and a sense of optimism. In some ways, she was very much a creation of the 1970s; the rock and pop era had progressed to a point where the public felt it needed royalty. At that point, Simon realized her success had come with a price tag attached. The problem was she didn't want to be a rock or pop music princess. Music wasn't a lifestyle to her, not the way it was to Janis Joplin or Linda Ronstadt, and the harder the public pushed her in that direction, the more she dug in her heels. To Simon, the song was what was important. Music was a vehicle though which she could express herself with the spoken word.

As the 1970s wore on, Simon focused less on public appearances and more on her songwriting. She decided to try her hand at writing songs for the movies. Her first was "Nobody Does It Better," which she wrote and sang for the 1977 James Bond film *The Spy Who Loved Me*. Years later, she would follow up with "Let the River Run," which she did for the movie *Working Girl*. Other movies followed, including the soundtrack for Nora Ephron's *This Is My Life*, which contained the song, "You're the Love of My Life." From movies, Simon moved on to books, writing a series of books for children, including *Amy the Dancing Bear*.

By 1980, Simon was a recluse, at least as far as the public was concerned. Her marriage to James Taylor had ended. Music styles were changing. Rather than slugging it out and jumping into the fray with an entirely new crop of female singers, she went into her private self and closed the door. No public appearances.

No sexy album covers. She didn't emerge until 1995 with a significant new album—and a willingness, after 15 years, to again take the stage. The album was *Letters Never Sent,* a collection of songs based on letters Simon had found and read during her withdrawal from public life. "Letters is the most personal album, in a sea of personal albums, I have ever made," she said upon the album's release. "The songs evolved from letters that I had squirreled away in the top of my closet. You know, the kind of letters you write in the heat of the moment, and then you have second thoughts and decide to 'sleep on it.' . . . Blowing off the dust, I massaged some of the letters into songs."

Simon said repeatedly during the 1970s that she didn't understand why people had labeled her with a "sexy" image. She was so convincing when she said it, it was difficult not to believe her. When she reappeared in 1995 at the age of 50, entertainment writers first focused more on her accomplishments and the fact that she'd recovered from her stage fright than on her old sexy image. Then, as she undertook more and more public appearances, a sense of amazement evolved among the 20- and 30-something music writers that Simon still had a sensual air about her—and at 50!

CHER: COMING OUT ON TOP

In the beginning, Cherilyn Sarkisian LaPierre thought she would be an actress. And why not? She lived in Hollywood, her mother was an actress, and she took acting lessons while attending high school. Everything pointed toward the movies as a career. Of course, something would have to be done about that name. It would have to be shortened to Cher.

When Cher first met Sonny Bono in a Hollywood coffee shop, he was 27 and she was 16, though she told him she was 18. He was working as a promotions man for record mogul Phil Spector. Sometimes Bono sang background on the records Spector produced. Bono took the high school girl to one of those sessions, and he thought it would impress her if he arranged for her to sing background vocals with him. For a time in the mid-1960s, Sonny and Cher performed as Caesar & Cleo.

Spector was impressed enough with Cher to produce a single, "Ringo, I Love You," with her using the name Bonnie Jo Mason. The record bombed. When Bono encouraged Spector to give her another shot, he declined. After several wrong turns, Bono persuaded Atlantic Records to sign them as a duet. As Sonny and Cher they recorded a song that Bono had written. "I Got You Babe" was paired with "It's Gonna Rain." When they sent it to Atlantic Records head Ahmet Ertegun, he thought "It's Gonna Rain" was the better side. Bono pleaded with him to release "I Got You Babe," but Ertegun was adamant.

Before the record could be released, Bono took "I Got You Babe" to a Hollywood radio station. He told them they could have it exclusively if they would play it once an hour. They did, and the song became an immediate hit.

Among teenagers, Sonny and Cher were one of the top acts of the 1960s. They followed up with "The Beat Goes On" in 1967 and "All I Ever Need Is You" in 1971. Not until Cher broke away as a solo act in 1971—and CBS Television was persuaded to air "The Sonny & Cher Show"—did adult record buyers begin to take her seriously. The same year the television show began, Cher racked up her first Number 1 hit with "Gypsies, Tramps and Thieves." She followed up in 1973 with another Number 1, "Half-Breed," then in 1974 with "Dark Lady," which would prove to be her last Number 1 single.

Sonny and Cher had been having marital problems for quite some time, but this didn't become public knowledge until 1974. One of the highlights of "The Sonny & Cher Show" were the verbal barbs they tossed at each other during the opening of the program. Viewers thought Cher's caustic digs at Sonny were humorous, but what they didn't know was that the couple had separated and were pretending to be happily married for the sake of their careers. After their divorce, they attempted a comeback show on CBS, but the show failed, with the audience apparently deciding that watching a divorced couple argue in public wasn't nearly as funny as it had been when they were married.

With her last Top 10 single, "Take Me Home," charting in 1979, Cher focused all her energies on her first love, acting. She was every bit as successful in the 1980s as an actress as she was as a singer in the 1970s. She appeared in such films as *Good Times* and *Chastity,* but she didn't blossom as an actress until *Silkwood.* Her role in that motion picture won her an Oscar nomination as Best Supporting Actress. With the release of her 1985 film *Mask,* Harvard University's Hasty Pudding Club named her "Woman of the Year," an honor that previously had gone to the likes of Jane Fonda and Katharine Hepburn.

Cher's public persona cast her as a strong female who, despite always getting into trouble, was able to somehow come out on top. But if she was perceived as a role model for other women, it was more along the lines of what not to do. By the mid-1990s, good acting roles had proved hard to come by, and comebacks on the recording front seemed even more elusive. Enormously talented as a singer and as an actress, Cher was never able to bond emotionally with her female public; she gave love, or so she felt, but it was never returned. As the end of the millennium approached, she bore a reputation—richly undeserved—as one of the woman most people loved to hate. When Sonny was killed in a freak skiing accident in January 1998, Cher attended his funeral and spoke briefly. Once again, she incurred the wrath of the tabloid media, which seemed to find fault with every comment she made about her late ex-husband.

Cher

TRANSCENDING THE RACE PROBLEM

There was more to the downturn female recording artistst experienced in the 1970s than would appear from an analysis of the numbers alone. In many ways, this was the most unusual, perplexing, and disheartening decade of the modern era. By the mid-1970s, America had come to terms with the "race problem" by enacting laws that protected the rights of African Americans to vote, assemble, and travel with equal protection of the law. What America hadn't done was change its way of thinking.

Despite all the gains that the civil rights movement made during the 1960s and early 1970s, black entertainers still found themselves segregated. It might never be clear now how much of that was by choice, and how much society forced upon them, but whatever the cause, black women in the music business lived an isolated existence, one marked by anger, frustration, and hopelessness. This is one of the reasons black female artists felt resentment toward their white sisters when they appeared together at outdoor venues and found themselves dressed so radically differently.

Black female artists felt they were at the bottom of the pecking order. At the top were white male stars, followed by white females, then black males, and, at the bottom, black females. In spite of all the hardships—the cheating managers and agents, the sexually demanding club and venue managers, a fickle public, and, perhaps worst of all, black boyfriends and husbands who demonstrated a preference for newly liberated white females—black female artists, projecting an indomitable spirit, produced a dazzling array of music during the decade. Diana Ross, Natalie Cole, Thelma Houston, Roberta Flack, and Gladys Knight & the Pips, all kept black women "staying alive" at the top of the charts.

Diana Ross Reigns Supreme

With four Number 1 hits during the decade, most people would consider Diana Ross to be one of the dominant female voices of that era, and certainly she was the dominant black female vocalist. As the lead singer of the Supremes, she'd participated in 12 Number 1 singles, so when she broke away to release her first solo project in 1970, she was under a lot of pressure to deliver. Thinking that Ross needed a new direction, Motown's Berry Gordy asked Bones Howe, an outside producer, to supervise the project. Howe was a proven hitmaker, with Number 1 singles by the Association and the Fifth Dimension to his credit. Midway through the project, Gordy realized that Howe saw Ross as a black Barbra Streisand. This vision didn't appeal to Gordy, so he dropped Howe from the project. Nickolas Ashford and Valerie Simpson, two Motown staffers, were asked to take over production. They'd written two hits for Marvin Gaye and Tammi Terrell, "You're All I Need To Get By" and "Ain't No Mountain

Nick Ashford and Valerie Simpson

High Enough." They decided to rework the latter song, changing it from a duet to a solo effort.

Ashford and Simpson produced the record, and Ashford, who had started out singing gospel in a Baptist Church in Harlem, sang the soaring backing vocals at the end of the song. Gordy hated it, saying that at 6 minutes, it was much too long to release as a single. He wanted to change the song around, but Ashford and Simpson stuck to their guns, and it was released as they'd recorded it. Six weeks after "Ain't No Mountain High Enough" was released, it went to Number 1, knocking another Motown record, "War" by Edwin Starr, out of the top slot.

Fifteen years later, Ashford and Simpson would record a Top 20 hit of their own as vocalists on 1985's "Solid," but their twin talents as songwriters and producers made them unique during the 1970s. Some of their songs became giant hits, including "Ain't Nothing Like the Real Thing" and "Let's Go Get Stoned."

With the success of "Ain't No Mountain High Enough," Simpson attracted attention for her contributions as a producer. She was the first woman to get production credits on a major hit. Unfortunately, she didn't want to pursue this facet of the music industry; she really wanted to become a solo artist. She attempted several solo projects and several duets with Ashford, but until the 1985 hit none of the projects lived up to expectations. With Simpson's incredible talents in the studio, it is tempting to ponder what she might have accomplished if she'd developed those talents and stayed the course as a producer.

Ross followed "Ain't No Mountain High Enough" with "Touch Me in the Morning," which went to Number 1 in August 1973. Between the release of the two songs, Ross made her acting debut in *Lady Sings the Blues*. Before the session for "Touch Me In the Morning," there was concern at Motown about the sexual implications expressed in the song's lyrics and about whether Ross's newfound career as an actress would divert her focus and energies from the work that would be required of her in the studio. As it turned out, she was asked to record the song 12 times. Afterward, according to songwriter Ron Miller, engineers spent 300 hours splicing the song together; the finished product didn't contain "three syllables" in sequence from the same recording. By then, everyone was experiencing frustration with Ross. This even carried over into the media. In a 1974 review of her album *The Last Time I Saw Him,* the *Rolling Stone* critic was brutal, calling the album "utterly facile" and "pretentious," and then observing that Ross was "capable of simply making a fool of herself."

Ross had two more Number 1 singles that decade—"Do You Know Where You're Going To?," the theme from the movie *Mahogany,* and "Love

Hangover"—but it was clear to everyone that Ross was more interested in her emerging movie career than her singing career. The glamour and the glitter associated with Hollywood, was all more than she could resist. Another problem was the complication of the personal relationship that developed between Ross and Gordy. Her last solo single to go to Number 1, and her last released by Motown, was "Upside Down," which peaked in September 1980.

Gordy has been criticized for his infatuation with—and sometimes blind devotion to—Ross, sometimes at the expense of his other female recording artists. But the fact remains that he was one of the decade's most outspoken proponents of female talent. He openly sought female talent for Motown, and he hired women on a consistent basis. Suzanne de Passe, one of his executive assistants, played a major role in the direction the label took. Later, she left the music business and focused her efforts on film and television production with equally impressive results, proving that she was more than a stand-in for Gordy.

Biographer J. Randy Taraborrelli maintains that Gordy had a plan right from the get-go. He was a big admirer of Debbie Reynolds and Doris Day and wanted to build his company around black women of similar talents. "Gordy wanted a female artist to be the focus of his company, but it would have to be someone whose style could appeal to both black and white audiences," wrote Taraborrelli in *Call Her Miss Ross.* "She would be a black woman who would make her race proud because they respected her worldly sophistication. She would also make whites comfortable because they understood her image and finesse. He certainly had nothing against black music, but [he] realized that it was limited mostly to blacks."

Roberta Flack: A Commercial-Success Miracle
In 1972, Clint Eastwood was filming *Play Misty for Me,* a suspense thriller about a disk jockey, played by Eastwood, who was targeted for revenge by a female stalker. When time came to choose a song to play beneath the love scene between himself and Donna Mills, he remembered a song Roberta Flack had recorded in 1969. The song, "The First Time Ever I Saw Your Face," had stuck with him. So he called Flack and asked for permission to use it in the movie.

After the movie's release, it took just six weeks for the song to go to Number 1. For Flack, who at 33 had never had a commercial success, it seemed like a miracle. Encouraged, she returned to the studio. The following year, she scored her second Number 1 hit with "Killing Me Softly With His Song." A third Number 1 followed in 1974 with "Feel Like Makin' Love."

Natalie Cole: Emerging from Her Father's Shadow

Natalie Cole, the daughter of crooner Nat King Cole, also made an impact in the 1970s. She had only three Top 20 hits that decade—"I've Got Love on My Mind," "This Will Be," and "Our Love"—but she received a great deal of media attention because of her lineage. Sometimes it went to absurd lengths, such as the time she sang at a restaurant in Greenfield, Massachusetts, near the college she was attending. The sign on the door read: "Nat King Cole's Daughter Appearing Here." Her name was never even mentioned. Natalie Cole scored several Top 20 hits in the 1980s, including "Miss You Like Crazy" and "Pink Cadillac." But Cole's biggest—and most memorable—hit was probably 1991's "Unforgettable," which she "sang" with her late father, courtesy of the magic of the new audio- and videotape technology.

If you're thinking at this point that the 1970s was an excellent decade for female solo artists—in view of all the incredible hits women turned out—then you would be right from a creative standpoint. Women made some incredible music throughout the decade, despite the many restrictions placed upon them. Unfortunately, for every success female artists enjoyed, males chalked up three successes. Since the business of music is one of numbers, they impartially indicate the progress of the sexes—and, on that basis, it is clear that women made the worst showing of the modern era during the 1970s.

CHAPTER 6

THE BALANCE OF POWER SHIFTS

THE 1980s

TOP 20 HONOR ROLL
1980–1989

Paula Abdul	The Go-Go's	Diana Ross
Anita Baker	Heart	Sade
Bananarama	Whitney Houston	Sheila E
The Bangles	Janet Jackson	Carly Simon
Pat Benatar	Joan Jett	Stacey Q
Blondie	Katrina & the Waves	Brenda K. Starr
Laura Branigan	Chaka Khan	Barbra Streisand
Edie Brickell	Carole King	Donna Summer
Irene Cara	Gladys Knight	Sylvia
Belinda Carlisle	Cyndi Lauper	Teena Marie
Kim Carnes	Madonna	Tiffany
Tracy Chapman	Melissa Manchester	T'Pau
Charlene	Mary Jane Girls	Tina Turner
Cher	Christine McVie	Bonnie Tyler
Neneh Cherry	Bette Midler	Tracey Ullman
Natalie Cole	Stephanie Mills	Suzanne Vega
Taylor Dane	Anne Murray	Dionne Warwick
Sheena Easton	Juice Newton	Jody Watley
Gloria Estefan	Olivia Newton-John	Karyn White
Expose	Stevie Nicks	Jane Wiedlin
Roberta Flack	Dolly Parton	Kim Wilde
Samantha Fox	The Pointer Sisters	Deniece Williams
Aretha Franklin	Regina	Vanessa Williams
Debbie Gibson	Linda Ronstadt	

As female rockers gained acceptance in the 1980s, two exclusively male alternatives, rap and heavy metal, increased in popularity. The lyrics of both musical forms expressed hostility toward women at the same time that theyrecruited them as fans and groupies. "The anti-female posturing of heavy metal stars relates less to misogyny than to a rejection of the cultural values associated with femininity," writes Denna Winstein in *Heavy Metal: A Cultural Sociology.* "Men act, women are acted upon—through sight, touch, or merely imaginative transformations. Power, the essential inherent and delineated meaning of heavy metal, is culturally coded as a masculine trait."

Toward the end of the 1970s, a feminist organization named Women Against Violence Against Women threatened to boycott Warner Communications because of album covers that the organization considered degrading to women. The dispute was resolved, but it came to a head again in 1984 over videos that MTV, another Warner-affiliated company, aired. Elayne Rapping, writing in *The Guardian,* complained that women were being depicted in the videos as "bitches, teases, castigators and all-around sex-things."

Rapping was right, but there was more to it than that. The war of the sexes, as it spilled over into the 1980s, was complicated by the acceptance of large numbers of women of what was admittedly anti-female music. Those women didn't gravitate to the music because they hated themselves; they did it because they were reacting to mothers and grandmothers who appeared weak and inadequate to them.

The gender tug-of-war that was beginning to take hold in the 1970s resulted in the best decade in modern history for solo female artists. In the years from 1980 to 1989, 73 female solo artists made the Top 20 charts. That translated to 31 percent of the total chart placements. Male solo artists received 69 percent of the total, a strong, dominant showing, but their worst numbers yet—and a harbinger of what was to come.

PAT BENATAR: A FEMALE ROCKER EMERGES

"Janis Joplin was dead. There were a lot of singers around, but they were doing different things than what I wanted," says Pat Benatar. "I wanted to do a certain kind of thing, and the people I was emulating were men." Benatar was among the first of the female rockers to adapt the hard-driving, guitar-propelled rock 'n' roll that had come to represent pop music's new direction for male artists. Mick Jagger and Keith Richards of the Rolling Stones. Robert Plant and Jimmy Page of Led Zeppelin. These were Benatar's heroes as she was learning the guitar during the 1970s. By the time her first album, *In the Heat of the Night,* reached Number 12 on the album charts, her male competitors—such bands as Queen and Pink Floyd—were hogging the singles charts with Number 1 hits like "Crazy Little Thing Called Love" and "Another Brick in the Wall."

Benatar responded with a second album later that year. *Crimes of Passion* generated a single, "Hit Me With Your Best Shot," that peaked at Number 9 and went on to become a million seller. The song created an image for Benatar: the sexy one. Not satin-dress sexy like Diana Ross. Not sweet-voiced sexy like Olivia Newton-John. Benatar's sexy image had a rough edge to it.

Benatar was the strongest, most aggressive of the female rockers to emerge from the 1970s, but she wasn't alone. Other female rockers were hitting the charts, including Deborah Harry of Blondie and Joan Jett and the Blackhearts. These artists discovered that the system was rigged so they had to compete with each other, not with their male competitors. Radio programmers wouldn't air records from female artists back to back. Often they wouldn't even air two female records in the same 30-minute segment. This situation made Benatar and the other female artists livid. "There were many times when clearly you had the record that was being requested the most, but they would say, 'We already have a girl on the playlist.' And if it was me on the playlist, then my other peer group would not get on. They would say things like, 'We can't play the Pretenders record because we just played you.' It was a constant problem—and it still happens," says Benatar.

Benatar's efforts were recognized at the 1981 Grammy Awards when she was given the first Grammy ever awarded in a brand new category, "Best Rock Vocal Performance Female." She took home the award every year for the next three years. In the early 1980s, Benatar was the epitome of what the industry thought a female rock star should be: bold, sexual, energetic (all 5 feet, 2 inches of her), and an advocate of in-your-face, guitar-driven music.

Unfortunately, by the time the industry decided that it was acceptable for women to project aggressive images, Benatar decided that was no longer what she wanted. She was approaching 30, had met the man of her dreams—she'd married guitarist/producer Neil Giraldo in 1982—and was looking for new challenges. "If you want to be sexual on stage, that's fine, but if you decide you don't want to do it anymore, people will refuse to let go of it," she says. "That was a big problem once I decided I had enough. I was 26 when I started. A young, single person. Very quickly I met my husband, and it changed the way I wanted to look as a performer. The problem was, I was already locked in peoples' minds."

Despite the Grammys, the hits, the million-selling records, Benatar wasn't immune to old-fashioned sexual harassment. "I had all kinds of radio

Pat Benatar

programmers saying, 'Come over here, and sit on my lap.' That sort of thing. 'Let's see if we can get that record played.' It was truly amazing. I felt like I was in a movie. You can't possibly allow that kind of thing to happen, but they have the power to make your life hell. You couldn't come right out and say, 'You fucker. Kiss my butt.' You had to say, 'Oh, no thank you,' because they were in positions of power. It was very demoralizing. People say, 'What's the big deal?' But it was a big deal. I'm a little person, but I am always ready for a fight, and when I was young, I was a maniac, constantly doing battles with people over those things."

The shortage of other women to talk to about the sexual harassment compounded Benatar's problem. Most of the people she worked with were males. The only women she came into contact with were usually publicists, not a group she could feel comfortable confiding in about problems with the media. She talked to her husband about the harassment, but there were limits there. Nothing can sabotage a relationship quite so much as a female complaining to a male that she is always fending off sexual overtures from other males. "This was a whole new thing for everyone involved, and there was very little support at the female end," says Benatar. "It would have been nice to have someone to commiserate with. It was always a struggle because I spent most of my time arguing. I think it would have been easier to explain what I wanted to another woman."

Benatar felt like she was part of a movement, though, in her own mind, it wasn't always easy to define what kind of movement. "My age group was probably the first true product of the women's movement," she says. "It had a great influence on women my age. We were 13 and 14 when it became full blown. But we had a lot of dissent, even within our own ranks, because we were afraid of being lumped together as feminists in negative ways. Even though we had a camaraderie among us, we tried to downplay the fact that we were female. Our attitude was, 'Let's just play the music, and get on with it.' It was about war, not refinement. There was a gauntlet. You were out there trying to get through the day."

Young women had few places for to turn. "It was my intention to have younger females relate to me because I hated it so much when I was young, with guys singing, 'Let me take you back to my room, little girl.' What do they think? That we have no feelings? I would like to take you back to my room. How about that? I don't think we could see clearly what it was we were trying to accomplish because we were being battered every single day," says Benatar.

Benatar's vision didn't improve until she became a parent. She has two daughters. Haley, her older child, was born in 1985, with Hana following eight years later. "Motherhood was the first step to dropping all the guards I had up from being so defensive," Benatar says. "Because you can't do that with children. It opens up everything. Your writing. Your perspective. Every aspect of your life. Raising daughters is not the same as raising sons. I teach my daughters about strength. There's not a question in their minds that they can't do things. Their gender never enters into it." The change in Benatar's life became apparent when she went onstage dressed to kill in rock 'n' roll black, only to look down to see the remnants of baby vomit clinging to her shoulder. So much for stardom.

"I believe that men and women are separate in the way we view things, not that we are not equal—just different," says Benatar. "With the group of women that I belonged to in the beginning, it was said we had a mostly male audience screaming, 'Take your clothes off!' But it was from the beginning a predominantly female audience who related to what we were doing. It was unique for them to see someone like themselves up there. My husband is my collaborator, my producer, but we view things differently, even when we write songs. When his influence is heavy into the lyrics, the song is another thing entirely. You can separate our songs by who wrote what."

DEBORAH HARRY: THE RAP REVOLUTIONARY

Ironically, it was a woman—a former Playboy bunny—who introduced white America to rap music. In 1980, Deborah Harry, the lead singer of Blondie, had already had two Number 1 hits. The first, "Call Me," was the title song for the movie *American Gigolo;* the second was "The Tide Is High." Blondie was already soaring when Deborah and band member Chris Stein decided to write a song based on the new music they'd been hearing in the Bronx and in Brooklyn.

For a native Southerner—Harry was born in Miami, Florida, but raised by adoptive parents in Hawthorne, New Jersey—the rap parties she and the other band members attended in New York City struck a familiar chord. One day, Stein suggested they write and record a rap song of their own. The result was "Rapture," the first rap song to ever make the pop charts.

Blondie did a follow-up album, *The Hunter,* but none of the singles released charted in the United States ("Island of Lost Souls" peaked at Number 15 in Great Britain). After the band broke up and Stein became ill, Harry attempted a solo career. Between 1982 and 1989, she charted two singles in the Top 20, but the magic was gone. A review of her 1987 album, *Rockbird,* was typical of the times: "The only drawback evident on *Rockbird* is the lack of commercially viable songs," writes Becky Russell in

Deborah Harry

Nine-O-One Network. "With the exception of hardcore Blondie fans, I doubt a very large percentage of the general public will hear her album." Everyone still loved Harry, or so they said, but without hit songs that love wouldn't translate into a long career.

JOAN JETT: LOVES ROCK 'N' ROLL

Taking up the slack was rocker Joan Jett. With her coal-black hair, brushed up to Sex Pistol-punk standards—and her heavy black eyeliner and her big, pouty, Mick Jagger look-alike lips—she projected a sense of drama and sex appeal. She played her Gibson guitar slung low, massaging its neck with nimble fingers that induced unavoidable phallic associations. For males in the audience, Jett's guitar playing engendered a hormonal surge. For women, it elicited knowing smiles because they knew what she was doing and why—and they approved.

Jett wasn't born that way. She picked it up out on the road, where from 1975 to 1978, she sang and played guitar with an all-girl group named the Runaways. She couldn't have picked a worse decade to be a female guitar player. That dawned on her and the other members of the band while they were touring in England, and they decided to call it quits. Jett stayed in England and started working with ex-Sex Pistols Steve Jones and Paul Cook, who decided to try their hand as producers. For their first recording, they chose a song that the Arrows had recorded several years earlier. Arrows band members Jake Hooker and Alan Merrill wrote "I Love Rock 'n' Roll" as a response to the Rolling Stones' "It's Only Rock 'n' Roll (But I Like It). The Stones' song offended Hooker and Merrill because rock 'n' roll was everything they lived for; they wanted to write a song in response.

Jett's version of "I Love Rock 'n' Roll" was released in Holland on the flip side of a remake of Leslie Gore's "You Don't Own Me." Meanwhile, Jett put together a new band in England. This time she chose only male musicians. The group became known as Joan Jett and the Blackhearts. Jett didn't bother taking the band to the United States because she felt no one would take her seriously. Europeans, she found out, were more accepting of women rock musicians.

Eventually, Jett returned to the States to perform on Staten Island. In the audience were "I Love Rock 'n' Roll" co-writer Jake Hooker and producer Roy Thomas Baker. After the show, they double-teamed Jett in an effort to persuade her to again record the song. Baker and Jett's manager, Kenny Laguna, agreed to co-produce it. She was reluctant at first, feeling that she'd already given it her best effort, but finally agreed to do a remake. When the record was released, it went nowhere, just as she'd feared. Undaunted, she undertook a dizzying schedule of one-nighters. She performed the song everywhere she went.

"I ain't no punk rocker," she screamed to the audience, a reference to criticism she'd received from radio program directors. "I play rock 'n' roll."

With Jett acting as a cheerleader for her own record, women by the thousands started calling radio stations to request the song. Program directors had no choice. They played the record and by March 1982, it was Number 1 on the pop charts. Reaction to the record astonished Jett. Nothing associated with her many years of one-nighters had prepared her for the success that followed. In a 1984 interview with *Bam* magazine, she said, "People might expect me to be sick of it by now, the title and all, but when you sit there and look at that gold record and you think of your accomplishments—I mean to come back and do what we did is so incredible in itself that I can't believe it sometimes."

Jett followed up the success of "I Love Rock 'n' Roll" with "Crimson and Clover," which peaked at Number 7 in June 1982. Six years would pass before she had another Top 20 record. Her last hit, "I Hate Myself for Loving You," barely made it into the Top 20 in September 1988, proving that, like Pat Benatar and Deborah Harry, Jett was about a decade ahead of her time.

TINA TURNER: OVERCOMING OBSTACLES

When teenager Annie Mae Bullock was picking cotton on a plantation east of Memphis in the 1950s, Ike Turner was one of the most successful and powerful black men in the mid-South. As a talent scout for West Coast record labels that specialized in R & B, he was allowed access to Sam Phillips's studio at Memphis Recording Service. At a 1951 session with his band, the Kings of Rhythm, Turner recorded "Rocket 88," a song that was subsequently released by Chess Records. The record went to Number 1 on the R & B charts, giving both Turner and Chess Records their first chart toppers. "Rocket 88" was the precursor to the first rock 'n' roll songs Elvis Presley recorded in Phillips's studio, and many historians consider it the first rock 'n' roll song ever recorded.

Bullock didn't meet Turner until she and her mother moved to St. Louis in the late 1950s. Bullock was at a nightclub with her sister one night to hear his band and started singing by accident when the drummer, who was dating her sister, came over to their table for a little jive talk with them. To the drummer's surprise, Bullock took the microphone away from him and started singing. Turner was so impressed with her spunk that he asked her to travel with the band.

Two years later, after Bullock became pregnant, they married, and she changed her name to Tina Turner because she and Ike thought it sounded better. Tina became the star of the Ike & Tina Turner Revue, a high-voltage R & B band that featured Ike on guitar, Tina on vocals, and a group of high-stepping, female background singers. Their first hit record, "A Fool in Love," made them stars on the black nightclub circuit. In the early 1970s, they extended their popularity to young, white rock 'n' roll audiences with a remake of Creedence Clearwater Revival's "Proud Mary." They did well as a touring band, and their records sold reasonably well, but none went to Number 1.

Finally, in 1976, after years of what Tina has described as an abusive relationship, she and Ike divorced. Tina Turner then pursued a solo career, but for years it looked as if her career was stalled. Then in 1982, she signed with Capitol Records. Her first single, a remake of Al Green's 1971 hit, "Let's Stay Together," charted, but failed to make the Top 20. She didn't record "What's Love Got to Do With It?" until the time came to do an entire album. When the song hit Number 1 in 1984, Turner was 45. The song not only rejuvenated her career, but also made her America's first middle-aged sex symbol.

© 1996 PETER LINDBERGH

Tina Turner

Turner became successful by overcoming every barrier put before her: age, sex, and race. Members of women's movements, who saw her as a modern-day, musical Joan of Arc, embraced her. All of this mystified Turner. "The first I heard of women's lib was when *Time* magazine ran this picture of some women waving their bras in the air," she says in her autobiography. "Great picture, but I didn't really get it. Was it supposed to mean that just because you took off your bra you were now using your mind? I couldn't really relate to that 'movement' kind of thing. They were talking about 'liberation'—but liberation from, like, housework. That was the least of my problems. My problem was simply survival."

The success of the hit single focused attention on the entire album, *Private Dancer*. Over the next two years, the album spawned two additional Top 20 singles—"Private Dancer" and "Better Be Good to Me"—and sold more than 10 million copies. At the 1984 Grammy Awards, Turner won awards for Best Female Rock Performance, Best Female Pop Performance, and Record of the Year. She'd proven that age had nothing to do with it. In the process, she became every woman's hero. "After I left Ike, I began to wonder about equality—socially, racially, spiritually, and between men and women," she writes in her autobiography. "Even knowing that men are physically stronger, I cannot believe that we women are not equal. . . . This is why I have not given up on men."

CYNDI LAUPER: A FREE SPIRIT

Sharing the spotlight with Tina Turner in 1984 was Cyndi Lauper, whose "Girls Just Want to Have Fun" peaked at Number 3 on the Top 20 early in the year. Male reviewers wrote Lauper off, poking fun at her lighthearted approach. *Newsweek* called her a "new-wave Gracie Allen." But Lauper's target audience—young women who felt that equality included the right to have as much fun as men—didn't write her off.

Lauper's follow-up song, "Time After Time," went to Number 1 in June 1984. She was 31 at the time, still young enough to be an effective salesperson for her eccentric, little girl persona. She dressed like a new-wave diva, but sang in a sing-song voice that always seemed only a step or two away from breaking out into laughter. Whatever the critics said about her—and male writers usually gave her the hardest time—it soon became evident that she wasn't posing as an eccentric. She truly was what she appeared to be: a free spirit, a little girl trapped in a woman's body. Lauper made history in 1984 when two additional singles, "She Bop" and "All Through the Night," made the Top 10, making her the first artist of the modern era to have a debut album that generated four Top 10 hits.

Unfortunately, Lauper's quirky light had a short wick. By 1989, her brief, flickering flame was extinguished. She made several comeback attempts, most recently in 1997 with a new album, *Sisters of Avalon*. Before its release, nervous record executives tried to put Lauper and her early success in perspective. "There are certainly some preconceived notions that we have to overcome," Epic vice president David Massey told *Billboard*. "We believe that with perseverance and the right exposure, we can gradually knock down any barriers ahead."

When Lauper hit the interview circuit to promote the album, both she and her interviewers honed in on the women's movement. *Interview* magazine asked her if she felt the music industry was sexist. "It is, but I don't dwell on it because my world isn't like that," she said. "I decided a long time ago the only way to change things was for me to change my environment."

Lauper might have been successful in changing her immediate environment, but as she made more and more personal appearances it became apparent that she wasn't going to blend into the environment at large. The market for her music was still the same—young girls and women in their early twenties—but

© ANNIE LEIBOVITZ

Cyndi Lauper

was she still the same? At 31, with her delightful persimmon hair, she was able to reach that market. At 44, she seemed less like a playful free spirit and more like the scary old woman who lives in the attic. Seeing her attempt to fit into the little girl persona she had worn so well in the 1980s was painful for most people, just as seeing Mick Jagger do the turkey strut at 54 was for many of his fans. Lauper's 1997 album never made the Top 20, proving that girls can't always have fun.

MADONNA: THE FEMALE ELVIS

Benefiting from Tina Turner's unrepentant sexuality and Cyndi Lauper's gender-bending experimentation was Detroit-born Madonna Louise Veronica Ciccone, a former doughnut shop clerk and ballet dancer who had a knack for the dramatic. As Turner and Lauper were topping the charts in 1984 and raking in handfuls of Grammy awards, Madonna was testing the waters with a series of singles, "Borderline," "Holiday," and "Lucky Star." It didn't become apparent until the release of "Like a Virgin" in December 1984, that she had a future in the music business. The song went to Number 1 on both the singles and the albums charts, establishing Madonna as a major player. She followed up in 1985 with "Material Girl," which went to Number 3, and "Crazy for You," which peaked at Number 2. At the same time, she tried her hand at acting with a role in the movie *Desperately Seeking Susan,* for which she received rave reviews.

Madonna blended her flair for the dramatic with a level of sexuality never before displayed in popular music. For the most part, her sudden ascent into stardom stunned the media. *Time* magazine called her the "sultriest of the video vamps." About her role as Susan in *Desperately Seeking Susan,* Madonna told the magazine she identified with the character: "She's a free spirit and does what she wants." In 1986, with the release of Madonna's third album, *True Blue, Newsweek* writer Cathleen McGuigan alluded to her "Marilyn Monroe look" with begrudging admiration: "Way back about sixteen or seventeen months ago, there were certain oracles of pop who predicted that Madonna was just a flash in the pan—a very hot flash, but no more authentic than the gaudy baubles she wore, draped by the yard across an expanse of bare flesh."

Madonna garnered her share of male record buyers with her willingness to exploit her sexuality, but she won the hearts of an even larger audience of women of all ages who admired her boldness. She had become the female Elvis. Critics could call her tawdry all they wanted (they'd called Elvis worse), but her message was getting through, and the more criticism she received, the more determined her audience became to adopt her viewpoint, style of dress, and attitude toward men. By 1987, *Rolling Stone* magazine was describing her

Madonna

as "something a bit better than another hot or controversial celebrity: she is an icon of Western fixations."

Throughout the 1980s, Madonna ruled the charts with a string of Top 20 hits, including "Papa Don't Preach," "Express Yourself," and "Who's That Girl?" She stayed in the tabloids with a marriage and a divorce to actor Sean Penn. Then she co-starred in another movie, *Dick Tracy*, with Warren Beatty, who she was linked romantically with. By this time, she'd fallen into a pattern of bad relationships and bad movie roles. But the more negative publicity she received, the more acceptance she received from her fans.

Madonna ended the decade and began a new one in controversy as MTV refused to air the video for her single "Justify My Love." Under fire from feminists over videos from male artists that critics said degraded women and advocated violence, MTV banned Madonna's video on the grounds that it was too sexually explicit. It was a bitchy way for the network to strike back at the feminists.

Madonna responded by hitting the interview circuit, milking the controversy for what turned out to be millions. *Time* called her efforts a "program of self-defense and self-promotion." In a masterful stroke, she appeared on "Nightline" with Forrest Sawyer, who aired the video on the pretense of examining the issue of censorship. So the video that was too lurid for MTV saw the light of day on a network news program. Sawyer knew that Madonna's appearance would only boost sales of both the video and the record, and he found the irony irresistible. "In the end, you're going to wind up making even more money than you would have," he said during the interview. "Yeah," Madonna replied. "So, lucky me!"

Madonna wasn't the only successful female voice of the 1980s, but she was the dominant one. Her iron-willed reluctance to accept neither her own defeats nor control from a male-dominated industry inspired a new generation of younger female artists to look for the flickering light at the end of the tunnel—no matter how dim it appeared in the distance.

DOLLY PARTON: A SELF-MADE SUPERSTAR

Ask people in the business who they think was the most successful woman in country music in the 1980s and invariably they'll answer Dolly Parton. Narrow that group down to a female-only audience and ask them who they most admire in country music, and, once again, the answer will be Dolly Parton. "You can't deny what Dolly has done," says BMI's Frances Preston. "Brains, drive, know how—you can talk about managers all you want to, and Sandy Gallin [Dolly's manager] is one of the best managers in the business—but when it comes to Dolly Parton, she has handled her own career. Dolly knows what Dolly wants to do and what Dolly wants to be. I have always loved her line, 'I paid a lot to look this tacky.'"

Parton was no overnight sensation. By the time her first Number 1 pop single, "9 to 5," topped the charts in 1981, she'd spent 14 years in the trenches of country music, first as a struggling new artist with Monument Records, then as a singer with Porter Wagoner. He succeeded in getting her signed to his label, RCA Records. She had a series of country hits during the 1970s—"Coat of Many Colors," "Jolene," and "Love Is Like a Butterfly"—but the audience for country music was limited and Dolly wanted more out of life. She set her sights on the bright lights of Hollywood.

With the release of the movie *9 to 5*, in which Parton co-starred with Jane Fonda and Lily Tomlin, Parton became an international star. Her acting won universal praise from magazines and newspapers that had a long history of ridiculing the women of country music. There was something about Parton that the public could identify with. All of this mystified Parton since she was admittedly a self-made woman: a big-breasted caricature of a Barbie doll dressed in a form-fitting dress and a fuzzy, big-haired wig. Other women had tried that approach, but Parton succeeded where the others didn't because she never took it seriously. She gave men what they said they wanted, and she laughed about it all the way to the bank. Her attitude made her especially endearing to other women. If men didn't get the joke, that was their problem.

"Many an old boy has found out too late that I look like a woman but think like a man," Parton writes in her autobiography. "It is a great mistake to assume that because I look soft, I do business that way. Just like the first prostitute who realized she as 'sittin' on a gold mine,' I know what I have to sell, and nobody goes prospecting in my gold mine without first buying the mineral rights."

Parton pursued a movie career throughout the 1980s, playing opposite Burt Reynolds in *The Best Little Whorehouse in Texas*, and opposite Sylvester Stallone in *Rhinestone*. But she stayed in touch with her music fans, scoring her second Number 1 in 1983 with "Islands in the Stream," a duet with Kenny Rogers. They followed up with a Christmas album in 1984 and a joint American tour the following spring.

The 1980s was an incredible decade for Parton, but by her own admission, the crowning achievement not just of the decade but of her entire career was the release of the album she'd recorded with Linda Ronstadt and Emmylou Harris. *Trio* was released in March 1987, to rave reviews. Parton told interviewers that she sounded better on that album with the other women than she'd ever sounded alone. Ronstadt and Harris were flattering in their comments about her as well.

The three women were unable to arrange their schedules to promote the album the way each wanted to, but it took off without much help and went platinum in July. Of the three artists, only Harris had never had a Top 20 hit on the pop charts. At times, Ronstadt and Parton seemed embarrassed that they'd achieved a level of financial success that Harris hadn't, and their public comments, awkward at times, reflected this sense of unease. Harris's career received a jolt from the album, but for some reason the public never took to her the way other country music artists have done and her career has yet to realize its true potential. If country music artists themselves were allowed to chose the industry's next megastar, they would undoubtedly select Harris.

REBA McENTIRE: THE NEW QUEEN OF COUNTRY MUSIC

By the mid-1980s, the major beneficiary of Dolly Parton's diversification into motion pictures was Reba McEntire. The unwritten law of country music was that a woman couldn't be both queen of country music and a pop megastar. So Parton's success meant that there was an opening for the job of queen of country music.

McEntire had been making records since the late 1970s, but with little success. In some ways, she was Parton's exact opposite. With her feisty red hair, she was distinctive like Parton. She was also attractive like Parton, though in more of a girl-next-door manner. But unlike Parton, McEntire continuously tried to divert attention away from her simmering sexuality. This was a struggle, however, because she didn't possess any of Parton's skills when it came to manipulating men and their fantasies. Parton is a brilliant, sophisticated woman who has made a career out of "talking country." McEntire, on the other hand, is a brilliant country girl who desperately wants to be acknowledged as a sophisticated woman. If she ever "talks country," it is a slip of the tongue.

Throughout the 1980s, McEntire released a new album each year. And some years, such as 1985, 1986, and 1987, she released two albums. She never had a crossover hit during that time, but she was consistently successful on the country charts. In 1984, she won her first Top Female Vocalist awards from the Country Music Association (CMA) and the Academy of Country Music (ACM). In 1986, CMA honored her with its biggest award, Entertainer of the Year.

From 1984 to 1986, McEntire won the top honors from both the Nashville-based CMA and the Los Angeles-based ACM. But when she received her first Grammy in 1987, both country groups started backing away from her, although the more conservative CMA shut the door on her first. When the 1997 CMA award nominations were announced, country music fans were surprised that McEntire's name was missing from the list. They shouldn't have been surprised.

She hasn't received a CMA award since 1987, when she was chosen Female Vocalist of the Year.

The CMA snub reportedly hurt McEntire, and who could blame her? She has had 14 platinum albums, 6 double-platinum albums, 5 triple-platinum albums, and 1 quadruple-platinum album. This represents sales of more than 35 million records. And her high-energy roadshows, which often seem more pop-oriented than country, are consistently among the top-grossing in the country. With this much success, why would CMA stop giving her awards in 1987 and stop nominating her by 1997?

By 1987, the country music establishment perceived McEntire as a woman with an attitude. Not content to record one or two albums a year and to follow up the albums with promotional tours, she started poking around in areas where other women hadn't gone before. She decided to become a businessperson. She purchased a building in Nashville across the road from the state fairgrounds, hired a staff, and set up her own management firm, named Starstruck Entertainment. She started up her own publishing company and decided to promote her own concerts. Most of the staff she hired were women.

Independence isn't a trait that is greatly admired by an industry whose unspoken motto is, "You scratch my back, and I'll scratch yours," especially when a female member of the species exhibits that trait. Coming from a redhead, you might suppose, only makes it harder to tolerate. McEntire's genius is that she built an enormously successful career by going around some of the traditional roadblocks. Her true-blue fans know her song titles by heart, but few people outside that circle would be able to name many of her hits. This is because the public doesn't associate any monster hits with her. By operating as a self-contained business and promoting her own work, she has been able to take her music directly to her fans, bypassing the industry and the media to a certain extent, and creating her own connection with the public.

By the 1990s, McEntire had diverted her energies into a movie career. Did she forget that she'd assumed the mantle from Parton for precisely the same reason? McEntire's acting debut came in 1990 as a survivor in the thriller *Tremors*. Then came acting roles in *The Gambler Returns: The Luck of the Draw* with Kenny Rogers and *North* with Bruce Willis and Kathy Bates. Concerned about what her fans would think about her new career interest, McEntire told *The Saturday Evening Post* that she chose roles that were consistent with her image as a country music entertainer. "I'm not going to strip off or do a sex scene," she said. "I'm not flirtatious and, goodness, I'm not an exhibitionist."

In 1995, McEntire and Norvel Blackstock, her husband, decided to relocate her business operations from the fairgrounds to a newly constructed, three-story building on Music Row. The "good ole boys" who said she was standoffish

Reba McEntire

when she set up shop near the fairgrounds would now get to enjoy her company smack dab in the middle of the sacred ground. Not much was said about her decision to move until it was announced that she was constructing a helicopter landing facility on top of her building. That was the last straw!

The country music establishment rose up in arms. Even the mild-mannered Chet Atkins came out against McEntire and her helicopter pad. Music executives petitioned the local government to stop her from going aerial. The idea of a hot-tempered redhead hovering over Music Row in a helicopter, stirring up the leaves, and making a lot of racket, was more than the "good ole boys" of the row could bear. With the mischievous little grin she has made famous, McEntire withdrew her request for authorization for a landing pad with an understanding that she could reapply at a later date. The men won—or did they? To the men, the only thing worse than having a redhead hovering overhead was a redhead who kept them waiting for her next move.

THE BANGLES: A VICTIM OF INFIGHTING

In the beginning, they were the Bangs. Getting a record deal was the furthest thing from their minds. With Annette Zalinakas on bass; Vicki Peterson on lead guitar; her sister, Debbi, on drums; and, standing a foot shorter than the rest, Susanna Hoffs on rhythm guitar and vocals, they enjoyed playing the southern California nightclub scene, where their hard-core audience was made up of horny high school and college age males who relished their in-your-face sexuality. When they wanted to put out a record, they pooled their savings and paid for it themselves. They did their own bookings and promotions. In short, the Bangs were having an estrogen blast—all without any males telling them what to do.

Then along came Miles Copeland, the chairman of I.R.S. Records and manager of the Police. After hearing the Bangs at a Los Angeles nightclub, he told them he wanted to be their manager. He had a plan. They listened, but their first thought was, "Oh, no," because of his previous association with the all-girl group, the Go-Go's. The Bangs considered the Go-Go's, which Belinda Carlisle fronted, as an uptown, bubble-gum exercise in feminine alter-ego. They wanted no part of that. Eventually, however, Copeland won them over. He booked them for a tour in Great Britain, and the women quit their day jobs and made a dash for the airport. When they arrived in Europe, they learned that another band already had established a reputation as the Bangs. No problem. They changed their names to the Bangles.

By 1983, the Bangles had released a self-titled EP album, but they weren't exactly causing riots with their public appearances. Zalinakas, the bass player, decided that she'd had enough. She really wanted to sing, but the Bangles already had a singer. This was about the time that Michael Steele heard that there was a room to rent in Vicki Peterson's house and a possible opening in the band. Steele had played in lots of bands. The daughter of a commercial pilot (her mother) and a car-wash magnate (her father), she'd grown up in Newport Beach in rich-girl isolation. She was painfully shy, preferring to shut herself up in her bedroom and read books rather than to associate with her drug-using, high-flying peers. After high school, Steele tried her hand as an artist. "Then I realized as I got further into it that there are so many rules," she says. "I was really attracted to rock music because there is a lot of freedom and no particular rules, and I like that kind of situation better."

Steele learned to play bass but soon found that rock bands had rules of their own. She played in many bands, almost too many to count—Boy's Ranch, Snakefinger, Slow Children—and even served a brief stint in the Runaways with Joan Jett. By the time Zalinakas made her decision to leave the band, Steele had moved in as Vicki Peterson's roommate. She auditioned for the job and was accepted, just in time as it turned out, to sign with Columbia Records. The Bangles recorded their first album for Columbia and continued playing nightclubs; they barely even noticed that the album didn't do well. It didn't become apparent that they had a future until 1986 when their second album,

The Bangles. Left to right: Vicki Peterson, Susanna Hoffs, Michael Steele, and Debbi Peterson.

Different Light, was released. The first single, "Manic Monday," made it into the Top 10, and the second single, a novelty dance tune titled "Walk Like an Egyptian," took off like a rocket, going to Number 1 in December 1986.

With the Bangles' sudden success came a change of audience. For the past five years, they'd appealed to a mostly all-male audience. "Manic Monday" and "Walk Like an Egyptian" changed all of that. When Steele first heard the latter song, she knew it would either be a big success or a big failure. What she didn't know was that it would open the door to a new audience of female fans. When they arrived, she rationalized their presence by saying they'd been there all along. They were "smarter than the guys, that's all, and they stayed on the back rows, where they wouldn't get smashed," she says.

Interviewed in 1987 at the height of Banglemania, Steele spoke with pride of her newfound female fans. "When I go out now, it usually is girls who recognize me," she says. "I've heard from some people that a lot of girls look to us as role models. I think that's great because we're basically well-adjusted people, and we're doing what we want to do, and there's nothing wrong with that."

The Bangles worked well together as a group when it was "us against them," but with success came internal cracks in their solidarity. Where once it was the girls against the guys, it soon became the girls against Hoffs and vice versa. She wanted to be a star and the more she wanted it, the less the Peterson sisters and Steele felt like a band. "Everyone in this band has to do what they want to do," said Steele in response to a question about the attention Hoffs was getting for her movie *The Allnighter.* "If people don't do what they want, they'll start getting frustrated. Some of us are interested in films. It's a free country."

The Bangles charted with "Walking Down Your Street" in 1987, with "Hazy Shade of Winter" and "In Your Room" in 1988, and with "Eternal Flame" in 1989. They didn't have any hits in the 1990s, the band disbanded, and Hoffs pursued a career as an actress and a solo artist. She was spotted in 1997 at a gritty Nashville nightclub fronting a new band. Steele, the quiet one, had seen the handwriting on the wall as early as 1986. "All my life I've wanted to do this, but you have to be a realist," she says. "You have to face the fact that rock 'n' roll is a loser's game. The people who set it up are the businessmen, and they are the ones who profit in the end. Musicians are basically used and thrown aside. I don't mean to sound overly cynical, but you have to enjoy it while it's there."

HEART: CAPITALIZING ON INTERNAL SEXUAL TENSION

"You can't take sex out of rock 'n' roll," said Ann Wilson, the raven-haired Heart sister who shares vocals with her blonde bombshell of a guitarist sister, Nancy. "If you do, you emasculate it," Ann said in a 1988 interview. "I suppose our image is largely visual at this point, but I think our success is much more dependent on our music. We can look like young love, perfect in every way, but if our music was bad, people wouldn't accept us. We can't just rely on looking good, looking the way young girls want the guys to look, and the way guys want Nancy and me to look. We just look the way we look and hope that's good enough."

Heart was the 1980s remake of the 1970s Fleetwood Mac, with Ann and Nancy playing the roles Stevie Nicks and Christine McVie abdicated, but with a major difference: the three male components of the band were glamour boys with long, well-styled, shoulder-length hair. As a band, Heart pleased female record buyers at both hormonal and gender-identification levels. Those are prized demographics. "There is a chemical balance, a sexual tension between the men and the women in the band. It makes the band more interesting, and we use it to our advantage," says Nancy.

When Heart first started out in the 1960s, the group was composed of Ann and Nancy, and four male musicians. Ann sang lead, and Nancy played guitar. They had a number of hits in the 1970s, including "Crazy on You" and "Magic Man," but they didn't extend their influence beyond the West Coast until the mid-1980s, when the band was pared down to three males (with Howard Leese, the only survivor of the original group). Beginning with 1985's "What About Love?" and then moving on to 1986's "Nothin' At All," Heart stayed on the charts for the remainder of the decade, although they were never able to find a Number 1 hit. Their 1987 album, *Bad Animals*, gave them two hit singles, "Who Will You Run To?" and "Alone." They finished out the decade with two hits in 1990, "Stranded" and "All I Wanna Do Is Make Love to You."

Both Wilsons are serious musicians and songwriters, but neither has ever apologized for exploiting their sex appeal. According to Ann, cleavage runs in the Wilson family, who doesn't apologize for it. "I've always been lucky to know men who have encouraged us for that," she laughs. Nancy is content to leave the sex appeal onstage. Her guitar comes closer to being a constant companion. Picture her onstage, dressed to the nines, blonde hair flying wildly in the hot passion lights, playing two hours a night before a live audience. Then picture her returning to her hotel room to kick off her shoes to do more of the same in the privacy of her room, alone, without the fanfare. "I do a lot of playing after the shows," she says. "In my room I keep a tiny guitar, a tiny keyboard, and a tiny amp. I don't really practice. I just play a lot."

Nancy's guitar became important to her while she was in her teens; it was a substitute for a boyfriend. "I was kind of an unpopular girl, kind of fat, and my guitar was, like, my man. I really didn't have any friends in school. They were all Ann's age, about four years older than me. My guitar was my secret love."

Heart broke up in the 1990s by mutual agreement. Nancy had married in 1987 and found herself thinking more about having children than making music. She toyed with the idea of doing a solo album and writing scripts for movies. Ann was in perfect agreement. The months of being out on the road had taken its toll. "Nancy and I both want to have families," says Ann. "But I believe strongly in fate. I'm not getting desperate for it. I know it will happen to me, and then they (the children) will have a mother with a lot of experience to hand down to them."

JANET JACKSON: BREAKING FREE

Janet Jackson's single, "Nasty," entered the Top 20 in June 1986. It was her first taste of success, and she was thrilled. If Madonna's "Live to Tell" hadn't been holding down the Number 3 slot, "Nasty" probably would have entered higher. Nevertheless, the promotions people at Jackson's label continued to work the record. The following month "Nasty" peaked at Number 2. There was hope it would move into the top spot, thus giving the new artist her first Number 1, but Madonna's newly released "Papa Don't Preach" overtook Jackson's record to top the charts in August.

In September 1986, Jackson released a new single, "When I Think of You." It entered the Top 20 at Number 14 and the next month it zoomed to the top, giving Jackson her first Number 1. Her label had hopes that it would stay in the top spot, but with the release of Madonna's "True Blue," the record sank like a rock, just barely staying in the Top 20.

A pattern was developing. In December 1986, Jackson released yet another single, "Control." It entered the Top 20 at Number 14. The next month, in January 1987, it peaked at Number 4. A month later, Madonna's new single, "Open Your Heart," pushed "Control" off the charts completely. Jackson fired back with "Let's Wait Awhile," which shot up to Number 2 in March, only to be brought down in April by Madonna's "La Isla Bonita."

Jackson sat out 1988. She wasn't able to top Madonna until October 1989, when her single "Miss You Much" topped Madonna's "Cherish." Knowing a good cat fight when they saw one, the music press nudged the two women into each other's face, like handlers taunting high-strung birds at a cock fight. Jackson said this. Madonna said that. Word went out that the two women hated each other.

In fairness to Madonna, it must be said that she was already an established artist when her 20-year-old rival entered the charts. At age 27, Madonna wasn't exactly approaching retirement age, but she was more experienced and more focused on her career than Jackson. For her part, Jackson had been performing

Janet Jackson

with her brothers since she was 7 years old. The success of the Jackson Five, then in later years the phenomenal success of brother Michael Jackson as a solo artist, placed a lot of pressure on her. She was reminded on a regular basis that the Jacksons were music royalty of sorts. If she came out hissing and clawing at Madonna, it was because it was expected of her, or—if not that—at least something.

Jackson had several things going for her. She was attractive and petite—although much was made of her oversized buttocks—and had dark, soulful eyes that loved the camera, and when she was at her best, a voice that was as good as anything else around. On the negative side, she was criticized as vapid, with nothing upstairs. People said she was a shell filled with public relations goodies. Cruel, insensitive comments were written about her. She responded by staying out of the public eye as much as possible. She did as few interviews as she could, offering herself up to the public in carefully choreographed videos; while these were effective, they did nothing to stifle the criticism. Often, when she did interviews—even with friendly supporters—her words seemed to work against her.

Jackson's biggest contribution in the 1980s, aside from a few hit singles, was to give other African America female artists their freedom. Until she came along, stuffy images of elegance and sophistication constrained black female artists. This was a reaction to generations of racial prejudice that perpetuated the myth that black women were free and easy, the moral equivalent of a dog in heat. The first female recording artists to emerge from the modern era felt that they had to rise above that and set an example. It was a matter of black pride. They couldn't be sexy or casual for fear it would reflect badly on their race.

For Jackson, who hadn't been raised like that, all the old sexual taboos were ridiculous. Most of the black people she knew were millionaires. She didn't accept the black community's old prohibitions. She was a visual artist, and videos were an important ingredient in her success. To her way of thinking, Madonna had lifted—well, stolen—black R & B to form the basis of her music. Madonna's mixture of sex and music was undeniably effective. Why, Jackson asked herself, couldn't she do the same?

Almost in the blink of an eye, Jackson threw out 200 years of racial caution. If fans wanted to see her bellybutton, they got their wish. If they wanted to be teased by quick glimpses of her breasts, well, here they are boys! Jackson made videos that were unprecedented for a black artist by virtue of their strong sexual content. This was a bold, courageous, gutsy step for her to take—and by doing it, she not only set herself free, but also released the inhibitions of an entire new generation of upcoming black female artists.

UPHOLDING TRADITION

As Janet Jackson was getting her first taste of the charts—and redefining sexuality limitations on African American female artists—Dionne Warwick, Anita Baker, and newcomer Whitney Houston carried on the more conservative tradition of delivering R & B interpretations of sophisticated pop compositions. When Baker's second album, *Rapture,* was released in the summer of 1986, it didn't generate a lot of hits—"Sweet Love" peaked at Number 16 in November— but it gave the black community a new heroine. Her first album had more or less fallen through the cracks. *Rapture* was packed with ballads and bluesy, clear-voiced vocals backed by real jazz-based instrumentation—not the synthesizer substitutes that many black music lovers felt had sucked the life out of R & B in recent years.

Baker eventually garnered a mainstream pop audience—not to mention a handful of Grammys—but her core audience remained in the black community, where older record buyers appreciated her devotion to the type of music that Sarah Vaughan had popularized with previous generations.

Dionne Warwick had seemingly been around forever when "Then Came You," which she'd recorded with the Spinners, went to the top of the charts in 1974. Ten years earlier, she'd made the Top 20 with "Anyone Who Had a Heart" and "Walk On By," but for some reason she found success hard to achieve— and even harder to hold onto. Encouraged by the success of "Then Came You," Warwick thought she'd turned a corner in her career. Unfortunately, this led into a dead-end street. She didn't have a hit until five years later when she was paired with singer/songwriter Barry Manilow on "I'll Never Love This Way Again." She followed that up in 1980 with "Deja Vu," which barely slipped into the Top 20.

Warwick's last hit—she eventually gave up music to create a profitable "psychic network" on television—came in 1985 with Elton John, Stevie Wonder, and Gladys Knight. "That's What Friends Are For," which Carole Bayer Sager and Burt Bacharach wrote and produced, peaked at Number 2 in 1986, edged out for the top slot by Lionel Richie's "Say You, Say Me." Ironically, this was Wonder's last showing on the Top 20. In addition to "That's What Friends Are For," he had a solo single out that peaked the following month at Number 14. The song proved to be Knight's next-to-last showing. Of the four artists who made up the "Friends" quartet, only John was able to keep his recording career intact into the 1990s.

Taking the baton from Warwick was Whitney Houston, her cousin. A slender, attractive woman with high cheekbones and an expansive smile, Houston bristled with style and energy. Sex appeal was an important component of her persona, but it was the old-fashioned type—what you see is what you don't get—that fit into the African American tradition for female performers.

Whitney Houston

Gloria Estefan

Houston first appeared on the Top 20 charts in 1985 with two singles, "You Give Good Love" and "Saving All My Love For You." She picked up momentum the following year with two more Top 20 hits, "Greatest Love of All"—her second Number 1 hit—and "How Will I Know?" Her 1987 album, *Whitney*, produced three Top 10 hits, although you would never know it from the *Rolling Stone* review that called it "a mess of an album" and made references to the producer working within her "limited parameters." The scathing review, which offered backhanded compliments, was typical of the reviews that female artists, especially African Americans, received at that time from the music press, which was published for a predominantly male readership.

The women fought back by appealing directly to their fans, primarily through the electronic media. In June 1986, despite all the hardships and roadblocks, they made history when Houston, Patti Labelle, and Janet Jackson held the top three positions on the Top 20 charts. Never before had three women done that. It was a harbinger of even bigger success to come.

THE DIVIDE-AND-CONQUER APPROACH

One interesting aspect of the direction female artists were taking in the 1980s was that they approached it from several different angles. This was the old divide-and-conquer routine. For years, the pop charts reflected only two variations: one was black, and the other was white. Gloria Estefan changed that by offering a Latino alternative.

Estefan and her band, the Miami Sound Machine, debuted on the charts in 1986 with three high-energy, Miami-salsa hits, "Words Get in the Way," "Bad Boy," and "Conga." They seemed to come from nowhere. Their catchy rhythms and Estefan's distinctive voice and sensual good looks touched a nerve with the public, and opened the door for other performers to incorporate Latin music into standard American pop and rock 'n' roll formats. More hits followed, with the Number 12 "Rhythm Is Gonna Get You" and the group's first Number 1, "Anything For You," which topped the charts in May 1988.

Also finding their way onto the charts were women like Aimee Mann, who after two years of exploring the punk/new wave scene in Boston with a band called the Young Snakes, regrouped with a new sound that wasn't exactly punk and wasn't exactly new wave. Mann's new band, Til Tuesday, became an instant hit in Boston, with Boston Phoenix critic Joyce Millman describing it as "very much the band of the moment."

Til Tuesday's first album, *Voices Carry*, produced a Top 10 single of the same name. With her snow-white, punkish hair, Mann seemed cold and untouchable on video; in person, she was often standoffish and irritable. One way to annoy her was to suggest she that wrote from a woman's perspective. "I try to explore the way people feel toward one another, whether it's a man towards a woman or a woman towards a man," she told writer Dawn Baldwin. "I don't believe that there are certain feelings inherent in one sex more than in the other." Mann also said she had no patience with people who couldn't accept her because she is female. "When we're working with someone who is sexist, I just say, 'Get him out of here,'" she says. "They need to get over it." This attitude was gathering steam as the decade progressed.

"Tina Turner really broke a lot of ice for women, but she was R & B, and Janis Joplin broke a lot of ice, too, but then she died," says Rebecca Russell, the vocalist for Reba and The Portables, a popular nightclub band in the 1980s. "First the heroes come up and prove that women can be accepted, then we sort of infiltrate. But still it's hard because you get called a wimp by the guys. Or if you're in a bar singing and shaking your ass, you're called a whore. Now we're accepted. No one ever questions it now."

Vicki Tucker, the daughter of Tina Brazil, a big band era singer, had to learn how to be aggressive. When she followed in her mother's footsteps, forming her own band in the 1980s, she found the footing a little precarious at times. "When you're dealing in a man's world and you're female, you can't be softspoken," she says. "If you push, then you are called a bitch. I've been called a bitch. Okay, I don't care. If I'm a bitch, then I'm a bitch. But I'm going to voice my opinion."

"The guys are there to look at you. They hear you with their eyes before they hear you with their ears," says Russell. "They're the ones who come up and say you're great and all that, but it's the women who come up to you, maybe in the restroom, and say, 'Oh, I really admire the way you sing" and "Does your throat hurt?'"

TIFFANY REVISITED: THE SHOPPING-MALL SENSATION

If you were young and female, and had a little cash in your pocket, the place to be in America in 1987 was one of the thousands of shopping malls that had sprung up across the country. Teenagers, especially, found the air-conditioned enclosures a life-support system that provided everything they needed for survival: entertainment, food, records, movies, clothing, and a place to hang out with other teenagers.

Shopping malls were a natural place to break in new recording acts. The fact that it had never been done before didn't dissuade executives at MCA Records in Los Angeles. In 1986, they'd signed 14-year-old Tiffany Darwish to a multi-album recording contract. Teenage girls had recorded hit records before—and everyone agreed that Darwish was destined for stardom—but they knew they

Tiffany

needed something different, something fresh and new, to get her name and face out before the public.

Behind-the-scenes goings-on at MCA made it even more critical that Darwish succeed. When Irving Azoff took over as label boss at MCA in 1983, the company was in big trouble. People jokingly called it the Music Cemetery of America. Of the 46 recording acts on the MCA roster, only Olivia Newton-John was bringing in money. Without warning, Azoff dropped 39 of the company's acts. It was a musical massacre. As Azoff struggled to rebuild the label's roster, the company came under scrutiny by the Federal government amid allegations organized crime had penetrated its operations. MCA was going under; it needed a hit act—and fast.

Into this buzzsaw walked Darwish, a pretty, redheaded teen who had a big, grown-up voice and ambitions to match. She was from Norwalk, California, a small town north of Los Angeles. She started singing when she was quite young, and by the age of 9 was a backstage regular at Los Angeles's Palomino nightclub, where she won several talent contests. At that time, her specialty was country music. She would perform any place that would give her the stage—bars, country hoedowns, you name it. She just wanted to sing. Her biggest supporter was her stepfather, who was with her one night at the Palomino when they learned that country star Hoyt Axton would be performing that night. "I'm gonna get you on stage with him," he told Darwish.

When Axton showed up at the night club, Darwish and her father were waiting backstage. "My daughter here is 9 years old, and she's won most of the contests here, and if she could just get up and sing one song with you, that would be wonderful," he said. Darwish looked up at Axton with a little girl smile—the one that all 9-year-old girls smile when they want something—and he had nowhere to go but on stage with his new discovery. He wasn't disappointed. Together they sang "Joy to the World." From that day on, every time Axton played the Palomino, he asked Darwish to sing with him.

The following year, Hoyt Axton introduced Darwish to his mother, Mae Axton, who knew a little something about the music business. She'd started her career doing promotions for Colonel Tom Parker and his new discovery, Elvis Presley. As the co-writer of Presley's first national hit, "Heartbreak Hotel," Axton went on to make a name for herself as a songwriter. She thought Darwish had a future in country music, so she took Darwish back to Nashville and worked with the 10-year-old girl for about six months. Darwish did interviews galore, including the major television shows on TNN. She even worked a booth at country music's biggest annual celebration, Fan Fair, where she signed autographs, and sold photographs and Tiffany T-shirts.

"Mae really inspired me," says Darwish today. "She knew everyone in Nashville, and she was a woman who had the key to the city basically. It was wonderful being her student." That arrangement fell apart later that year when it became apparent that Darwish's parents and Axton had opposing ideas on how to further her career. "I loved Patsy Cline and Loretta Lynn, but that was not what I really wanted to sing," says Darwish."I was a big fan of the Eagles and Linda Ronstadt. I wanted something edgier."

Darwish returned to California with her parents. There she met, Jane Beaver, a publicist, who took Darwish under her wing and used her contacts to help find the budding star a manager. She introduced the then 12-year-old Darwish to George Tobin, a former staff producer at Motown. He was producing a Smokey Robinson album at the time in his North Hollywood studio, and during a break in that session that he first heard Darwish sing. He was ecstatic. He told his friends that she had a voice like taffy. You would pull it in any direction, and it would still be delicious. Tobin signed her to a seven-album exclusive production and management contract.

Once Tobin had placed Darwish with MCA—and her uptown country style had been pulled, taffy-style, into a pop format with an R & B groove— the problem of how to break her in became paramount. For months, her completed albums sat in the warehouse. Radio was cool to her, and the media was expressing burnout over the career of teen sensation Shaun Cassidy. Finally, someone came up with the idea of a national mall tour. MCA approached Shopping Center Network, a marketing company that specialized in mall-based events; it already had a tour underway called "Beautiful You: Celebrating the Good Life Tour." Darwish was booked for 10 malls, beginning at the Bergen Mall in Paramus, New Jersey. The routine was the same at each mall: Darwish would sing on a small stage in a center area of the mall, accompanied by recorded instrumentals. Corporate giveaways and contests were also part of the package.

MCA publicist Susan Levy was put in charge of making the tour a success. There was no handbook for her to go by; no one had ever had a successful mall tour because no one had ever undertaken a mall tour. So Levy had to follow her instincts. Whether it was blind luck or creative genius born of quiet desperation, she succeeded in whipping the local media into a frenzy as Darwish's mall appearances became events that hundreds of screaming teenagers attended. "Susan and I used to hang out a lot during the downtime, and we talked about clothes and stuff like that, things that interested me at the time," says Darwish, adding with just a hint of hindsight embarrassment, "Of course, she was hanging out with a kid."

Most of the teens who turned out for the mall tour were female. In later years, Darwish was always shocked when men approached her and said they'd been fans. "I had some guys who came to my concerts, but it was mostly a sea of girls," she says. "Now as time has gone on, guys come up to me and say, 'I had a big crush on you when I was 16.' I go, 'Really!' It embarrasses me. I didn't know guys thought I was attractive. Most of the guys who came to my concert, I didn't see them liking me as a girlfriend or anything."

The mall tour succeeded beyond anyone's expectations. Part of that success was a result of Darwish's charismatic personality and her youthful energy; the other ingredient was Levy's considerable skills as a publicist. "I Think We're Alone Now," the first single from Darwish's debut album, *Tiffany*, entered the Top 20 in October 1988, and peaked at Number 3 in November. The follow-up single, "Could've Been," peaked at Number 2 early in 1988. As Darwish's career rocketed upward, her private life spiraled downward. In the midst of all her success in 1988—*Tiffany* had sold 4 million units—she hired a lawyer and filed for legal emancipation from her mother, who already had received a divorce from Darwish's stepfather.

At the age of 17, Darwish moved out of her mother's apartment, and the Los Angeles County sheriff's office classified her as a runaway. Everyone in her life, it seemed, followed her lead and hired lawyers of their own. Her last hit record, "All This Time," made the Top 20 in February 1989. By that time, Darwish had had enough. The fight with her mother. The pressure from Tobin. The constant media attention. She just up and walked away from it all.

CHAPTER 7

THE NEW ROCK 'N' ROLL BILL OF RIGHTS

THE 1990s

TOP 20 HONOR ROLL
1990s

Aaliyah

Paula Abdul

Tori Amos

Fiona Apple

Irykah Badu

Anita Baker

Mary J. Blige

Brandy

Toni Braxton

Mariah Carey

Mary Chapin Carpenter

Deana Carter

Tracy Chapman

Natalie Cole

Sheryl Crow

Celine Dion

En Vogue

Gloria Estefan

Melissa Etheridge

Fleetwood Mac

Amy Grant

Heart

Whitney Houston

The Indigo Girls

Janet Jackson

Jewel

Alison Krauss

K. D. Lang

Annie Lennox

Madonna

Reba McEntire

Sarah McLachlan

Natalie Merchant

Bette Midler

Missy Elliott

Alanis Morissette

Alannah Myles

No Doubt

Sinead O'Connor

Joan Osborne

Dolly Parton

Wilson Phillips

Bonnie Raitt

Leann Rimes

Linda Ronstadt

Sade

Selena

The Spice Girls

Lisa Stansfield

Barbra Streisand

Tina Turner

Shania Twain

Suzanne Vega

Vanessa Williams

Wynonna

Trisha Yearwood

The type of change that is happening now could not be realized overnight. It has taken two generations," says Pat Benatar. "The first generation, they were the pioneers. The next generation were the people who got the benefits. For second- and third-generation females, this is law for them. They look back at what happened to their mothers and say, 'How could that ever have happened?'" Benatar laughs. It is the laugh of a battle-scarred veteran of many hard-fought campaigns. "Well, they weren't there. My mother was a working mother at a time when everyone else stayed home. That is one reason I was so open to the women's movement. It was the way I was raised."

"When I first started in 1990, they said women didn't sell," says Decca Records publicist Anita Mandell. "They said they had a hard time placing women. They said that since all the record buyers were women, they were going to buy men, not women. Now it's turned around. Women are starting to look at themselves more and be more accepting of themselves. They are rallying together."

As women have assumed increasingly larger roles behind the scenes of the music industry, they've begun to question the rules of the game. Are boardroom and marketing aggression male qualities, or are they gender-free qualities defined by the nature of the work itself? "I think they are male qualities because when women work together, they don't work under the same rules," says Curb Records executive Claire Parr. "When I work with a team of female executives who are secure in what they do, they are more team oriented. There is a loss of the sense of 'I' and more of a team attitude. They are more willing to help other women succeed. I have had men be incredible mentors to me, but the men who have been mentors have at times been threatened by me. The women who have been my mentors have been more willing to hold me up and say, 'You really did a great job.'

"I would like to see more women in the business because women are primary consumers in this business. Men are selling music to a market they don't have a tie to. They are trying to sell music to women, but they don't want women making decisions about how things are put together. That has always amused me, all those guys trying to capture the female consumer. I don't get it," continues Parr. She compares the approach to women trying to sell duck decoys to men. "I respect a man who wants to sell duck decoys to other men. But I'm not out selling duck decoys. I don't think women want to be separate from men. They just want a level playing field."

One of the troublesome facets of the debate about women in music is the realization that men and women do have well-documented differences when it comes to music. They look for different things when they select music, and they hear different things when they listen to the music. "I was at a panel discussion in New York on the sonics of music," says Decca Records head Sheila

Shipley Biddy. "They had done research and found that the female ear is different as to how it hears sounds sonically. They used the example of a man and a women together in a car. The music is playing loud, and the woman will take it down a notch because it vibrates her eardrum differently. The researchers speculated that females, brought along genetically to hear children cry, hear lower and higher frequencies better. Men hear the middle range better, and they'll listen to it real loud. Women listen to lyrics first, melody second. Men listen to the melody and rhythm and beat—and that catches them first. They might have listened to a song six or seven times and you ask them something about it, and they will say, 'What?' They might not get the lyrics until they have listened many times."

This subject prompts laughter from RCA Records executive Renee Bell. "I think women are so different," she says. "I still don't know how we ever got together. Women are very complicated creatures. It is incredible that men can write songs about what women are going through and don't have a clue how to deal with women. I'm sure that most of the [successful] songs written by men are by happily married men who have been in long relationships."

To anyone who lived through the 1950s, the 1990s are deja vu—all over again. But instead of guys singing about cars and surfing and making it with chicks on the backseats of cars parked on the levee, it was girls singing about menstruation, date rape, and making it with other girls on the backseats of cars parked on the levee. It was the same, and it was totally different. Girls were coming out of the woodwork, like in those old, cheesy monster movies where green slime is oozing out of everything in sight. Only it wasn't slime, and it wasn't oozing. It was just girls everywhere you looked—behind the microphone, slashing away at the drums, riding their guitars like they were something wild coming out of chutes at the rodeo.

Never known for their civic pride or cultural leadership, record companies looked for ways to translate the emerging girl pride into cold hard cash. They began to make up for four decades of neglect. They actively looked for female musicians and artists.

MELISSA ETHERIDGE: SUCCESSFULLY COMING OUT

As the 1980s came to a close, one of the most interesting and dynamic entertainers on the rock-club circuit was Melissa Etheridge. Her self-titled 1988 album failed to generate any hit singles, but album-oriented radio stations picked up several cuts on the album for airplay: "Similar Features," "Chrome Plated Heart," and "Bring Me Some Water." Etheridge's music was straightforward, high-energy rock 'n' roll, punctuated with tasty guitar licks—nothing fancy. Even so, there was something curious about Etheridge.

Melissa Etheridge

Shortly after the release of Etheridge's first album, a male radio syndication producer went to a hotel to pick her up for a scheduled interview. Already, the producer had gone to the hotel to pick up two other guitarists, Stevie Ray Vaughan and Jeff Healey, both of whom rode in the front seat of the car with the producer. When the producer, thinking one guitarist was like another, opened the passenger door for her, she sniffed, tossed her hair like guitarists are apt to do when they're irritated, opened the door to the backseat herself, and without saying a word, jumped into the car. The surprised producer later swore he heard hissing sounds as she straddled the middle hump.

Once Etheridge arrived at the studio and saw that she would be interviewed by a female co-host, she relaxed and loosened up; she started cracking jokes and acting like one of the guys. Asked to perform live, she did so without a moment's hesitation. On the way back to the hotel, perhaps sensing that she might have been unduly rude to her host, she invited the producer to her concert that night—and to a backstage party after the show. Several hundred women showed up for the concert, but only a few men were in the audience. Once the music began, the producer leaned against the wall and watched with amazement as Etheridge gave a frenzied performance that delighted the women in the audience. "I'll be damned," he muttered. "She's a lesbian." He looked about the roomful of women. "They're all lesbians."

After the show, the producer went backstage and was warmly greeted by Etheridge, who was accompanied by a golden-haired female friend. Etheridge extended her hand to the producer and asked what he thought of the show. Oddly, she didn't withdraw her hand after the handshake. She talked to the producer, still holding his hand, tightly, the way politicians do in receiving lines. Why is she doing this? the producer wondered. Then he glanced at the musician's companion, who was glaring at the lingering handclasp as she seemed to ponder the significance of her friend cavorting with the enemy. Etheridge was just having a little fun at the expense of her secret, sexual-id persona; her gesture reflected what lesbian performers—and there were plenty, both in rock and country music—were experiencing on a day-to-day basis. "People think I'm really sad—or really angry," she said, explaining her music. "But my songs are written about the conflicts I have. . . . I have no anger toward anyone else."

Etheridge was well known in the underground gay community, which was why her roadshows were always so well attended, but that didn't become common knowledge until the 1990s were well underway. She didn't attain the level of success she deserved until she publicly acknowledged her sexual orientation.

K. D. Lang had a similar experience. When she first appeared on the country music scene, dressing like a man, looking a little too much like Elvis Presley, music fans shrugged and attributed it to her Canadian upbringing, as

K. D. Lang

if all Canadians were like that. Once country music insiders learned she was a lesbian, the discovery didn't really affect her career since country music has always had a larger percentage of gay performers than pop or rock. In fact, a favorite pasttime of Nashville songwriters is writing witty songs about homosexual country performers. Once Lang publicly acknowledged that she was a lesbian, her country music associations seemed to fall to the wayside, but that probably had more to do with the new direction her music was taking—toward the pop side—than to any backlash attributable to irate, homophobic country music fans.

In the early years of Lang's career, her interest lay more with traditional country singers, such as Patsy Cline. The changes Lang's music underwent in the 1990s took her in a different direction and enabled her to win a Grammy in the Best Pop Vocal category (something that never would have happened had she continued to target a country music audience).

What Etheridge and Lang went through was in some respects a crucial ingredient of the impending women's revolution. It is as if someone somewhere said, "Okay, we're all set to go, but first we gotta take care of that lesbian thing." None of the lesbians who came out of the closet in the early 1990s suffered career-wise because of their announcement; in some respects, their honesty opened new doors for them.

SELENA: THE MEXICAN MADONNA

One of the female artists SBK Records, a division of the internationally powerful EMI Records Group, signed in 1993 was Selena Quintanilla, a 21-year-old Hispanic singer who already had a sizable fan base in the Tejano music community. "I don't like to compare artists, but Selena is the closest artist I've got to Madonna," said EMI head Daniel Glass. "She's definitely a pop star."

Nancy Brennan, vice president of A & R at SBK Records, had a dazzling track record with male artists, Jon Secada among them, and she was put in charge of guiding Selena through the musical minefield that lay between Tejano adoration and mainstream pop stardom. Brennan was sent to a showcase in Las Vegas, where all the stops were pulled out for Selena. This was Brennan's first taste of Tejano music, and she walked away from the showcase gushing with enthusiasm. "I was just so impressed," she told Joe Nick Patoski, author of *Selena: Como la Flor*. "I think she has every element for international success: an amazing voice, a phenomenal stage presence, gorgeous looks, and a great personality."

Within three months of Selena's signing with SBK, her album, *Selena Live,* was topping the Latin American charts. In March 1994, she was awarded a Grammy for Best Mexican American album. Two months later at the *Billboard* Latin

Music Awards in Miami, she took home honors for Best Regional Mexican album. For the remainder of the year, her *Selena Live* album stayed at the Number 1 or Number 2 slots of the Latin charts. By spring 1995, Brennan had Selena poised on the brink of pop stardom; everything was in place for her to make her crossover to a mainstream American audience.

If everything went as planned and Selena became the new Madonna, it would be a first for a Hispanic female and for a female A & R executive. Women had topped the charts for years, but a female executive had never before been instrumental in guiding another woman's ascent on the charts. On March 31, 1995, all the hopes and dreams for Selena came to a sudden end when Yolanda Saldivar, Selena's 34-year-old bookkeeper shot the 24-year-old singer to death. Ironically, the publicity resulting from the murder and the subsequent trial sent Selena's album zooming up the charts. In life, she'd never placed in the Top 20. By September 1, 1995, *Selena Live* was the Number 1 album on the pop charts. She became in death what everyone knew she was in life, a star. *Selena Live* is thought to be the first Number 1 hit ever achieved by a female who had a female A & R executive at the helm. The fact that it was accomplished in death took some of the luster off the victory, but it didn't lessen its importance.

COURTNEY LOVE: BAD GIRL MAKES GOOD

In 1994, the year before Selena's death, Kurt Cobain's mysterious—and, some would say, suspicious—suicide had shocked the music world. Throughout the 1950s, 1960s, and 1970s, sudden death had become a way of life for rock musicians. Then, in the 1980s, the sudden death syndrome seemed to wane as the illegal drug use of older artists and musicians tapered off; it was no longer the popular thing to do. But it returned with a vengeance in the 1990s, first with the fatal helicopter crash of blues guitarist Stevie Ray Vaughan, followed by Cobain's shotgun suicide, and then Selena's pointless murder at the hands of another woman.

Rising out of this chaos was Courtney Love, who in addition to being Cobain's widow, also held the title of First Lady of Grunge and was the leader of a band called Hole. To the dismay of Cobain's fans, Love hit the road after his death, performing at every opportunity. Almost overnight, she replaced Cher as the woman America most loved to hate. She was crude, rude, overbearing, and disdainful of criticism. She was careless about her appearance, often seen with lipstick smeared over her face, unbrushed hair, and out-of-control acne. Then, in a move that was as surprising as it was brilliant, she played the role of Althea Leasure Flynt in the hit movie *The People vs. Larry Flynt.* As a result of the film's success, Love underwent a makeover, re-emerging as a serene, tastefully dressed—pearl earrings, for heaven's sake—respectable woman any mother would be proud to embrace.

Love never really had a hit record and was a rock star only by the loosest definition of the term. Nevertheless, she became one of rock's biggest, international female celebrities and made the covers of every major magazine. She became the first visible evidence of the theory that American girlhood—all of American girlhood—was beginning to think of itself in new terms. This was the new Rock 'n' Roll Bill of Rights: Each girl a star in her own right.

LIZ PHAIR: A CUTTING-EDGE VOICE OF GENERATION X

Hearing that clarion call was Liz Phair, who, like Courtney Love, was someone people loved to hate, although for different reasons. She was perceived to be a rich girl who wanted to play around at being a rock star. Her very existence was a real slap in the face to the tens of thousands of rock fans who take it all very seriously. When she wrote songs that had lines like "I want to be your blowjob queen," some fans were offended because they sensed she might be insincere.

To quell the rumors, *Details* magazine writer Rob Tannenbaum once asked Phair why she wrote that particular line. There was no mystery, she said, pointing out that she was in college—and drunk—when she wrote it. "I had this big crush on a younger man, and I was so frustrated. I felt like a man dealing with a young fawn of a girl," she explained. "I'd been dancing around him in ways that he wasn't even aware, of and all I wanted to do was get down and bone." Tannenbaum asked Phair if she did. "We never did," she said. "God, he even came over and slept in my bed one night and just snoozed there. It was ridiculous."

With the album *Exile in Guyville,* Phair established herself as one of the cutting-edge voices of the girls of Generation X. She explicitly addressed the needs and wants of a new generation of women who felt they'd gotten a raw deal. In 1993, *Rolling Stone* magazine named her Best New Female Artist. *Newsweek* listed her as one of the 25 "must hear" voices of her generation. Toward the end of 1994, sales of *Exile in Guyville,* which had been released by a small, independent label, soared past 200,000, establishing Phair as a commercial success. Her second album, *Whip Smart,* continued the momentum, spurred on by the approval of feminist rock critics who saw her as the voice of the future.

Phair seemed to relish the attention, especially from her male fans. The tables had turned, and she marveled at the ease with which guys assumed roles that girls formerly held (she confessed to interviewers that she prefers "girl' to "woman" because that is the way her fans think of her: as a girl). Phair found she could sing to them, excite them with promises of everlasting love and backseat sex, then turn around and deny the entire experience. Poor guys!

Don't they know it's only rock 'n' roll? "I know what I'm doing when I use the word fuck, but I think it's termed explicit because I'm a girl," she told *US* magazine. "The thrill of it is like, your little sister could be up there having these thoughts and you wouldn't know it. That's the titillation. It makes you look around at all the good girls and wonder what's going on in their heads."

Phair shocked her fans in 1996 by getting married and buying a house in Chicago. Then she shocked them further by becoming a mother. By midsummer 1997, she was spending her days at home in front of the television, rocking her baby and watching the Weather Channel. Especially gratifying were the days when storm fronts marched up and down the American heartland, spawning tornadoes and sending earthlings scurrying for cover. Phair surprised her fans even further with her new album, *Whitechocolatespaceegg,* which was released later that year; the album's tracks had a distinctive country feel to them.

ANI DIFRANCO: AN INDEPENDENT SUCCESS

Ani DiFranco was equally prone to experimentation. She'd been performing forever, or so it seemed to her, without much success when she decided to shave her head. "Men don't smile at you as much," she explained to a *Boston Globe* reporter, "But at least when they do smile, you know it's genuine and not necessarily a come-on." DiFranco decided to grow her hair back after noticing that conversations stopped cold when she entered a room. That was a little more attention than she really wanted.

DiFranco never registered during the 1980s because she didn't fit. The 1990s, however, were a different story, and she was embraced as the mirror image of disaffected womanhood. In 1994, after she'd put in a good 12 years of barroom picking and singing, as well as released six albums on her own label named Righteous Babe Records, *Guitar Player* magazine anointed her the hottest young performer in folk. She recorded a live double album, her first, in 1997. Critics highly praised the album, entitled *Living in Clip.* In 1998, DiFranco released an album, *Little Plastic Castle,* that was recorded in Austin, Texas.

DiFranco once told an interviewer that she considered herself a vehicle through which women could project their own goals of self-empowerment. This image doesn't bother her until she considers her own self-described "goofyness," then she questions the entire system of offering up role models on the basis of a song. In truth, this tendency to waffle about the perimeters of reality is part of DiFranco's allure. Her songs can be fierce, and her stage persona can be unsettling (even to herself, she once admitted), but when she sets all that aside, the 5-foot, 2-inch Beatles fan becomes the type of woman older men like to pat on the head.

Because DiFranco writes and publishes her own songs, produces and sells her own records, and utilizes a network of distributors—and has managed to sell more than 100,000 tapes and CDs without the help of the majors—she is sometimes asked to wear her businessperson hat and participate in dead-serious analyses of the music industry. During an interview with the *Financial News Network,* DiFranco was put behind a desk with her guitar and bombarded with statistics—until she reacted to one question with the observation that the interviewer was missing the point. The interviewer paused, as if hit in the face by a pie, then moved on to other statistical questions.

The point that the interviewer missed—and the one that all the statistics in the world can't address—is that what sets DiFranco's music apart the moment it is created until the moment it reaches the marketplace, is that it is largely untouched by male hands (unless DiFranco so instructs). No "big boys" are pocketing money earned by the sweat of her brow—and to young women on the way up, it just doesn't get much cooler than that.

GWEN STEFANI: PLAYING WITH STEREOTYPES

It was becoming clear that female artists on the way up were not only learning the ropes, but also swinging on them like playground toys. "I'm just a girl—all pretty and petite," sings Gwen Stefani in No Doubt's hit single, "Just a Girl," then counters with "so don't let me have any rights." *Newsweek* probably spoke for a lot of people when it wrote of Stefani: "One of the most endearing things about Stefani is the way she simultaneously apes both feminist and bimbo stereotypes." With her bleached blonde hair; her muscle-hard, bare midriff; her stripper-next-door, onstage whirls; and her eat-your-heart-out-and-die smile, Stefani has tweaked the concept of sex appeal with a new post-feminist twist. She is the wild child who brings the teenagers in the audience to their feet with chants of "I'm just a fucking girl! I'm just a fucking girl!" She is the wild child who prances, skips, and whirls about the stage, taunting authority and social convention, only to go home that night with her parents. Her teen audience appreciates the contradiction.

Strictly speaking, Stefani isn't a solo female performer—she has actual guys playing the instruments in her band—but the guy profile of a No Doubt performance is so minimal it qualifies Stefani as a solo artist on a technicality. The guys in the band don't necessarily like that. In fact, some of them have complained to inquiring reporters that the rock 'n' roll business isn't exactly what they expected, but they are, if anything, staunch California-bred realists. So what if they aren't girls? They're making damn good money: their second album, *Tragic Kingdom,* sold more than 5 million copies. They're also enjoying all the perks of being a girl, so who among them is going to rock that boat? Besides, someone has to be the girl.

THE SPICE GIRLS: REDEFINING "GIRL POWER"

Wanted: Streetwise, outgoing, ambitious, and dedicated girls to play in a band. With that ad, Bob and Chris Herbert, a British father/son team who thought the charts were primed for an injection of tag-team estrogen, set out to put together a supergroup of pop-savvy young women. The Herberts didn't care whether the women played musical instruments; they simply had to look damned good, and they had to be able to carry a tune. That was all that mattered.

Five women made the final cut: Victoria Adams, Melanie Brown, Emma Bunton, Melanie Chisholm, and Geri Halliwell. They came from varying backgrounds. Adams's parents are wealthy; her father an electrical retailer. She rode to school in a Rolls Royce. Bunton's father is a milkman, and her mother is a martial arts instructor. She worked as a child model. Halliwell's father was a car salesman; her mother, a cleaning lady. By age 19, Halliwell had found her niche as a nude photographer's model. Chisholm's mother is a singer, and her father works as a travel agent. She has a tattoo on her upper right arm of a woman and the Japanese symbol for strength. Brown's father is a blue-collar worker, and her mother is a department store sales clerk.

For months, the five women worked together under the instruction of the Herberts, then, abruptly, the women broke it off. They spent the next year working together, writing, recording, and trying out various dance steps. In March 1995, the women met Simon Fuller, Annie Lennox's manager, and signed a new management agreement. Five months later, calling themselves the Spice Girls, they signed a record deal with Virgin Records. The Spice Girls' debut single, "Wannabe," went to Number 1 in Great Britain, making them the first girls group in history to top the charts. The single eventually sold 4 million copies. Throughout 1996 and into 1997, the Spice Girls solidified their fan base in Great Britain. Then they set their sights on the most important market of all: America.

The Spice Girls' music is a mixture of dance, hiphop, R & B, and smooth-as-silk pop ballads. Technically solid. Middle of the road. Nothing extreme. But their music isn't the foundation for the success the group had in Britain. It is their sexy, bare-midriff attitude, their ability to give new meaning to the phrase "Girl Power," that made them instant celebrities. In many ways, the Spice Girls were caricatures of America's 1950s pinup queen Betty Page. She was outrageous, naughty, and totally devoid of sexual pretension, and she delighted in showing off her body. Once, when asked who she most admired, Halliwell chose Margaret Thatcher. She called the former prime minister the "first Spice Girl."

Would "Girl Power" transfer to America? That was the question that echoed in the corridors of Virgin Records. The label's first major decision for an American campaign was to put the Spice Girls in the hands of another woman. It wouldn't do at all to have a man in a three-piece suit telling Americans what

Spice Girls. Left to right: Melanie Brown, Victoria Adams, Melanie Chisholm, Emma Bunton, and Geri Halliwell.

to think about Britain's proud export. Virgin turned to Suzanne MacNary, the vice president of publicity at Virgin's New York City office. It was her job to make the girls spicy, but not too spicy for American sweet-and-sour musical tastes.

MacNary had her work cut out for her. In *Rolling Stone*'s March 1997 review of the Spice Girls' album, the magazine gave it only 1$^1/_2$ stars, calling the music a watered-down mix of hiphop and pop. "Despite their pro-woman posing, the Girls don't get bogged down by anything deeper than mugging for promo shots and giving out tips on getting boys in bed," wrote reviewer Christina Kelly. The negative review didn't concern MacNary—*Rolling Stone* seldom gives good reviews to female artists—but it was very helpful to her and other Virgin executives in that it showed them where they could and couldn't go with the Girls.

The Spice Girls' strongest point was their video. Hip. Colorful. Sassy. Sexy. MTV would go for the Girls in a big way. Television in general was good, but it would have to be careful not to put the Girls in situations where they would be asked a lot of questions about "Girl Power." Unlike Brits, Americans don't have much of a sense of humor about feminism. They either embrace it and don't see anything funny about it, or despise it and don't see anything funny about it. Either way, feminism wasn't anything to laugh at.

MacNary's campaign, which was based on accentuating the visual, meant high profiles for MTV, short interviews for television, and staged events where cameras could get passing glimpses of the Spice Girls in controlled situations. What she positively couldn't do was put the Girls in the hands of the print media. They would only ask embarrassing questions and then sit there, with the clock ticking, waiting for the Girls to answer. MacNary not only avoided setting up interviews with the print media, but also refused to return reporters' telephone calls, with few exceptions. "She's not in; she's out with the Spice Girls," said her assistant. It was true; from the day the Girls arrived in America, MacNary stuck to them like glue.

By midsummer, it became apparent that MacNary's hide-and-run strategy was going to pay off. Newsmagazines ran photos of the Girls in their People sections. Television talk show hosts David Letterman and Rosie O'Donnell had them on their programs. MTV went all out for "Girl Power," showing the Girls' nipple-friendly video at every opportunity (it was banned in some Asian countries because censors felt it was too explicit).

In its July 10, 1997, issue, *Rolling Stone*—the very magazine that had panned the Girls' debut album, practically slapping them silly with its catty review—ran a cover story on the group, with the headline "Spice Girls Conquer the World." The massive nine-page article, complete with 10 photographs, told readers everything they could possibly ever want to know about the Spice Girls.

Little was said about their music, but plenty was said about their private lives. Chisolm told interviewer Chris Heath: "I haven't had sex since we've been successful. It's over a year. It doesn't bother me, though. I'm not really interested in sex and stuff. Not at the moment, anyway. I went through a phase where I had boyfriends, so I've kind of been-there-done-that kind of thing. Men bore me. I'm not saying women excite me, but men bore me."

The same month that the Spice Girls were featured on the *Rolling Stone* cover, their album went to the top of the album charts. They were the Number 1 act in America, yet they'd never played a concert, and never played anywhere live except on "Late Night with David Letterman," a performance most critics agreed was disastrous. Also, the Spice Girls had given only a handful of interviews, all to people MacNary had handpicked.

The Spice Girls can pontificate all they want about "Girl Power." MacNary gave the term real meaning in America with her efficient, sometimes brilliant, management of their frequently unmanageable image. The Girls came, they conquered—then they left. MacNary stayed.

THE INDIGO GIRLS: AMBASSADORS OF "RESPONSIBLE GIRLISM"

The Spice Girls weren't the only women banding together in the 1990s. The Indigo Girls, Amy Ray and Emily Saliers, had been around since the mid-1980s and developed a loyal following, especially on college campuses. The duo released a new album in 1997—its seventh—entitled *Shaming of the Sun*. The Indigo Girls not only hit the road to promote the album, but also participated in a talent search, sponsored by Scholastic Inc., for the best new lyric writer in the country. They also supported Women's Action for New Direction, a grassroots organization made up of retired schoolteachers, college students, and stay-at-home mothers. By the mid-1990s, the Indigo Girls had become the elder statespersons of girl groups—ambassadors for "responsible girlism."

Luscious Jackson, four New York women—Jill Cunniff, Gabby Glaser, Kate Schellenback, and Vivian Trimble—who actually play musical instruments, emerged as an alternative version of the Spice Girls, without the glitz, the dance routines, or the in-your-face sex appeal. The Beastie Boys signed the Big Apple band to their label, an association the women thought would help them. It didn't. No sooner was their third album, *Fever In Fever Out* headed toward the stores than they found themselves on soapboxes defending their womanhood. No, they insisted to reporters, the Beastie Boys didn't produce their albums. "We produced ourselves," one irritated band member said to reporters, "so why don't you look at the credits on the records?"

SHANIA TWAIN: THE SEXIEST WOMAN IN COUNTRY MUSIC

Sex is to country music what apple pie is to a Rotarian. Not the main course, but an essential component of the meal. Ask most country music fans who the sexiest woman in country music is and most will say Shania Twain. Ask most country music insiders who the most hated woman in country music is, and they will give the same answer. Those who are down on Twain explain their opinion by saying she alienated the Nashville music community by using her sexuality to sell herself as a performer. The real reason, however, has more to do with the incredible success she had with her second and third albums—any woman who holds the sales records she does is going to find herself unloved by those who don't—but the too-sexy-for-her-clothes criticism is easier to apply since it doesn't reflect nearly as badly on the critic. It would be a fair criticism if it were true. It isn't.

Talk to any male reporter who has covered the music scene since the mid-1980s, and he'll tell you a different story. Of all the female country music stars sliding up and down today's charts, Twain probably uses her sexuality to her advantage the least. It isn't unusual for other female stars to show up for interviews braless in tight-fitting T-shirts, or even in a revealing aerobics outfits, but Twain is always well-dressed and well covered up. It also isn't unusual for female country music artists to begin interviews by giving male reporters "big ole breast-to-chest" hugs, but Twain would die—literally die—if anyone suggested that she should do that. Twain never dated music executives who could help her career—a common practice—and she has never come close to being tainted by scandal.

If Twain is due for some criticism, it would be for not using her sexuality. Sure, she has made videos that display her board-flat abs or the outline of her perfectly rounded buttocks—but they are nothing compared to what other women have done. For example, Tanya Tucker once went to a restaurant near the Vanderbilt University campus, stripped buck naked and streaked through the main dining area. On another occasion, she went to a broadcasters convention, accompanied by NBC newscaster Stone Phillips, mounted the stage, whipped open her shirt, and flashed her bare breasts to the audience.

Deana Carter, whose "Strawberry Wine" was a Number 1 hit in 1997, once stopped a concert cold when she was asked to leave the stage to put on a pair of panties. It seems the blonde bombshell likes to wear short skirts without panties. No problem. It is easy to see why she would like to do that: it has advantages on a hot day. But on this particular day, Carter created a near riot as photographers clawed and scrambled to get a keepsake shot.

Not even Dolly Parton, the former queen of country music, is immune to the sudden urge to exert her sexuality. In her autobiography, she discusses the time during the filming of *Nine to Five* that she was riding past Tom Jones's house in a limo. "He was hotter than a firecracker at the time, and I said, 'I wonder how Tom would feel if I just got stark naked and streaked right through his front yard?'" she writes. "Well, I was just talking, but before long people started to say 'dare' and 'double dare,' words like that make me lose control. . . . 'Jason, stop the car,' I said, and before I knew what was happening, I felt the cool grass of Tom Jones's yard on my bare feet. Of course, that was a perfect complement to my bare ass parading around in the swankiest part of L.A. for all to see."

If you're feeling a tinge of moral outrage at the antics of Tucker, Carter, and Parton, stop it. This isn't about morals. It is about the freedom to be themselves. They are no different than 99 percent of the other women of country music (Reba McEntire representing the remaining 1 percent). They've got the power, and they know how to use it. In 1993, *Playboy* magazine sent a talent scout to Nashville to scope out the potential for a major pictorial on the "Girls of Country Music." When he arrived at the hotel, dozens of hopeful country music starlets greeted him in the lobby. They formed a line a mile long to wait for interviews in the hotel suite, exchanging tips on the music business as they waited their turn.

Some of the more interesting interviews, reports the scout, were with the big-name stars who pondered baring all for the magazine. He recalls one meeting in particular in which he sat on a sofa with one star, a *Playboy* magazine opened up across their laps to the centerfold section. "I could do that," the sultry star said, pointing to a photograph, "and that one—but, oh, not that one." The plug was pulled on the *Playboy* project after nervous label executives put out word that they thought a nude pictorial was more liberation than they could handle.

Twain understands the sexuality inherent in country music as well as anyone. In the beginning of her career, by reversing the process—being demure, almost puritanical, in her private life and then letting it all hang out in her public persona—she capitalized on an element of country music that everyone has known and understood for ages. This was a stroke of genius. With the late 1997 release of her third album, *Come on Over*, Twain continued to stress the appeal of rock-tinged, high-voltage country music and the blinding power of womanhood (one of her favorite themes from day one). "I spent my whole teenage life flattening my breasts, wearing triple shirts, always worried about those things," she told Associated Press. "Teenage girls, they need to learn to grow up confident about these new things that are growing on their chests. It's very important that girls grow up with a sense of confidence about the fact that they're women."

Twain introduced the first single from her new album at the 1997 CMA Awards. "Love Gets Me Every Time" is an upbeat tune with a catchy hook that seems unintentionally reflective of her private personality. She sang it on live television using a prerecorded track. She looked like a million dollars. She had a form-fitting knit that clung to her curves like wet paper, but no bare midriff. She nailed the song, displaying polished dance moves that would have sent Patsy Cline into a tizzy. When the song ended, the camera pulled back to show Twain on stage facing the audience. The audience members responded with polite applause, but no one rose to their feet. She is the hottest selling act in country music, but the establishment couldn't bring itself to its feet. After the show, local television reporters lined up the stars and trotted them past the cameras. Twain was nowhere to be seen. She was probably on a plane back to her farm in New York. Who could blame her?

KATHY MATTEA: QUIETLY GOING GOLD

Kathy Mattea was sitting inside her tour bus at the Nashville fairgrounds. The bus was pulled up next to the stage at the 1994 Fan Fair celebration, a week-long event that draws about 24,000 country music fans each June. Across the field and on top of a hill—are the old headquarters of Reba McEntire's Starstruck Entertainment. Fan Fair offers record labels an opportunity to showcase their rosters, and it offers fans the opportunity to see and hear many of their favorite stars perform in an outdoor arena. Mattea was scheduled to go on stage next. She likes to perform, and the excitement showed in her eyes. "Sometimes I wake up and say, 'I live in Nashville, and I'm a country music star,'" she says, breaking into a wide grin. "I want to grab someone and say, 'Is that a hoot or what?'"

Mattea isn't your typical country singer. There is something terribly middle class about her despite her working-class, Italian-American upbringing in rural West Virginia. Something organized and efficient despite her creative attraction to the fanciful. Something almost sisterish despite her girl-next-door sex appeal. If you met her and didn't know she was a country singer, you might think she was a bookkeeper, a physician, or a school teacher. She has one of those unpretentious voices that critics love to rave about—and they have, lavishing praise in ways rarely done for female country vocalists.

When Mattea moved to Nashville in 1978 at the age of 19 to pursue a career in country music, she didn't have a clue, or a contact in the music business. For several years, she waited tables and worked as a secretary, writing songs and singing on demos and advertising jingles, hoping against hope for a break. Finally, she attracted the attention of Mercury Records, which signed her to a recording contract in 1983. Her first two albums, *Kathy Mattea* and *From My Heart,* produced four songs that charted and earned her a nomination from the Academy of Country Music as New Female Vocalist of the Year.

Throughout the 1980s, Mattea released a string of singles that did well, but she didn't attract major attention until she released "Eighteen Wheels and a Dozen Roses." In 1990, she won a Grammy for "Where've You Been," a song about a salesman and his wife and their final meeting in a nursing home. Two years later, Mattea faced a crisis when a blood vessel in her vocal chords burst, threatening to end her career. But after taking a little time off, she rebounded, her voice as strong and passionate as ever.

Mattea attributes the success female country artists enjoyed in the 1990s to the fact that record labels have given the women more rope. "Women don't have as much pressure to conform," she said in a 1997 interview. "They leave us alone more than they do the guys. No one is breathing down your neck saying, 'You know, you have to wear a cowboy hat.' I've talked to more than one male artist who has gotten that kind of pressure from the labels. When I first started, there were not very many women around. You would look at the Top 10 and there would be, like, one female, sometimes two, and that was it. It's much different now.

"I'm one of those people who, through all the changes in country music, has quietly done my own thing. I never had a huge spike in sales that a lot of people have had. I sort of quietly go gold. I've never had a platinum studio album, so my take on it is a little different because I haven't ridden that wave. There were times when I felt frustrated for not selling more, but for the most part I feel glad to have my own niche. I don't know if that is because I was taught not to expect more because I am a woman or if it's just my nature as a person. It's hard for me to be objective about it."

Mattea would like to see change in some areas. Little things, she admits, but things that would make life sweeter if they never came up. "If a guy walks out on stage in jeans and a T-shirt, no one says anything. If a woman walks out on stage in jeans and a T-shirt, people go 'and she could be such a pretty girl, too.' . . . There's more pressure on us to glam up. Part of that is cultural across the board, but I think we feel more pressure to think about how we look. I would like to be able to walk out there in overalls if I felt like it and it not become an issue."

DEANA CARTER: A MIND OF HER OWN

Deana Carter grew up in a musical household. Her father, Fred Carter, Jr., was one of country music's most sought-after session guitarists from the 1950s

Deana Carter

through the late 1970s; he started out on the Louisiana Hayride and later played with a variety of artists, including Willie Nelson, Roy Orbision, Bob Dylan, and Waylon Jennings. For Deana Carter, this meant two things. First, there was never a shortage of music around the house. She tells the story that at family reunions, she had the option of washing dishes or singing harmony—and she usually steered clear of the kitchen. Second, it meant music had a male scent to it. It was what her father did for a living, a male profession like truck driving or farming. She eventually changed her perception of what was male, what was female, and what was open to both. But in the early years, music was pretty much something men did with other men for other men—at least in her eyes.

At the age of 17, Carter asked her father to help her get a record deal, and he did, taking her around to the record labels and studios and introducing her as his daughter. With Dean Martin as her namesake—her father once wrote a song for the crooner—she felt it was her destiny to be in the music business. When no one showed any immediate interest, she started having second thoughts about a career in music. At the time, her grandmother was suffering with a disabling illness and Carter, seeing what she was going through, decided to go to the University of Tennessee to study rehabilitation therapy. Part of doubt, too, was seeing the pain Carter's mother was experiencing over her inability to help the grandmother. "My mom was the Rock of Gibraltar in my family," she says. "She came from a generation when the female was, like, the mom. She is the biggest influence in my life, and I love her with all my heart. If I could be one-fifth the person she is, I'd be happy."

After graduation, Carter worked for a time helping stroke and head-injury patients in recovery, but her interest in music eventually resurfaced. Anyone standing outside the door while she was caring for her patients would have realized that right away. One of the relaxation tools she used for her patients was the music of Fleetwood Mac.

At age 23, Carter decided to give music another try. She left her job working with stroke patients and took a series of odd jobs—waiting tables, teaching preschool children, and cleaning bathrooms—while she wrote songs and made demos to pitch to record labels. One of her demos made its way to Willie Nelson, who remembered her father. He was impressed with the tape and set up a meeting with her. They talked and sang and passed the guitar back and forth, a ritual as old as country music itself, and when it was over, Nelson asked her to perform with him at an upcoming Farm Aid concert.

Doors were beginning to open for Carter. Soon she had a record deal with Capitol Records, the home of Tanya Tucker and Garth Brooks. The first thing Capitol did was to pair Carter with Susan Levy, its brilliant vice president of artist development. Following her wildly successful Tiffany mall tour, Levy had moved to Nashville to head up MCA's publicity department and then—after six years at that job—moved over to Capitol in 1995. As head of artist development, Levy oversees everything that influences an artist's image: hair and makeup, photography, packaging, advertising, and video production.

Capitol's instructions to Levy were simple: Make Carter a star. Levy had plenty to work with, but right from the beginning Carter made it clear that she had a mind of her own. She co-wrote 6 of the 11 songs on the album. The first issue that arose was over the title. She wanted to use the title of one of the tracks she had co-written, "Did I Shave My Legs for This?"

"There was some thought at the label that people wouldn't take me seriously as an artist with that title—that people would think I was a comedian or a novelty act," says Carter. "But it was something I wanted to do. When we wrote that song, I said that if I ever had an album, that was what I wanted it called. That was before I was even signed with Capitol." With Levy's backing, Carter won the argument. "It wasn't much of a battle," she says with a laugh. "My argument was, 'Well, come up with a better title'—and that was kinda' hard to do. As hard as I have worked to be taken seriously as a songwriter, I also wanted to show that I have a sense of humor. It's like swan diving. If people can do it well, you've got to respect it whether you dig it or not. That song said that about me, about my personality."

The first hit from *Did I Shave My Legs for This?* was "Strawberry Wine," a first-love reminiscence written by Gary Harrison and Matraca Berg. With that song—and Levy's guidance—Carter metamorphosed from a pretty, earnest-to-the-hilt singer/songwriter with a singsong voice, to a timeless beauty, a siren of lost love whose plaintive call was filled with promise. As music, the song was solid. As imagery, when paired with the video, it was masterful. *Did I Shave My Legs for This?* was a female concept from start to finish. Female singer and songwriters (only one song on the album wasn't written or co-written by a female). Female label executive in charge of developing the concept. And, most important, female record buyers who bought the premise.

By February 1997, to the surprise of no one, least of all Carter, the album was in the Top 10 on the pop charts. The lesson is clear: women reward other women who tell it straight. It doesn't matter how they dress or how little they wear. It isn't the medium; it's the message. "It's important to gain the respect of other women," says Carter. "Women have a very good sense of honesty and bullshit—not to be crude—so a woman knows when she's being snowed. Women have this checks and balance system, where they can communicate about their problems.

By mid-1997, Carter was still pretty much in a daze. It was all still happening—and so fast. The fame. Nominated for two Grammys. The constant stream of television shows: "The Tonight Show with Jay Leno," "The Late Show with David Letterman." They didn't even have to pronounce her name right, just keep it coming.

Carter is appreciative of the work her label put into her project—not all labels go to the mat for their artists—but she is especially appreciative of what Levy has done for her. "She's very talented," Carter says. "I'm fortunate to be on a label that has people like that. She has a vision for the artists—and she's been a good friend to me, too."

There is no doubt in Carter's mind that things are changing for women. She is living proof of that. She credits some of that success to men who had the courage to let women in the door. "Women will always have their perception of men, and men will always have their perception of women," she says. "As long as we try to understand one another and be respectful of one another, then I think it will be a better place. There were times when people were condescending to me because I was a young woman . . . or maybe it was because of my youth. . . . I have tried to live my life non-genderized. It keeps you like one of the guys, but not threatening." Carter laughs, softly, almost teasingly, pausing in all the right places. "It's really important to accept people for what they are instead of what they have . . . physically or otherwise."

TERRI CLARK: ANOTHER "OVERNIGHT SENSATION"

Terri Clark is tall and slender, and she carries herself like royalty. Her sculptured face is flawless, and her almond eyes are intense. She wears T-shirts and rolls the sleeves up to show off her toned upper arms. Another time, another place, wearing a frilly dress and an uptown hairdo, she could be mistaken for one of those New York supermodel types. But Clark isn't like that. She is a country singer, she wears cowboy hats and boots, and she lives in Nashville, thank you—and if you mess with her, she'll kick your citified butt all the way to New York City.

Like Deana Carter, Clark became an "overnight sensation" in 1997—after several years of hard work in the trenches. Her debut album sold more than a million copies. Her debut single, "Better Things to Do," went to Number 1 on the country charts. *Billboard* magazine named her Top New Female Vocalist of 1995. Singles like "Poor, Poor Pitiful Me," "If I Were You," and "Suddenly Single," have endeared her to a new generation of women who see her as one of the new role models for the 1990s. The appreciation and respect are mutual. What Clark looks for first when she walks out on a concert stage are the faces of those women.

Terri Clark

"They've got their fists in the air, and they're screaming, 'You go girl! You go girl!,' and they're holding up signs, and they're wearing cowboy hats with their T-shirts sleeves rolled up, and it's so flattering," says Clark. "They relate to me somehow. When I perform, I never put myself on this pedestal because I could just as easily be one of them watching the show. Just because I sing doesn't make me any more different. I don't feel any better, and I think they know that, and I think they feel like I'm their best friend."

Clark arrived in Nashville by way of Medicine Hat, Alberta, where she grew up, a little girl with big dreams of making it in Music City. She was 18 when she pulled into town with her mother and strolled into Tootsie's Orchid Lounge. Clark asked a guy playing for tips if he minded if she did a little singing when he went on break. He didn't mind—Why would he? He had no time clock to punch—and Clark, fresh and young and fearless, did so well that the management offered her a job singing every night. She thought she had it made. She didn't, of course. Eight years later, eight hard years of waiting tables and selling cowboy boots, eight years later and pushing 30, she landed a recording contract with Mercury Records.

Today, Clark finds her image as a tough babe amusing. "I take it as a compliment," she says. "I do have another side to me. I have become known as the dirt-kicking, aggressive, in-your-face, don't-take-no-BS-off-of-anybody— but there is a softer side there." She is amazed at the success that women, in general, are having in music. "They're kicking everyone's butt. I love it," she says. "I think that women are making some of the most unique music. They all sound completely different from each other. Women want to hear songs they can relate to. I've never been into doing male bashing music. I've never been into bashing any particular gender. A lot of guys like my music, too. They turn it around with 'I've been there before.'"

WOMEN DOMINATING THE CHARTS

Country singer Doug Supernaw couldn't figure it out. Early in 1995, he slammed into a stone wall of protest with the release of his record "What'll You Do About Me." It was about a woman who invited a man into her life, changed her mind, and sent him on his way. The trouble was the man didn't want to leave. Women's groups came out in force to protest the song because they considered it pro-stalker. BNA Records, Supernaw's record label, heeded the protests and wrote out a statement of apology for Supernaw to sign.

"I got really upset when they did that," says Supernaw. "It was like nothing I would have said. I said, 'That's bullshit.' They said, 'We don't want you to talk about it because you'll make it worse than it is.'" As a result of the controversy, Supernaw and BNA severed their relationship. Supernaw said he thought that the song was humorous and that the reaction to it was unfair. "It's sad when just a few people can dictate what the rest of the country can hear," he says. What Supernaw learned—the hard way—was that country music was changing. Right or wrong, women reacted to his song in a negative way, and when push came to shove, their economic clout mattered more than his pride or even his career.

Country Music Successes

Shania Twain, Terri Clark, Kathy Mattea, and Deana Carter were just the tip of the iceberg. Women were destined to dominate the charts throughout the 1990s. One of the women who began the decade strong, sat on the sidelines for the middle years, and then made a successful return was Trisha Yearwood. Other women, such as Lorrie Morgan, Wynonna, Shelby Lynne, Alison Krauss, Faith Hill, Martina McBride, Mindy McCready, and Linda Davis, also had a significant impact.

Lorrie Morgan is the daughter of Grand Ole Opry star George Morgan and the widow of country singer Keith Whitely, who died in 1989 of alcoholism. Her albums include *Something in Red, Watch Me,* and *Leave the Light On.*

Wynonna Judd is the daughter of country singer Naomi Judd and the sister of actress Ashley Judd. Wynonna began her career as a member of the duo the Judds—Naomi was the other member—but pursued a solo career in the early 1990s after her mother was diagnosed with chronic hepatitis. Her albums include *Wynonna, Revelations,* and *Collection.*

Trisha Yearwood began her music career as a receptionist with the now defunct MTM Records. Although she enjoyed a strong beginning as a recording artist in the early 1990s, her career fizzled by mid-decade and then received a boost in 1997 with a new album, *How Do I Live,* which was awarded a Grammy in 1998. Yearwood's other albums include *Hearts in Armor* and *The Sweetest Gift.*

Mississippi-born Faith Hill, who first attracted attention for her stunning looks, made good use of the media play to promote her first release, *Take Me As I Am.* Now married to country singer Tim McGraw, she was nominated for a Grammy in 1998 for a duet with her husband titled "It's You Love."

Linda Davis, who began her recording career in 1982 as a member of Kip and Linda, didn't attract much attention until she recorded a duet in 1993 with Reba McEntire, "Does He Love You?" Davis was working as McEntire's backup singer at the time, a position she still holds. She followed up the duet with an album of her own titled *Shoot for the Moon.*

Martina McBride went from selling T-shirts at Garth Brooks's concerts to being inducted into the Grand Ole Opry. To date, she is probably best known for her "Independence Day" video, which depicts the trauma of domestic violence. Her albums include *The Time Has Come*, *The Way That I Am*, and *Wild Angels*.

Mindy McCready's 1996 debut album, *Ten Thousand Angels*, produced several hits, including "Guys Do It All the Time" and "Maybe He'll Notice Her Now." However, she has been slow to capitlaize on the success of that album, and dropped from view during the summer and fall of 1997 to work on new material.

Alison Krauss has breathed new life into bluegrass in recent years by incorporating snappy production values and a female perspective into recordings that have sold moderately well and attracted critical acclaim. Her albums include *Too Late to Cry* and *So Long So Wrong*.

Janet Jackson: Setting Herself Completely Free

By 1997, female artists were busting out all over, not just in country music; it was like a virus sweeping the country. As a movement, it was very different from the feminist movement of the 1960s and 1970s: it had none of the rough edges. For all its false starts, it was a glorious, if not sometimes entertaining, event to watch from the sidelines.

Janet Jackson released her seventh album, *The Velvet Rope*, and watched it debut at Number 1 on the Top 20 album charts. Her preceding album, *janet*, released in 1993, had also debuted at Number 1, and it ultimately sold more than 6 million copies. But it was obvious from the start that *The Velvet Rope* was about more than money. It was about Jackson setting herself free, not just in a creative sense, but in a personal way. On *janet*, she toyed with her sexuality, like a giggling schoolgirl flashing her class and then running away to hide in the gym. On *The Velvet Rope*, Jackson is standing stark naked in the spotlight singing the hiphop equivalent of "It's My Party." This album is about girl-fun with sex, the nastier the better. When she sings about screaming and moaning in "Go Deep," she isn't referring to the effects of deep-sea diving. For its review, *Entertainment Weekly* used a headline that asked the question, "What's a (relatively) nice girl like Janet doing on the erotic Velvet Rope? She's making sex sound brazen—and beautiful."

According to some reports, Jackson hasn't spoken to her brother Michael since 1993. Who could blame her? Sex scandals are nothing new to the music business, which thrives on rumors of who is doing the nasty with whom. But rumors of sex scandals involving children are something else. How is a sister supposed to feel when the media is publishing stories that call her brother a pedophile? By exerting her own sexuality—the nasty girl kind—Jackson drew an imaginary line in the dirt, not just with her fans but with her own family.

She needed some distance. No one could empower Jackson but herself. This took courage, but she did it.

Jackson also seemed to have set herself free from her obsession with Madonna. In 1994, *Vibe* magazine asked Jackson if it was true that she hated Madonna. "Hate is a strong word," she said. "I never said 'hate.' But if I did hate her, I'd have valid reasons."

Madonna: A True Pioneer

The millennium isn't likely to provoke additional comments from Janet Jackson about Madonna. As Jackson's popularity has risen, Madonna's has fallen, at least as a sex-symbol recording artist. Her future seems to involve her roles as a business executive and as an actress than as a singer. Despite all the media hype over her 1996 movie, *Evita,* the past few years haven't been easy on the Material Girl. She has learned that the Bible knew what it was talking about when it said prophets were without honor in their own country.

Madonna is a true pioneer, not just in music but also in the arena of women's rights. She has made lots of money, and she has influenced popular culture in myriad ways, yet she has few friends and women of the 1990s view her as something of a public nuisance. She can't figure it out. "There's a whole generation of women—Courtney Love, Liz Phair, even Sandra Bernhard to a certain extent—who cannot bring themselves to say anything positive about me even though I've open the door for them, paved the road for them to be more outspoken," she told Sheryl Garratt in an interview for *The Face.* "[Liz Phair] doesn't have the power I have, so people are amused by it. But none of these women would want to recognize that. In fact, they slag me off any time anybody asks what they think of me or compare them to me. It's kind of like what a child does to their parent: they denounce you. They want to kill you off because they want their independence from you."

Mariah Carey: Reinventing Herself

If an award is given to the 1990s diva with the most humongous balls, it will have to go to sweet little Mariah Carey. In 1997, she not only celebrated the release of a new album, aptly titled *Butterfly,* but also boldly publicized the end of her marriage to Sony Music head Tommy Mottola in a series of television and print interviews. This was an expression of woman power to the max. In some ways, the two events were related.

When Carey and Mottola first met in 1988, she was an 18-year-old waitress who had hopes of becoming a singer, and he was the 30-something head of Sony Music. Mottola was looking for a pop star, someone along the lines of Whitney Houston, and Carey wanted to be a star—any kind of a star—so it

Mariah Carey

was a perfect match. His vision for her success had her playing the role of the virgin next door, the squeaky clean, velvet voiced angel of every man's wildest dreams. This vision easily translated into big bucks. Her 1990 debut album, *Mariah Carey,* went to Number 1, as did her 1995 album, *Daydream.* By 1997, her albums had sold more than 8 million copies and brought in more than $200 million.

Carey's working relationship with Mottola turned into a romance during the production of her first album, and evolved into marriage in 1993. When they announced that they were separating in May 1997, the music world was stunned. The shock wasn't so much because people were surprised that the marriage didn't work out—that was pretty much a given from the start in the eyes of most people—but because they naturally assumed neither Carey nor Mottola would ever do anything to jeopardize their working relationship.

With the release of *Butterfly,* the public was treated to the new Mariah Carey. Replacing the sweet little girl image was the startling image of a 30-year-old woman in her sexual prime. There was lots of flesh in her personal appearances and in her first video, and lots of nasty talk and sexual references in her music. Carey was seen darting about New York City on the arms of healthy, young, black rappers and models—and she was wearing next to nothing. It was all deliberate, calculated to win her independence (this is where the award for the most humongous balls comes in).

With the exception of Carey, Celine Dion, and newcomer Fiona Apple, Sony Music has had little success with solo female artists during the 1990s. In fact, the label probably has the worst track record of any of the majors when it comes to female artists. Carey is Sony Music. Fighting the divorce, which Carey wanted, or tampering with her career would be professional suicide. Above all else, Carey is aware of that. By airing the dissolution of her marriage in a very public way, she gave Mottola only two options. He could accept her newfound freedom and back out of the way, or he could challenge her declaration of independence and set her free to move on to a new record label (and him to find a new job). It takes courage for a woman to play that sort of game, but Carey did it—and she won.

Toni Braxton: Exploring New Territory

Breaking new ground is what it is all about. No area of music was immune. One of the most important breakout R & B artists of the 1990s was Toni Braxton. Women have been the backbone of R & B, almost from the beginning, but they've been expected to find success within the conservative, gospel-influenced traditions of the black community. Until Braxton came along, that meant downplaying their sexuality and femininity.

Braxton was studying to become a teacher when Babyface discovered her in 1991 and signed to his Atlanta-based LaFace Records. With Babyface writing songs for her and producing her projects, no one was surprised to see Braxton's self-titled debut album rack up sales of $10 million and earn the singer three Grammy Awards. Babyface supplied his protege with lush, synthesizer-laced ballads that pushed her R & B intonations into the realm of pop acceptance, but it was Braxton's break from the R & B tradition in the area of her personal image that insured her long-range success. "She may be the daughter of a preacher man, but R & B's sultry new star is definitely no choir girl," said a headline atop a profile of the singer in *US* magazine.

"You're Makin' Me High," the first hit single from Braxton's second album, *Secrets,* was all about sexual desire and masturbation, two subjects entirely foreign to traditional R & B. When Braxton first heard the Babyface-penned song, with lyrics about her lover being inside her all night, "doin' it again and again," it made her uncomfortable, and she worried about what the black community would think of her. "I'm very comfortable with my sexuality, but the lyrics in that song are so overt," she told Cheo Hodari Coker in an interview for *The Los Angeles Times.* "There were times when I was singing it when I felt I was letting the whole world know my thought about that subject."

Braxton broke new R & B ground with explicit lyrics. She also allowed herself to be photographed in her bare feet (a longtime no-no for black women) and in revealing clothing that displayed her body. She let her hair down, literally, and she wore a wig that accentuated her silky smooth sexuality.

THE GANGSTA RAP CONTROVERSY

What Toni Braxton did for R & B, other women, such as Queen Latifah and the rap trio known as Salt-N-Pepa, attempted to do for that most anti-female music of all, gangsta rap. Sometimes called the "Queens of Rap," Salt-N-Pepa turned heads in 1986 with their debut album, *Hot, Cool & Vicious,* which sold more than a million copies. For more than a decade, the group turned out a series of rapper hits, causing more than a few critics to scratch their heads. Why would women participate in an art form that is synonymous with unrepentant misogyny?

The short answer was that their songs didn't attack or berate women. The long answer is that eventually the genre seemed to get to them. In 1997, Salt-N-Pepa broke away from the man who had discovered them and produced their work for 11 years. They produced their new album, *Brand New,* themselves.

Toni Braxton

It reflected the gospel influences that had been a part of the group all along. The women called it their declaration of independence.

Gangsta rap itself raises interesting questions about how women perceive themselves. "If the music has become synonymous with profound misogyny, its artists can also boast a huge female following attracted by its energy and sexuality," writes Helen Kolawole in *Girls! Girls! Girls!* "Women's role in rap is largely to appear as 'video hoes' placed on the screen for the titillation of the male audience. Very often the misogyny and violence become intermingled and indistinguishable."

Ironically, the first rap hits were released by Sugarhill Records, an independent label owned by Sylvia Robinson, an African American, and her husband, Joe. Their 1979 release, "Rapper's Delight," was the first rap hit. Another rap record, "White Lines," was the first to deal with drug use. Yet another, "The Adventures of Grandmaster Flash on the Wheels of Steel," was the first to utilize a DJ's "scratch 'n' cut" skills. Without Sylvia Robinson, rap might never have gotten off the ground.

The answer as to why women seem attracted to gangsta rap can be found in the larger question of why some women pursue self-destructive relationships. The reality of it is that a sizable percentage of women are attracted to the danger that accompanies bad-boy behavior. Al Capone never did without sex that we know of. Neither do any of the drug dealers who inhabit the street corners of every American city. Ask any of them if their particular line of work limits their ability to find sexual partners, then step back and have a good laugh with them. Women, for all their healing, nurturing attributes, aren't without their disciples of the dark side. So it is with rap.

SHERYL CROW: MAKING COMPROMISES

Sheryl Crow grew up in Kennett, Missouri, a small town where entertainment possibilities are limited if you don't have the capacity to entertain yourself. Her father, a lawyer, played the trumpet; her mother, a music teacher, played piano. When Crow wasn't entertaining her sisters and brother, she led the football team in cheers, twirled a baton—one of the highest aspirations available to prepubescent girls in the South—and learned all she could about music.

By the age of 22, Crow had acquired both a degree in education from the University of Missouri and a day job teaching music to elementary school students in St. Louis. At night, she sang and played keyboards in the city's beer joints, leading a double life that would eventually send her packing to the bright lights of Los Angeles in 1986. She waited tables for a while and did radio jingles, then was hired as a backup singer for a Michael Jackson tour,

Sheryl Crow

the high point of which was a duet with Jackson on "I Just Can't Stop Loving You." When Jackson's "Bad" tour ended in 1989, Crow was exhausted, uncertain about her future, and suffering from chronic depression. She'd made it to the fringe of the big time, but her only celebrity came from tabloids that said she was Jackson's lover. Later that year, she sang backup on a Don Henley project, but nothing was working out the way it was supposed to, and she lapsed into long periods of depression.

As a child, Crow had lain awake at night, afraid to go to sleep, afraid something dreadful would happen. She called it "sleep paralysis," an affliction she thought she'd acquired from her mother. For three years, she went day to day, singing backup and doing jingles. She even recorded an album for A&M as a solo artist, but the record company decided not to release it. Then she fell in with a group that was eventually called the Tuesday Music Club. The group included Kevin Gilbert, who she had a romance with, David Baerwald, bassist Dan Schwartz, drummer Brian MacLeod, David Ricketts, and producer Bill Bottrell.

Some women, particularly those prone to depression, aren't at their best in an all-male environment. If they are goal oriented, as Crow is, they bitch and complain and argue over small details, then in the end they compromise and go home and sink into a well of depression. It is a no-win situation for all involved. When *Tuesday Night Music Club,* the Tuesday Music Club's debut album was released in 1993, everyone was optimistic. It just had that good sound.

The first single, "Leaving Las Vegas," was an instant hit, earning Crow an appearance on television's "Late Show with David Letterman." When Letterman asked her if the song was autobiographical, she answered "yes," thinking that was the easier answer. If she'd answered "no," then she would have to explain more than she was prepared to explain. In truth, she'd never lived in Vegas. The song had sprung from a friendship between Baerwald and his friend, John O'Brien, who had written the novel *Leaving Las Vegas.* Everyone in the band knew the true source of the song.

When O'Brien and Gilbert heard Crow's response to Letterman, they hit the ceiling. It was a guy thing. It had to do with male honor, territory, and a sense of duty to friends. Crow wasn't opposed to any of those things; she simply gave a one-word answer to an unimportant question, for Christ's sake! Gilbert telephoned Crow immediately after the show and blew his top, thereby permanently severing his relationship with her. O'Brien fumed and fretted for three weeks, and then blew his brains out. O'Brien's family absolved Crow of any responsibility for his death—it had been a long time coming—but Baerwald flipped out and wrote a piece for *L. A. Weekly,* accusing Crow of making him betray his friend. By the time "All I Wanna Do" was released, the group had already gone down in flames. The song turned Crow into a star and earned her three Grammys, including Best New Artist.

Crow was on top of the world, but her problems were just beginning. The O'Brien incident became the betrayal that wouldn't die. His novel was made into a motion picture starring Nicolas Cage and Elisabeth Shue. *Leaving Las Vegas* was everywhere she looked. She couldn't go outside her door or turn on her radio without being reminded of O'Brien's suicide. The saga took another bizarre turn in May 1996, when Gilbert was discovered dead at his home in Eagle Rock, California. He was wearing a black hood and a woman's skirt. The coroner listed his cause of death as autoerotic asphyxiation.

Later that year, when the time came to begin work on Crow's follow-up album, *Sheryl Crow*, only Bottrell, the producer, remained from the original group. Two days into the session, he walked off the job. Crow was stunned. She blamed it on bad communication. Rather than look for another producer, she produced the album herself.

When the album was released in September 1996, it ran into immediate difficulties when Wal-Mart refused to distribute it. One of the songs, "Love Is a Good Thing," had a line that suggested that Wal-Mart sold firearms to children. It was just another throwaway line like her "yes" comment to Letterman, but the store chain wasn't amused. Wal-Mart could have sued. Songwriters sometimes forget they are just as responsible for their words as any other writers. Instead, the retail chain was content to deprive the album of 500,000 or so in sales.

In an interview with *Newsweek*, Crow said, "I've said that it's really great for other female artists to look at me and know what not to do." Fine, but having said that, the backpedaling began: Crow retreating to a compromise. "Part of it was my own fault. I'm an accessible person. I'm willing to do whatever. Not for the fame, but I just kind of went along with it." Then came the comment the interviewer thought surely was a misstatement: "I'm not at all happy with the success I've had."

JEWEL: A SLOWLY RISING STAR

Jewel Kircher didn't have a typical upbringing. Her parents, Atz and Nedra, were Swiss singers who fled to Homer, Alaska, to escape the Nazi reign of terror overtaking Europe in the late 1930s. Jewel and her two brothers were raised on a farm, where milking cows and riding horses were as much entertainment as chores. She was eight years old when her parents divorced. She stayed with her father when her mother moved to Anchorage and often accompanied him to seedy barrooms, where they sang together to earn a living. Male patrons sometimes put a dime in her hand, with the suggestion that she give them a call when she turned 16. She knew what it meant.

By the time Jewel turned 16, she'd moved in with her mother, the person she always considered her best friend—and still does. She stayed in touch with her father, and once took her black boyfriend home to meet him. Her father broke out into tears at the sight of the rapper. At first, Jewel didn't understand. Then her father explained that he was crying out of pride that he'd raised such an open-minded daughter.

Jewel wasn't in Anchorage long before she and her mother moved to Seward, a small town about 2 miles away. According to Jewel, the move was prompted by the sudden appearance of FBI agents who were investigating the business dealings of her mother's business partner. When the agents started showing up at Jewel's school, Nedra figured it was time they got a fresh start somewhere else. Mother and daughter eventually ended up in southern California, although they arrived at different times from different directions. Jewel had taken a detour to Michigan to attend an art school. She sang in coffeehouses and, for a time, lived with a guy who operated an escort service out of his house.

By the time Jewel was 19, she'd landed a deal with Atlantic Records. The album, *Pieces of You,* was recorded in the Innerchange Coffeehouse in San Diego, where she frequently sang. When the album was released in 1995, the critics largely ignored it. *Pieces of You* was an acoustic, folk-influenced album by an unknown girl from Alaska. How much more out of the mainstream could you get?

With Nedra's help—by then Nedra and a friend, Inga Vainshtein, had signed on as Jewel's managers—Jewel stayed out on the road, promoting the album with a fierceness that could be understood only by someone who has lived in her car, as Jewel did on more than one occasion). Atlantic followed up with a series of videos that capitalized on her extraordinarily cool beauty. On screen, her face seemed flawless, as pure as an Alaskan stream.

It took a year and a half, but by the end of 1996 there was a definite Jewel buzz on the music pipeline. Jewel, Nedra, and Vainshtein had accomplished the impossible. In April 1997, *Pieces of You* peaked at Number 4 on the Top 20 charts, making Jewel a contender for stardom and Nedra a contender for manager of the year. It was a girl thing from start to finish, with Jewel's success largely untouched by male hands. The album also set a record for Atlantic: no artist had ever taken longer to break.

"The creative process is not just about writing songs," Jewel told Paul Zollo of *Acoustic Guitar* magazine. "It's about approaching your life creatively, so

Jewel

that you are not a victim of circumstance; so that you are creating your life and it's not creating you."

ALANIS MORISSETTE: THE SKY'S THE LIMIT

When the smoke cleared on the 1996 musical battleground of the sexes, Alanis Morissette was standing head and shoulders above the rest; 14 women to 9 men was the final tally. This was the first time in history that female solo artists had out-charted their male competitors. As it became more and more apparent that Morissette was going to be regarded as the most successful female artist of the 1990s, people began to get a little uneasy about the Madonna factor. Was Morissette a Madonna stand-in? Was the Material Girl lurking in a back room somewhere, calling the shots? Was Morissette a cruel joke the increasingly reclusive and isolated Madonna was playing on the public?

During an interview with radio station WHTZ in New York, Morissette was asked how involved Madonna was in planning release dates or songs mixes. "I think, to her credit, she's more of a hands-off person," said Morissette. "I think because she's an artist, she appreciates the fact that we don't want people breathing down the back of our necks. So, if anyone would know how that feels, she would." Morissette was asked if she had much communication with Madonna. "Some," she answered, the tone of her voice indicating she was tired of fielding Madonna questions.

Rolling Stone magazine asked Madonna much the same question, though the emphasis was on how she thought Morissette was holding up under the pressure. "She reminds me of me when I started out: slightly awkward but extremely self-possessed and straightforward," Madonna replied. "There's a sense of excitement and giddiness in the air around her—like anything's possible, and the sky's the limit."

While Morissette was responsible for all the lyrics on *Jagged Little Pill,* Glen Ballard, her male collaborator, was responsible for much of the music. A Mississippi boy who had found success in Los Angeles as a songwriter and producer for the group Wilson Phillips, he was an unlikely partner for a groundbreaking feminist icon. Shortly after Ballard took home three Grammys, as did Morissette, for his work on the album, someone in the Mississippi legislature introduced a resolution praising him for his accomplishments. But the resolution was killed after the lyrics of Morissette's songs were made known to the lawmakers. No one was surprised. Only recently the Mississippi legislature had voted to ratify the Nineteenth Amendment to the Constitution, thereby giving women the right to vote. Most other states had ratified the amendment before 1920.

Morissette might have offended the Mississippi legislature, but she encouraged the loyalty of a fan base that, at times, seemed almost fanatical in its devotion. Alicia Silverstone, Generation X's most ambitious movie icon, saw fit to send Morissette a fan letter. Even Morissette found all the attention overwhelming at times. "It was like God's way of saying to me, 'You've been working your ass off, and I'm going to give this to you—enjoy it, please,'" she said to Jeff Spurrier in an interview for *Details* magazine. She was talking about the mysterious process by which the inspiration for *Jagged Little Pill* landed unannounced on her doorsteps, but she might as well have been talking about the revolution itself. If God was listening, She probably smiled.

TIFFANY: REVIVING HER CAREER

Tiffany Darwish had been living in Nashville about a year when her husband, a makeup artist who is frequently called on location for video productions, came in from work one day with the news that he'd run into someone on location who knew her. "Who was it?" she asked. He didn't know, but if she wanted to find out she could go with him on location. Whoever it was, was sure to return. Tiffany accompanied him to the video shoot. The mystery woman wasn't there when she arrived, so she waited around. It was 1997, nearly 10 years since her last hit record.

When the mystery woman arrived, Tiffany knew in an instant who she was. Susan Levy walked in the door, paused, looked at Tiffany, then excitedly said, "I remember you." It had been a decade since they had hung out together at the mall—and Tiffany had been America's star of the moment. In the years since, Levy had turned her fortuitous association with Tiffany into a career that at the time of their meeting on the video location had blossomed into a high-flying display of executive acrobatics that required her to perform without a safety net. It was now her job to hoist such new acts as Deana Carter up onto the high wire—and to keep others, such as Garth Brooks, from falling to a certain death. Just as Levy had assumed new responsibilities, Tiffany had found new direction by signing a management deal with Pam Lewis, Brooks's former manager.

"I didn't realize how hard it would be to get back into the business," says Tiffany of her decision in 1997 to jumpstart her career—only this time in the direction of her first love, country music. "It's so easy when you're working to get burned out and to say, 'I'm going to take a break.' I was young, and it was a little overpowering. Even if you are on top, if you take two or three years off, that could really set you back, no matter who you are."

At first, Tiffany wasn't sure putting her career in the hands of another woman was the right thing to do. The only manager she'd ever known was a male. All the people associated with her career, with the exception of Levy, were males. A part of her was questioning whether she would be able to work with another woman. Then she and Lewis got together for an introductory meeting. They clicked and formed an instant bond. It was a female thing, an experience she hadn't shared with her male manager. "There are times when she may be struggling through something and I can lift her up," Tiffany says. "Same thing for me. Just to know that she's there and believes in the project."

Lewis feels the same way. "I feel very alone at times," she says. "I don't feel I have very many close friends. I am like Garth in that way—I don't trust that many people, and I have been burned, and I have been hurt, and I have had people I don't even know be mean to me. But I'm a fixer—I gotta nurture. I'm surprised there are not more women managers because they are naturally suited."

LILITH FAIR: A COAST-TO-COAST CELEBRATION

You can't have a decent revolution without a party afterward. In the case of the women's revolution of 1996, it seemed only fitting that the victors let down their hair and throw a whiz-bang of a celebration. They could have called it anything, but they called it Lilith Fair. It began the day after Independence Day, July 5, 1997, and continued for six weeks, offering nearly 40, coast-to-coast concert performances featuring more than 60 female artists.

Participating in the series of concerts were: the founding mamas of the revolution, the Indigo Girls, Pat Benatar, Emmylou Harris, Suzanne Vega, and Tracy Chapman; such field commanders as Sarah McLachlan, Joan Osborne, and Sheryl Crow; and the flower-child newcomers who are the future of the movement, Fiona Apple, Abra Moore, and Jewel. Some women played a few of the dates; others played a dozen or more. The lineup was always different, but the essence of the concerts was the same: female artists, female musicians, female stage crew—and, for the most part, female audiences. Lilith Fair was an enormous success, artistically as well as financially.

Lilith Fair was the brainchild of Sarah McLachlan, the 29-year-old, Canadian-born daughter of American expatriate parents who moved to tranquil Nova Scotia, Canada, during the crazed, violent years of the Vietnam War era. Since so many of the big guns in the revolution were Canadian—Shania Twain, Alanis Morissette, K. D. Lang—it was entirely appropriate that a Canadian plan the victory celebration. McLachlan chose the name "Lilith" because, according to Hebrew folklore, Lilith was Adam's first wife. McLachlan tacked "Fair" onto it because "it means beautiful, it means equal, and it means a festival or celebration."

There is no mystery to McLachlan's activism. She was discovered at the age of 17 fronting a new-wave band named October Game. Nettwerk Records, a Vancouver-based record label, offered her a recording deal. But she waited two years before accepting because she knew it would mean relocating to Canada's West coast.

McLachlan's first album, *Touch*, was released by Nettwerk in 1988 in Canada, and by Arista Records the following year in the United States. The musician's followup album, *Solace*, released in 1991, marked the beginning of her working relationship with producer Pierre Marchard, who encouraged her songwriting.

© ARISTA

Sarah McLachlan

Over the years, McLachlan discovered to her dismay that no matter how hard she worked or how well she performed, her achievements were restricted by radio programmers who followed the "we already have a girl" system of putting together playlists. McLachlan thought that was unfair. The success of the 1996 revolution proved she was right, and what better way to celebrate than to throw the biggest girl party ever held?

When the Lilith Fair tour began, McLachlan was a well-regarded singer/ songwriter, a 10-year veteran of the club and concert scene. She wasn't a major star, however, even though she had a strong, cult-like following, and her most recent album, *Fumbling Toward Ecstasy*, released in 1994, had sold more than 2 million units. Two weeks out into the tour, McLachlan's fifth album, *Surfacing*, was released. Like her three previous efforts, Marchard produced it. Unlike the other albums, though, *Surfacing* took off during the summer at blazing speed, finally peaking at Number 2 on the pop charts in September 1997.

McLachlan began the Lilith Fair tour as a devout believer in the power of the feminine mystique, and she ended the tour a recording star of the first order. The financial success of Lilith Fair didn't seem to faze her. Other aspects of the tour were more important. "You know what the bottom line was?" McLachlan asked Roger Catlin of *The Hartford Courant*. "I just thought it would be really fun to put a whole bunch of women on stage—all the women I loved. To be able to play with them on the same stage and be able to put on a show like that—for us and for the audience."

The tour was so successful that plans began immediately for a 1998 tour. At first, McLachlan thought she would invite male performers to join the 1998 tour—"I'm no man hater," she says—but then the more she thought about it, the more she realized that would defy the reason for having the tour. So she decided she wouldn't invite men. Even so, she likes seeing men in the audience. "Most of the guys I've met on the road have been really sweet," she told Ann Powers of *US* magazine. "Sometimes they get their asses dragged there by their girlfriends. That's fine, as long as they're having a good time. And maybe they'll learn something."

For Pat Benatar, who played two dates with the tour, it was "the best 48 hours" she'd ever spent. "These women were totally empowered, as we were not," Benatar says. "It was remarkable. There is a total difference between their generation and our generation. We didn't have that feeling of friendship. We felt like we were competing against each other. We were terrified to let our guard down, of being gentle, kind, any of those things—because it wasn't about that. It was about being as strong as you could to get through it. These women are the product of what we did to get through it. It was so amazing to see the difference. It was like a toddler trying to learn to walk. Then the toddler at 3½ refining her motor skills. That was what those women were doing—refining their motor skills, because they did not have to run through the gauntlet. It was so emotional for me to be there. For them, it is not a question of, 'Do we deserve it? Can we have it?' In their mind, it's, 'Yeah, we deserve it,' and, 'Yeah, we want to have it.' I was just so proud of them. It was amazing."

THE REVOLUTION CONTINUES

The future looks to be in good hands. On the country side, 27-year-old Sara Evans, RCA Records executive Renee Bell's discovery, 31-year-old Anita Cochran, Warner Brothers' executive and producer Jim Ed Norman's discovery, seem to have the inside track on stardom: Evans, because of her incredible, silky-smooth voice, and Cochran, because of her overall musical talents. On Cochran's debut CD, *Back To You,* she wrote the songs, did the vocals, played all the lead instruments, and co-produced. LeAnn Rimes is a teenage wunderkind who seems a sure bet for stardom unless she self-destructs along the way. On the pop side, 20-year-old Fiona Apple and 29-year-old Abra Moore appear to be the strongest contenders for leaders into the new millennium. Both are inventive songwriters who often look up from their interpersonal travels to find themselves in the "strangest places" imaginable.

Abra Moore: The Metaphorical Wanderer

Moore now calls Austin, Texas, home, but she arrived via a circuitous route that took her from her childhood home in Hawaii to New York, where she studied piano in her teens, to Europe, where she performed in small clubs along the coast of England, then back to Hawaii, where she became one of the founding members of Poi Dog Pondering, only to leave just as the band was about to ink its first recording contract. With guitar in hand, Moore became the metaphorical wanderer. Perhaps because her mother died when she was four and her father was an artist in the Beat Generation mode—her childhood was filled with the music of Bob Dylan, Billie Holiday, and the Beatles—finding herself wasn't easy for the 5-foot, 6-inch, waif-thin brunette with a face like a Generation X fashion model and a lifelong penchant for fearless introspection.

For a time, Moore settled into a folkie acoustic style, her playful, lighter-than-air voice reminiscent of such 1980s artists such as Edie Brickell and Rickie Lee Jones. Moore released a critically acclaimed album, *Sing,* on a

Abra Moore

small, independent label. Despite enthusiastic reviews, the album never received radio airplay and quickly disappeared from store shelves. It did, however, attract the attention of Arista Records, which signed Moore to a recording contract. The label sent her back into the studio with producer Mitch Watkins, who encouraged her to pursue a harder, more contemporary sound.

Moore emerged from those sessions with a string of songs that suddenly made sense of her life and her wandering. When the album, titled *Strangest Places,* was released in 1997, "Four Leaf Clover," the first single, attracted immediate attention from alternative-music radio stations, and the video fell into heavy rotation on MTV. In addition to the success of the album, she made an impact on the movie industry by contributing songs to three motion pictures: *Excess Baggage,* starring Alicia Silverstone; *Matchmaker,* starring Janeane Garafolo, and *The Newton Boys,* starring Matthew McConaughey and Ethan Hawke. Moore even made a cameo appearance in *The Newton Boys* as a chanteuse who croons the blues classic, "Millenburg Blues," in a seductive barroom scene.

"My introduction into the music business has been in baby steps," says Moore, her early-morning voice as breathy and melodic as the recorded version. "As far as feeling like I had to prove something, I may have felt that a little bit on the latest record because of all the hype on the FEMALE . . . so I came into it feeling like, 'Oh, well, here comes another one, but give me a chance.' It's a good record aside from being from another girl." Moore is delighted with the success of the women's revolution, but she thinks people who focus on the femaleness of it all are missing the point. "Maybe it's just about the music," she says. "Know what I mean? I think women are having success because they are making really nice records, and people are appreciating them. People go, 'I wonder why there are so many? What's the deal? It must be some sort of fad!'"

Just hearing herself say the word "fad" makes Moore break out into laughter. "Maybe it's just balancing out. You know? I think if there's a good record out there, it deserves to be heard, whether you're a boy or a girl." She is like many other female singers and songwriters who have spent a lifetime suppressing the influences of their gender on their music and concealing their appreciation of other female performers, only to suddenly be told that it is all right to be female—and all right to appreciate the work of other women. As a veteran of the 1997 Lilith Fair, Moore was astonished at the reception the tour received. "There was a balance of people—a lot of boys, too," she says. "And backstage, everyone was rooting the other one on, you know. It was nice meeting Sarah (McLachlan). She's a very inspiring, steady, supportive person, and Jewel, she's great . . . and Emmylou Harris, she's the queen."

Fiona Apple: A Complex Shining Star

Fiona Apple was one of the shining stars of the 1997 Lilith Fair tour, but at age 19 she was so overpowered at discovering her own identity that she was barely able to appreciate the depth of womanpower that surrounded her. Six months before the tour, she was the opening act for Counting Crows. Although she'd toured for a year in Europe and released her first album, *Tidal,* her career was still in the very early stages . . . and she was still ever so green. Critic Kristin Whittlesey, writing for *The Nashville Banner,* describes one of Apple's performances with Counting Crows: "It was truly jarring when she opened her mouth between songs. That's when you realized that, yes, she really is all that young. Her stage demeanor was girlish, slightly goofy and clumsy. Her apparent lack of stage experience was all the more jarring because of her polished, professional performance."

By year's end, Apple had grown up, as girls are apt to do. Her album had cracked the Top 20, spurred by the success of the haunting single, "Criminal," in which she sings about being a "bad, bad girl" who has been "careless with a delicate man"—and a Best New Artist award from MTV. If Apple was still "slightly goofy," this was as endearing in its own way as was the dark, brooding power of her music. This contradiction is one of the fascinating aspects about Apple because it intimates that either she'll become one of the biggest stars in pop music history—or she'll self-destruct and vanish, James Dean-like, in a puff of smoke.

Apple herself seems to understand that. Once, while out on the road, she read a scathing review of one of her concert performances and went back to her hotel room and scratched her hand until there was no skin left. Her cries of "Listen to me but don't hurt me" can probably be traced back to the time she was raped at the age of 12 in the hallway outside her mother's New York apartment. "How much strength does it take to hurt a little girl?" she asked Terry Richardson of *Spin* magazine. "How much strength does it take for the girl to get over it? Which one of them do you think is stronger?"

Apple has answered that question with her work, which offers a blend of musical sophistication and existential detachment that is sometimes staggering in its complexity. How is it possible for a young woman, who just the year before had never worked with other musicians, to write such powerful, jazz-influenced songs? And how is it possible for a young woman who still lives at home with her mother to be so savvy about the gender battles that made the women's revolution of 1996 possible?

If you have to ask, says Apple, then please don't. This is a generational thing. If you think she is too young to have such serious thoughts about

Fiona Apple

complicated relationships, then you don't understand her generation. "A lot of people who are saying that [I'm too young] just don't know today's world," she told the Associated Press. "I've been in therapy my whole life—and it's the same with a lot of kids today."

With Apple's oversized, blue-gray eyes; her long, blonde hair; and her awkward woman-body, she has been made into a sex symbol, one that takes well to television's hit-and-run mode of operation. Brave and defiant, she paraded about in her underwear for the video of "Criminal," a video some critics said bordered on child porn. But Apple is quick to tell interviewers that walking around in her underwear is something she would never do in her own home because she hates the way she looks in her underwear.

Apple has promised herself that she'll give her fans, the record label, the video makers—the entire world—what it wants, even if this means showing herself in a bad light (if she hates the way she looks in underwear, why should they like it?). This is only fair, she reasons; she owes them that. But the day will come, she promises, when the prettiness, the bare skin, and the pouty looks will get lost in the power of the music. That is when she'll have you. That is when she'll twist the knife.

APPROACHING THE MILLENNIUM

"I encourage women not to be bitter, but to just keep working," says Parr. "Men have their own clubs, but women have their clubs, too. They have a shared perception of what it is like to work in a chauvinistic industry. Entertainment is about ear candy and eye candy. There are certain areas where we will see progress and areas where we will have to fight because there are areas in which we are genetically disabled—well, maybe not disabled—but not on the same rules, the same playing field. It's confusing to women now. We've been taught to want the same things our male counterpoints want, yet no one has taught us how to balance those things."

"I think on the business side and on the artist side, women are definitely evolving into power positions," says Tracey Edmonds, president and chief executive officer of Yab Yum Entertainment. "On the artist side, right now the Mariah Careys and the Whitney Houstons are selling multitudes of albums their male counterparts are not selling. And the same thing is happening on the business side. Women are evolving from being assistants to running the show." Many women feel the trend will continue. "I think the longevity is there for the women," says Brenda Lee. "What's happening is no fluke or overnight thing. Women are taking more control of their careers, and they are having a say in the business."

TAKING POPULAR MUSIC TO A NEW LEVEL

Fiona Apple's piano-based music might be an indication of where rock 'n' roll is going. People have taken popular music for granted, particularly rock 'n' roll. They forget that big band music and jazz went through the same process. In May 1964, when the Beatles, Mary Wells, and the Dave Clark Five were tearing up the charts, the Number 1 record in America belonged to Louis Armstrong. His version of "Hello, Dolly!"—arriving 10 years into the rock era—can be viewed as the last gasp of a dying art form. The same thing is happening to rock 'n' roll. The Rolling Stones are in the same place today that Armstrong was in 1964.

This isn't to say that rock 'n' roll—and male artists in general—are washed up. Just as Armstrong extended jazz 10 years into the new rock era, rock will continue to produce flashes of brilliance—and male artists will continue to have hit records well into the new millennium. But if you play the odds, you have to put your money on the women. They have history on their side—and they have birth rate demographics. Women might not outscore men on the charts every year for the next decade, but they are certain to outscore them for at least 6 of the next 10 years. You can count on that.

CHARTS

TOP 20 CHART HITS

YEAR(S)	NUMBER OF MALE ARTISTS	NUMBER OF FEMALE ARTISTS	PERCENTAGE (MALE ARTISTS)	PERCENTAGE (FEMALE ARTISTS)
1954-1959	108	45	71	29
1960s	221	71	76	24
1970s	208	62	77	23
1980s	164	73	69	31
1990	24	17	59	41
1991	20	11	65	35
1992	17	10	63	37
1993	27	14	66	34
1994	25	16	61	39
1995	19	14	58	42
1996	9	14	39	61
1997	17	25	40	60

TOP 20 ALBUM CHARTS FOR 1986

Male/Female Ratio: 23 to 11
Percentage of Top 20 Solo Albums in 1986 By Gender:
68 percent were by male artists; 32 percent were by female artists

MALE SOLO ARTISTS

Bryan Adams
Jackson Browne
Phil Collins
Elvis Costello
Peter Gabriel
Billy Joel
Huey Lewis
Paul McCartney
John Cougar Mellencamp
Eddie Murphy
Billy Ocean
Jeffrey Osborne
Ozzy Osbourne
Robert Palmer
Prince
Lionel Richie
David Lee Roth
Bob Seger
Paul Simon
Bruce Springsteen
Rod Stewart
Sting
Steve Winwood

FEMALE SOLO ARTISTS

Anita Baker
Whitney Houston
Janet Jackson
Patti LaBelle
Cyndi Lauper
Madonna
Stevie Nicks
Sade
Barbra Streisand
Tina Turner
Dionne Warwick

TOP 20 ALBUM CHARTS FOR 1987

Male/Female Ratio: 24 to 12
Percentage of Top 20 Solo Albums in 1987 By Gender:
67 percent were by male artists; 33 percent were by female artists

MALE SOLO ARTISTS

Gregory Abbott
Bryan Adams
David Bowie
Robert Cray
Kenny G
Peter Gabriel
Sammy Hagar
Bruce Hornsby
Michael Jackson
Billy Joel
Huey Lewis
John Mellencamp
Alexander O'Neal
Ozzy Osbourne
Prince
Lionel Richie
Paul Simon
Bruce Springsteen
Sting
Randy Travis
Luther Vandross
Billy Vera
Bruce Willis
Steve Winwood

FEMALE SOLO ARTISTS

Anita Baker
The Bangles
Emmylou Harris/Dolly Parton/Linda Ronstadt
Heart
Whitney Houston
Janet Jackson
Cyndi Lauper
Madonna
Carly Simon
Barbra Streisand
Jody Watley
Suzanne Vega

TOP 20 ALBUM CHARTS FOR 1988

Male/Female Ratio: 28 to 10
Percentage of Top 20 Solo Albums in 1988 By Gender:
74 percent were by male artists; 26 percent were by female artists

MALE SOLO ARTISTS	FEMALE SOLO ARTISTS
Rick Astley	Belinda Carlisle
Bobby Brown	Tracy Chapman
Robert Cray	Gloria Estefan
Terrence Trent D'Arby	Debbie Gibson
George Harrison	Whitney Houston
Bruce Hornsby	Joan Jett
Michael Jackson	Madonna
Huey Lewis	Joni Mitchell
Ziggy Marley	Sade
Richard Marx	Tiffany
Bobby McFerrin	
John Mellencamp	
George Michael	
Ozzy Osbourne	
Robert Palmer	
Robert Plant	
Prince	
Keith Richards	
Robbie Robertson	
David Lee Roth	
Bruce Springsteen	
Rod Stewart	
Sting	
Keith Sweat	
James Taylor	
Luther Vandross	
Steve Winwood	
Stevie Wonder	

TOP 20 ALBUM CHARTS FOR 1989

Male/Female Ratio: 18 to 14
Percentage of Top 20 Solo Albums in 1989 By Gender:
56 percent were by male artists; 44 percent were by female artists

MALE SOLO ARTISTS	FEMALE SOLO ARTISTS
Rick Astley	Paula Abdul
Bobby Brown	Anita Baker
Elvis Costello	Edie Brickell
Bob Dylan	Tracy Chapman
Danny Elfman	Cher
Kenny G	Gloria Estefan
Peter Gabriel	Melissa Etheridge
Don Henley	Debbie Gibson
Richard Marx	The Indigo Girls
Elton John	Madonna
Ziggy Marley	Stevie Nicks
Paul McCartney	Bonnie Raitt
George Michael	Jody Watley
Roy Orbison	
Tom Petty	
Prince	
Lou Reed	
Luther Vandross	

TOP 20 ALBUM CHARTS FOR 1990

Male/Female Ratio: 24 to 17
Percentage of Top 20 Solo Albums in 1990 By Gender:
59 percent were by male artists; 41 percent were by female artists

MALE SOLO ARTISTS
Babyface
Michael Bolton
David Bowie
Garth Brooks
Bobby Brown
Eric Clapton
Phil Collins
Harry Connick Jr.
Bob Dylan
Kenny G
Johnny Gill
M.C. Hammer
Don Henley
Bruce Hornsby
Billy Idol
Billy Joel
George Michael
Van Morrison
Tom Petty
Robert Plant
Prince
Keith Sweat
Vanilla Ice
Neil Young

FEMALE SOLO ARTISTS
Paula Abdul
Anita Baker
Kate Bush
Mariah Carey
Tracy Chapman
Cher
Gloria Estefan
Heart
The Indigo Girls
Janet Jackson
Madonna
Alannah Myles
Sinead O'Connor
Wilson Phillips
Bonnie Raitt
Linda Ronstadt
Lisa Stansfield
Suzanne Vega

TOP 20 ALBUM CHARTS FOR 1991

Male/Female Ratio: 20 to 11
Percentage of Top 20 Solo Albums in 1991 By Gender:
65 percent were by male artists; 35 percent were by female artists

MALE SOLO ARTISTS
Bryan Adams
Clint Black
Michael Bolton
Garth Brooks
Phil Collins
M.C. Hammer
Ice-T
Chris Isaak
John Mellencamp
George Michael
Ozzy Osbourne
Tom Petty
Prince
Bob Seger
Paul Simon
Rod Stewart
Sting
Ralph Tresvant
Luther Vandross
Vanilla Ice

FEMALE SOLO ARTISTS
Paula Abdul
Mariah Carey
Natalie Cole
Gloria Estefan
Amy Grant
Whitney Houston
Janet Jackson
Madonna
Bette Midler
Wilson Phillips
Bonnie Raitt

TOP 20 ALBUM CHARTS FOR 1992

Male/Female Ratio: 17 to 10
Percentage of Top 20 Solo Albums in 1992 By Gender:
63 percent were by male artists; 37 percent were by female artists

MALE SOLO ARTISTS	FEMALE SOLO ARTISTS
Bryan Adams	Paula Abdul
Michael Bolton	Mary J. Blige
Garth Brooks	Mariah Carey
Bobby Brown	Natalie Cole
Eric Clapton	En Vogue
Harry Connick Jr.	Amy Grant
Billy Ray Cyrus	Wynonna Judd
Peter Gabriel	Wilson Phillips
Vince Gill	Bonnie Raitt
Hammer	Vanessa Williams
Michael Jackson	
Elton John	
Mr. Big	
Prince	
Lionel Richie	
Bruce Springsteen	
Stevie Ray Vaughan	

TOP 20 ALBUM CHARTS FOR 1993

Male/Female Ratio: 27 to 14
Percentage of Top 20 Solo Albums in 1993 By Gender:
66 percent were by male artists; 34 percent were by female artists

MALE SOLO ARTISTS	FEMALE SOLO ARTISTS
Babyface	Mary J. Blige
Clint Black	Toni Braxton
Michael Bolton	Gloria Estefan
Garth Brooks	Melissa Etheridge
Bobby Brown	Amy Grant
Eric Clapton	Janet Jackson
Billy Ray Cyrus	K. D. Lang
Neil Diamond	Madonna
Donald Fagen	Reba McEntire
Kenny G	Dolly Parton
Johnny Gill	Sade
Ice-T	Barbra Streisand
Alan Jackson	Tina Turner
Michael Jackson	Wynonna
Mick Jagger	
Billy Joel	
Lenny Kravitz	
Kriss Kross	
Paul McCartney	
Meat Loaf	
John Mellencamp	
Jon Secada	
Rod Stewart	
Sting	
George Strait	
James Taylor	
Luther Vandross	

TOP 20 ALBUM CHARTS FOR 1994

Male/Female Ratio: 25 to 16
Percentage of Top 20 Solo Albums in 1994 By Gender:
61 percent were by male artists; 39 percent were by female artists

MALE SOLO ARTISTS	FEMALE SOLO ARTISTS
Bryan Adams	Tori Amos
Michael Bolton	Anita Baker
Garth Brooks	Toni Braxton
Jimmy Buffett	Mariah Carey
Eric Clapton	Mary Chapin Carpenter
Harry Connick Jr.	Sheryl Crow
Coolio	Celine Dion
Vince Gill	Gloria Estefan
Hammer	Melissa Etheridge
Alan Jackson	Amy Grant
Billy Joel	The Indigo Girls
Gerald Levert	Janet Jackson
Tim McGraw	Madonna
Meat Loaf	Reba McEntyre
John Mellencamp	Bonnie Raitt
John Michael Montgomery	Barbra Streisand
Steve Perry	
Tom Petty	
Prince	
Bob Seger	
Frank Sinatra	
Snoop Doggy Dogg	
Keith Sweat	
Luther Vandross	
Neil Young	

TOP 20 ALBUM CHARTS FOR 1995

Male/Female Ratio: 19 to 14
Percentage of Top 20 Solo Albums in 1995 By Gender:
58 percent were by male artists; 42 percent were by female artists

MALE SOLO ARTISTS	FEMALE SOLO ARTISTS
Michael Bolton	Mary J. Blige
Garth Brooks	Brandy
Jimmy Buffett	Mariah Carey
Kenny G	Sheryl Crow
Michael Jackson	Melissa Etheridge
Elton John	Janet Jackson
Montel Jordan	Alison Krauss
Lenny Kravitz	Annie Lennox
Tim McGraw	Madonna
John Michael Montgomery	Reba McEntyre
Ozzy Osbourne	Natalie Merchant
Tom Petty	Alanis Morissette
Prince	Selena
Seal	Shania Twain
Bob Seger	
Frank Sinatra	
Bruce Springsteen	
2 PAC	
Neil Young	

TOP 20 ALBUM CHARTS FOR 1996

Male/Female Ratio: 9 to 14
Percentage of Top 20 Solo Albums in 1996 By Gender:
39 percent were by male artists; 61 percent were by female artists

MALE SOLO ARTISTS	FEMALE SOLO ARTISTS
Garth Brooks	Tori Amos
Vince Gill	Toni Braxton
Alan Jackson	Mariah Carey
Tim McGraw	Tracy Chapman
John Mellencamp	Sheryl Crow
Sting	Celine Dion
George Strait	Janet Jackson
Keith Sweat	Madonna
2PAC	Natalie Merchant
	Alanis Morissette
	Joan Osborne
	Leann Rimes
	Shania Twain
	Wynonna

TOP 20 ALBUM CHARTS FOR 1997

Male/Female Ratio: 17 to 25
Percentage of Top 20 Solo Albums in 1997 By Gender:
40 percent were by male artists; 60 percent were by female artists

MALE SOLO ARTISTS	FEMALE SOLO ARTISTS
Michael Bolton	Aaliyah
Garth Brooks	Fiona Apple
Bob Carlisle	Erika Badu
Kenny G	Mary J. Blige
Warren G	Toni Braxton
Sammy Hagar	Mariah Carey
Hanson	Deana Carter
Heavy D	Celine Dion
Billy Joel	Missy Elliott
Tim McGraw	En Vogue
Alan Jackson	Amy Grant
Notorious Big	The Indigo Girls
Busta Rhymes	Janet Jackson
Snoop Doggy Dog	Jewel
George Strait	Madonna (Evita)
Keith Sweat	Reba McEntire
James Taylor	Sarah McLachlan
	Alanis Morissette
	No Doubt
	LeAnn Rimes
	Selena
	Spice Girls
	Barbra Streisand
	Shania Twain
	Trisha Yearwood

NOTES

CHAPTER 1

Tena Clark was interviewed by the author in 1997.

Terri Clark was interviewed by the author in 1997.

Debe Fennell was interviewed by the author in 1997.

Kathy Mattea was interviewed by the author in 1988, 1989, 1995, and 1996.

Sandy Neese was most recently interviewed by the author in 1997.

Frances Preston was interviewed by the author in 1997.

Shania Twain was interviewed by the author in 1993 and 1996.

All chart information in this book was derived from charts originally published by *Billboard* magazine and reprinted by *Rolling Stone* magazine. The information was tabulated and compiled by the author, who is responsible for its accuracy.

The author first wrote about the women's 1996 revolution in music for the July 1997 issue of *Glamour* magazine.

CHAPTER 2

Marilyn Arthur was interviewed by the author in 1997.

Estelle Axton was interviewed and photographed by the author in 1995.

Renee Bell was interviewed and photographed by the author in 1997.

Sheila Shipley Biddy was interviewed and photographed by the author in 1997.

Garth Brooks was interviewed for the radio syndication "Pulsebeat—Voice of the Heartland" in 1988.

Tracey Edmonds was interviewed by the author in 1997.

Pam Lewis was interviewed and photographed by the author in 1997.

Anita Mandell was interviewed and photographed by the author in 1997.

Claire Parr was interviewed and photographed by the author in 1997.

Mark Rothbaum was interviewed by the author in 1997.

CHAPTER 3

June Carter Cash was interviewed by the author in 1985.

All of the quotes in this book from the late **Marion Keisker** in this book not otherwise identified were taken from interviews in the Jerry Hopkins Collection at the University of Memphis. The collection is part of the Mississippi Valley Collection in the university library.

Information about **Sam Phillips**'s electroshock treatments at a mental hospital can be found in Peter Guralnick's *Last Train to Memphis* (1994). Additional information about Phillips and the early days at Sun Records was obtained from interviews with Phillips in the mid-1980s, and from Scotty Moore in interviews that took place from 1995–1997.

CHAPTER 4

Rita Coolidge was interviewed by the author in 1985.

The author first met **Bobbie Gentry** in the early 1950s when her name was Roberta Streeter; she was interviewed by the author in 1967 at a homecoming celebration in Houston, Mississippi.

Brenda Lee was interviewed by the author in 1997.

Tracy Nelson was interviewed by the author in 1996.

Carla Thomas was interviewed by the author in 1988 and 1989.

Mary Wilson was interviewed by the author in 1986.

Tammy Wynette was interviewed by the author in 1996.

CHAPTER 5

Laurie Lewis was interviewed by the author in 1995.

Bonnie Raitt was interviewed by the author in 1985.

Tanya Tucker was interviewed by the author several times in the 1980s and in 1995.

CHAPTER 6

The Bangles were interviewed and photographed by the author in the late 1980s.

Pat Benatar was interviewed by the author in 1997.

Tiffany was interviewed by the author in 1997.

Ann and Nancy Wilson of Heart were interviewed by the author in 1988.

CHAPTER 7

Deana Carter was interviewed by the author in 1997.

Melissa Etheridge was interviewed by Kelly Cruise and George Hays for the radio syndication "Pulsebeat—Voice of the Heartland."

Abra Moore was interviewed by the author in 1997.

Doug Supernaw was interviewed by the author in 1995.

BIBLIOGRAPHY

BOOKS

Aquila, Richard. *That Old Time Rock & Roll: A Chronicle of an Era.* New York: Schirmer Books, 1989.

Bego, Mark. *Linda Ronstadt: It's So Easy!* Austin, TX: Eakin Press, 1990.

Bindas, Kenneth J. *All of This Music Belongs to the Nation.* Knoxville: University of Tennessee Press, 1995.

Bronson, Fred. *The Billboard Book of Number One Hits.* New York: Billboard, 1985.

Chase, Gilbert. *America's Music: From the Pilgrims to the Present.* New York: McGraw-Hill, 1955.

Cooper, Sarah, ed. *Girls! Girls! Girls! Essays on Women and Music.* New York: New York University Press, 1996.

Cusic, Don. *Reba McEntire: Country Music's Queen.* New York: St. Martin's Press, 1991.

Dannen, Fredric. *Hit Men: Power Brokers and Fast Money Inside the Music Business.* New York: Times Books, 1990.

Denisoff, R. Serge. *Inside MTV.* New Brunswick, NJ: Transaction Books, 1988.

Dickerson, James. *Goin' Back to Memphis: A Century of Blues, Rock 'n' Roll, and Glorious Soul.* New York: Schirmer Books, 1996.

————. *Coming Home: 21 Conversations About Memphis Music.* Memphis: Scripps Howard, 1985.

Gruber, J. Richard. *Memphis 1948-1958.* Memphis: Memphis Brooks Museum of Art, 1986.

Gubernick, Lisa Rebecca. *Get Hot or Go Home.* New York: St. Martin's Press (1993).

Hopkins, Jerry. *Festival: The Book of American Music Celebrations.* New York: Macmillan, 1970.

Leamer, Laurence. *Three Chords and the Truth.* New York: HarperCollins, 1997.

Lynn, Loretta. *Coal Loretta Lynn: Coal Miner's Daughter.* Chicago: Henry Regnery Company, 1976.

Morrison, Craig. *Go Cat Go!: Rockabilly Music and Its Makers.* Chicago: University of Illinois Press, 1996.

Muirhead, Bert. *The Record Producers File.* Dorset, England: Blandford Press, 1984.

McAleer, Dave. *The All Music Book of Hit Singles.* San Francisco: Miller Freeman Books, 1994.

Nash, Alanna. *Behind Closed Doors.* New York: Alfred A. Knopf, 1988.

Nite, Norm N. (with Ralph M. Newman). *Rock On: The Illustrated Encyclopedia of Rock 'n' Roll.* New York: Thomas Y. Cromwell, 1978.

Oermann, Robert K., and Mary A. Burwack. *Finding Her Voice: The Saga of Women in Country Music.* New York: Crown Publishers, 1993.

Parton, Dolly. *Dolly: My Life and Other Unfinished Business.* New York: HarperCollins, 1994.

Patoski, Joe Nick. *Selena: Como la Flor.* New York: Boulevard, 1997.

Reynolds, Debbie, and David Patrick Columbia. *Debbie: My Life.* New York: William Morrow and Co., 1988.

Reynolds, Simon, and Joy Press. *The Sex Revolts: Gender, Rebellion, and Rock 'n' Roll.* Cambridge, MA: Harvard University Press, 1995.

Shaw, Arnold. *Dictionary of American Pop/Rock.* New York: Schirmer Books, 1982.

Smith, Joe. (Mitchell Fink, ed.). *Off the Record: An Oral History of Popular Music.* New York: Warner Books, 1988.

Tarabororrelli, J. Randy. *Call Her Miss Ross.* New York: Carol Publishing Group, 1989.

Turner, Tina. *I, Tina.* New York: Avon, 1986.

Weinstein, Deena. *Heavy Metal: A Cultural Sociology.* New York: Lexington Books, 1991.

Weissman, Dick. *The Music Business: Career Opportunities and Self-Defense.* New York: Crown Publishers, 1979.

Wynette, Tammy (with Joan Dew). *Stand By Your Man.* New York: Simon & Schuster, 1979.

ARTICLES

Aletti, Vince. "Whitney Plays It Safe." *Rolling Stone* (August 13, 1987).

Ali, Lorraine. "Backstage at Lilith." *Rolling Stone* (September 4, 1997).

Andrews, Suzanna. "Changing Nashville's Tune." *Working Woman* (August 1995).

Axthelm, Pete. "Lookin' at Country with Loretta Lynn." *Newsweek* (June 18, 1973).

Baldwin, Dawn. "Aimee Mann Not Waiting 'Til Tuesday." *Nine-O-One Network* (January/February 1987).

Brown, Foxy. "Cyndi Lauper." *Interview* (May 1997).

Browne, David. "Winging It." *Entertainment Weekly* (September 19, 1997).

Catlin, Roger. "McLachlan's Lilith Fair." *The Hartford Courant* (August 1997).

Clift, Eleanor. "Songs of Non-Liberation." *Newsweek* (August 2, 1971).

Cocks, Jay. "Madonna Draws a Line." *Time* (December 17, 1990).

Coker, Cheo Hodari. "Taking a Deep Breath, Again." *The Los Angeles Times* (June 16, 1996).

Considine, J. D. "Luscious Jackson." *Entertainment Weekly* (October 1997).

Dickerson, James. "Memphis Women Rockers." *Nine-O-One Network* (January/February 1987).

———. "Tanya Tucker: Good Friends Make the Best Records." *Nine-O-One Network* (April 1988).

———. "Pop Music: Now a Woman's World." *Glamour* (July 1997).

———. "The Bangles." *Nine-O-One Network* (December 1987).

———. "Hard-Working Tanya Tucker Zooms Career Back Into Gear." *CoverStory* (August 1994).

———. "Carol Decker Puts 'Heart and Soul' Into This British Group's Music." *Nine-O-One Network* (December 1987).

———. "Chickasaw County Child." *Mississippi* magazine (Winter 1968).

———. "Heart: You Can't Take Sex Out of Rock 'n' Roll." *Nine-O-One Network* (February 1988).

———. "A Taste of Pure Country." *CoverStory* (June 1994).

———. "Kathy Mattea: The Singer-Next-Door Who Won Nashville's Heart." *Nine-O-One Network* (April 1988).

Dunn, Jancee. "Cosmic Girl (Jewel)." *Rolling Stone* (May 15, 1997).

Elder, Renee. "Reba May Hover Over Music Row." *The Nashville Tennessean* (January 4, 1995).

Flick, Larry. "Is the World Ready for a Serious Cyndi Lauper?" *Billboard* (February 21, 1997).

Flynn, Brown Alan. "Petula Says Working Here Is Like Having a Party." *Memphis Press-Scimitar* (February 25, 1970).

Fong-Torres, Ben. "Linda Ronstadt: Heartbreak on Wheels." *Rolling Stone* (March 27, 1975).

Garratt, Sheryl. "Madonna." *The Face* (1996).

Garvin, Glenn. "Bobbie Hopes Film Will Relaunch Recording Career." *Delta Democrat-Times* (June 6, 1976).

Gersten, Russell. "Records." *Rolling Stone* (March 28, 1974).

Hannaham, James. "Alanis in Wonderland." *Spin* (November 1995).

Heath, Chris. "Spice Girls." *Rolling Stone* (July 10–24, 1997).

Heiman, Andrea. "Film Stars Decry Sex Harassing." *The Los Angeles Times* (1992).

———. "Facing Up to Sexual Harassment in Hollywood." *The Los Angeles Times* (February 15, 1992).

Hesbacker, Peter, and Bruce Anderson. "Hit Singers' Careers Since 1940s: Have Women Advanced?" *Popular Music & Society* (1980).

Honick, Bruce. "Why Country's Getting Sexier." *Country Music* (July 1996).

Kahn, Sheryl. "Reba's Rules." *McCall's* (September 1996).

Keel, Beverly. "The House That Reba Built." *New Country* (June 1994).

Kroll, Jack. "Wannabes (Spice Girls)." *Newsweek* (July 1997).

Ladouceur, Lisa. "Sarah McLachlan." *Pulse* (July 1997).

Laskow, Michael. "Nancy Brennan." *A&R Insider* (1995).

Lubenow, Gerald C. "The God of Grace." *Newsweek* (March 15, 1971).

Madden, Mike. "The Beat Is Latino." *Gannett News Service* (August 1997).

Meisel, Steven. "The Misfit." *Vanity Fair* (April 1991).

Michener, Charles. "The Divine Miss M." *Newsweek* (May 22, 1972).

Noyer, Paul Du. "Music, Maestress, Please!" *Q* magazine (December 1994).

Oermann, Robert K. "Shania Twain: More Than Meets the Eye." *The Nashville Tennessean* (February 28, 1996).

———. "Hunger Puts Janis Ian Back in the Spotlight." *The Nashville Tennessean* (October 4, 1997).

Orlean, Susan. "California Girls." *Rolling Stone* (March 26, 1987).

Orth, Maureen (with Janet Huck). "No Fear of Flying." *Newsweek* (February 23, 1976).

Pareles, Jon. "Forget the Hard Rock: It's Support for Sisterhood." *The New York Times* (July 7, 1997).

Pener, Degen. "Butterflies Aren't Free." *Entertainment Weekly* (September 1997).

Phillips, Chuck. "Geffen Firm Said to Settle Case of Sex Harassment." *The Los Angeles Times* (November 17, 1992).

———. "Anita Hill of Music Industry Talks." *The Los Angeles Times* (March 5, 1992).

Randall, Nancy. "Sexual Harassment: Women by the Thousands Are Fighting Back-And They Are Winning." *Nine-O-One Network* (February 1988).

Rapping, Elayne. "Empty vs. Mindless, Sure But Vicious, Too." *The Guardian* (February 8, 1984).

Robicheau, Paul. "Taking Aim (Ani DiFranco)." *The Boston Globe* (May 12, 1994).

Roland, Tom. "CMA Show Launch Pad for Twain." *The Nashville Tennessean* (September 23, 1997).

Saal, Hubert. "Bonnie and Blue." *Newsweek* (November 6, 1972).

———. "Singing Is Better Than Any Dope." *Newsweek* (October 19, 1970).

———. "The Girls-Letting Go." *Newsweek* (July 14, 1969).

Schleier, Curt. "Nancy Sinatra." *The Detroit News* (November 8, 1995).

Schmitt, Brad. "Starstruck Trims Clients, Narrows Focus to Reba." *The Nashville Tennessean* (May 29, 1997).

Schoemer, Karen. "Alternative Divas Luscious Jackson Break Out." *Newsweek* (March 31, 1997).

———. "The Malling of Shania." *Newsweek* (February 26, 1996).

Schruers, Fred. "Sheryl: She Only Wants to Be With You." *Rolling Stone* (November 14, 1996).

Smith, Danyel. "Janet Jackson." *Vibe* (1994).

Spurrier, Jeff. "The People's Courtney." *Details* (October 1995).

Tannenbaum, Rob. "Liz Phair." *Details* (June 1994).

Unknown author. "Rebirth of the Blues." *Newsweek* (May 26, 1969).

———. "Where She Is and Where She's Going." *Time* (March 20, 1972).

———. "The Spector of Payola '73." *Newsweek* (June 11, 1973).

Verna, Paul. "Abra Moore's Profile Sprouts with 'CLover.'" *Billboard* (May 1997).

Waller, Don. "Sylvia Robinson: Godmother of Street Music." *Pulse* (October 1997).

Whittlesey, Kristin. "Fiona Apple." *The Nashville Banner* (October 3, 1997).

Wild, David. "The Adventures of Miss Thing." *Rolling Stone* (November 2, 1995).

———. "Alanis Morissette." *Rolling Stone* (November 2, 1995).

Winegarner, Beth. "Cyndi Lauper." *The San Francisco Chronicle* (March 30, 1997).

Yampert, Rick de. "Emmylou Sings the Praises of Women." *The Nashville Tennessean* (August 3, 1997).

Zollo, Paul. "Jewel: Songs of Hope For the Next Generation." *Acoustic Guitar* (July 1997).

INDEX